CW00370090

GERMAN UNIFICATION IN EUROPEAN PERSPECTIVE

German Unification in European Perspective

Published by Brassey's for
Centre for European Policy Studies
33 rue Ducale, B - 1000 Brussels

Director
Peter Ludlow

GERMAN UNIFICATION IN EUROPEAN PERSPECTIVE

edited by

Wolfgang Heisenberg

Centre for European Policy Studies, Brussels

BRASSEY'S (UK)

(A Member of the Maxwell Macmillan Group)

LONDON * WASHINGTON * NEW YORK

| UK | Brassey's (UK) Ltd., |
| (Editorial) | 50 Fetter Lane, London EC4A 1AA, England |

Orders *(all except*   Brassey's (UK) Ltd
North America)   Headington Hill Hall, Oxford OX3 0BW, England

USA   Brassey's (US) Inc.
(Editorial)   8000 Westpark Drive, First Floor
                         McLean Virginia 22102, USA

Orders *(North America)*   Macmillan, Front and Brown Streets,
                          Riverside, New Jersey 08075, USA
                          Tel (toll free): 800 257 5755

Copyright © 1991 The Centre for European Policy Studies, Brussels

All Rights Reserved. No part of this publication may be reproduced, stored on a retrieval system or transmitted in any form or by any means: electronic, electrostatic, magnetic tape, mechanical, photocopying, recording or otherwise, without permission in writing from the publishers.

First edition 1991

Library of Congress Cataloguing-in-Publication Data available

British Library Cataloguing in Publication Data available

ISBN 0 08 041339 0

Printed in Great Britain by BPCC Wheatons Ltd, Exeter

Contents

Part IV: Challenges for European Integration

List of Contributors

Giorgio Basevi is Professor of Economics at the University of Bologna, Italy.

Lammy Betten is Professor of Law at the University of Utrecht, The Netherlands.

Rudolf Brauer is Director of the Deutsches Institut für Marktforschung, Berlin, Germany.

Koldo Echebarria is a consultant with Arthur Andersen, Bilbao, Spain.

Renata Fritsch-Bournazel is Chargée de Recherches at the Fondation Nationale des Sciences Politiques-CERI, Paris, France.

Albrecht Frohnmeyer is Adviser to Directorate-General VII of the Commission of the European Communities in Brussels.

Paul De Grauwe is Professor of Economics at the University of Leuven, Belgium, and Senior Research Fellow at CEPS.

Daniel Gros is Senior Research Fellow at CEPS.

Wolfgang Heisenberg is Senior Research Fellow at CEPS.

Charlotte Höhn is Director of the Bundesinstitut für Bevölkerungsforschung, Wiesbaden, Germany.

Jürgen Kröger is Head of Unit, National Economies of Member States (I), Directorate-General II of the Commission of the European Communities in Brussels.

Anne-Marie Le Gloannec is Chargée de Recherches at the Fondation Nationale des Sciences Politiques-CERI in Paris.

Peter Ludlow is Director of CEPS.

Roger Morgan is Professor of Political Science at the European University Institute in Florence, Italy.

Günther Schäfer is Professor of Public Policy at the European Institute of Public Administration, Maastricht, The Netherlands.

Horst Schilling is a researcher with the Gesellschaft für Koordinierung von Arbeitsmarktförderung und Strukturentwicklung in Berlin.

Helmuth Schreiber is the Director of the Ost-West Abteilung, Institut für Europäische Umweltpolitik, Bonn.

David Spence is Secretary to the Task Force on German Unification at the Commission of the European Communities in Brussels.

Gerhard Stahl is Adviser to the Socialist Group in the European Parliament.

Alfred Steinherr is Director of the Financial Research Department at the European Investment Bank in Luxembourg.

Ernst Ulrich von Weizsäcker is Director of the Europäische Institut für Umweltpolitik in Bonn.

Introduction

Wolfgang Heisenberg

In modern European history, references to the "German question" denote two different but related problems. In a broad sense, there is the view that, because of Germany's geographical position at the centre of Europe, the country's political structure, its role and status have always been of crucial importance for the equilibrium (or disequilibrium) of the European state system.[1] According to this view, the German question was at the centre of the two world wars of this century, but was not "solved" by them. Because the victorious powers were unable to agree on a political restructuring of Central and Eastern Europe, the military status quo, and with it the division of Germany and Europe, became the basis of the post-war political system. More usually, however, the German question is a more specific reference to the division of Germany after the second world war, and the political, social and humanitarian problems resulting from it.

In the broad sense, the German question, according to Michael Stürmer's popular formulation, does not belong to the Germans alone:[2] it can only be solved in a European context. From the late 1960's to the late 1980's, there was a near-universal consensus within European political élites that a solution was only conceivable in the context of pan-European unification. This consensus was helped by the fact that the division of Europe appeared so stable that the German question did not warrant any specific political action.

---

1 In Michael Stürmer's formulation, German history has always happened "where all the peninsulas of Europe are linked to each other and to the Eurasian landmass, where all highways meet, where all ideas fertilise each other, and where all economic forces have their hub. Germany was therefore for centuries, from the Peace of Westphalia to Bismarck, the counterbalance and guarantee of the European power system, and became - when Hitler's tyranny brought about the downfall of Bismarck's state, and Germany's new role in Europe broke down the European state system - the centre and hinge of the world system in which we live today." Michael Stürmer, "Deutschland? Aber wo liegt es? Die Bundesrepublik Deutschland in der Pax atlantica" in **Bundesrepublik Deutschland: Geschichte, Bewußtsein** (Bonn: Bundeszentrale für politische Bildung, 1989).

2 Ibid.

Whether there was a solution to the more specific aspects of the German question was a more controversial issue. While Germans themselves had little influence after the war on the political evolution of Europe and the escalating East-West conflict, US-Soviet differences about the political future of Germany were at the centre of that conflict, particularly during the two Berlin crises. However, because the balance of terror precluded a military "solution", the division of the world between East and West, and with it the division of Germany, became accepted facts of life. German opinion polls of the 1970's and 80's showed that, although support for reunification remained strong, the idea of Germany as a nation-state had receded. This led some observers to argue that the two Germanies had acquired national identities of their own, and that the question in its specific sense had largely been solved by (German) adaptation to the status quo.[3]

The surge of national feelings, however, associated with the opening of the intra-German border in 1989, and the first free elections in the GDR, showed that this was a superficial judgment. In spite of the long process of adaptation to the reality of two states, German nationalism proved strong enough to make unification nearly inevitable once the East's political and economic system had begun to disintegrate and the border was opened.

German unification was an important national event. It is likely to have satisfied what was left of pan-German national ambitions. This does not mean, however, that unification has also settled the German question. It is still true that the question in its broad sense can be solved only within a process of pan-European restructuring. The political revolutions of 1989 in Central and Eastern Europe have opened the door for the development of a new pan-European state system, and German national unification has made an adaptation of the existing system inevitable. But this is still an open-ended task, as it was in the years before German unification. There is still no agreement about the goals of this process, and it will certainly be more than a decade before it is possible to speak of a "new" political system in Europe.

---

3   See, for example, Gebhard Schweigler, "German questions or the shrinking of Germany" in F. Stephen Larrabee (ed.), **The Two German States and European Security** (New York: Institute for East-West Security Studies, 1989).

On the national level, the socio-economic situation in Eastern Germany after German economic and monetary union is only the most obvious indication that German unity has not yet abolished all the negative consequences of division. According to most recent studies, it will take at least five to ten years before Eastern Germany achieves a level of economic development comparable to that of the Western part, and it would be naive to assume that political integration will work much faster.

It is, however, important to recognise that not even this apparently "internal" process belongs to the Germans alone. Because Germany is already a closely-integrated part of the European Community, "national" adaptation is also a European task. It creates a broad range of problems which cannot be dealt with on the national level alone. It is even possible to argue that German unification was only possible, without causing serious rifts in and over Europe, because the "old" Federal Republic was already closely integrated into the EC and NATO, and because the momentum of European integration was strong enough to open up perspectives of a pan-European settlement of the German question.

CEPS' project on German unification is based on these considerations. It was planned long before the political revolutions of 1989, but at a time when it was clear that **perestroika** in the Soviet Union, particularly the new Soviet foreign and arms control policy, had led to a rather fluid political situation in Europe, and that in the resulting process of change the German question would again play a decisive role. At that time, it seemed important to show that the re-emerging German question was at least as much a European as a national German problem.

The events of 1989 made adjustments to the shape of the project inevitable, but did not change its basic focus. It was not difficult to see that, in contrast to the enormous speed of German national unification, the inevitable restructuring of the European political system would take time. Moreover, the integration of the former GDR into the Federal Republic and the EC was a challenge not only for the process of West European integration but also for relations between the EC and the countries of the Warsaw Pact (soon to be formally dissolved as a military alliance). Because of the popular, though mistaken, belief that German unification had solved the central issue of the German question, the project appeared to be even more important than before unification.

The book is divided into four parts. In part I Peter Ludlow and David Spence chart the main official negotiations which contributed to German unification: the intra-German negotiations, the "Two-Plus-Four" talks and the preparation of German unification within the European Community. This is more than merely an academic exercise, because it shows that, in spite of the fact that German unification was primarily determined by events in Germany and the intra-German negotiations, the European Community was able to adapt its procedures to the extraordinary speed of unification and to play an important and constructive role in the diplomatic preparation of German unity.

Part II focuses on the changing political landscape of Europe. One of the central questions in this context relates to the new Germany and its future international role. Anne-Marie Le Gloannec argues that, although in a legal sense no successor state to the two Germanies was created, "the new Germany will not be just a Federal Republic writ large". She analyses the possible impact of unification on the Federal Republic's political system and its future **raison d'état**.

On the international level, the prospect of German unification has led to strong emotional reactions in some of the neighbouring countries and raised concerns about the future political and economic power of a reunited Germany. Renata Fritsch-Bournazel investigates these reactions and concludes that, in spite of a temporary revival of old fears and old clichés, there are positive signs that European governments are aware of the unique opportunity to balance the increasing power of a united Germany with qualitatively-new developments in Community policy.

Roger Morgan investigates these implications for the European Community in detail. He expects an adjustment in the representation of Germany in some Community institutions, probably a slowing-down of European defence co-operation, and - as a result of the creation of five new German **Länder** - a powerful impetus to existing pressures for a more decentralised Community.

Finally, Wolfgang Heisenberg analyses the implications of German unification for European security. He argues that German unification has destroyed the foundation of the "old" European security system without replacing it with a new one. European security is therefore in a transitional phase, in which military security has lost some of its former importance, but reliance continues to be placed on the Atlantic Alliance, while measures such as the intensification of European **political** integration, particularly in the field of security co-operation, and the establishment of pan-European security institutions, have become decisive for the future security of the continent.

Part III deals with the economic and social problems associated with German unification. Giorgio Basevi's paper surveys the answers economic theory can give to the question of how German unification will influence European economic integration and progress towards monetary union.

Daniel Gros and Alfred Steinherr investigate macroeconomic management in the new Germany and its implications for the European Monetary System. They argue that starting German economic integration with a currency union was probably the best economic choice, and that concerns about the risks of monetary destabilisation and exchange-rate repercussions are not supported by economic analysis. They fear, however, that the process of privatising real assets in Eastern Germany will be too slow or that economic rationality will suffer, and that a sell-out to external owners may result. To avoid such consequences they elaborate alternative proposals which would respect the previous social contract of the GDR.

Paul De Grauwe discusses German economic unification on the basis of two different economic theories, the "comparative advantage model" and the "increasing returns model", which lead to very different predictions of how the integration process will take place. He argues that labour is and probably will remain relatively expensive in Eastern Germany, and that there is, therefore, a real danger of a developing core-periphery arrangement in Germany, as predicted by the "increasing returns" model. The German authorities, in his view, can probably avoid such a development in some parts of Eastern Germany by a transfer of substantial resources, while other regions may have protracted problems in catching up with the rest of the German economy.

Paul De Grauwe's cautious assessment of the chances for East German economic development is complemented by four papers dealing with the adjustment problems of the East German economy. Jürgen Kröger gives a broad overview of these problems. Ernst-Ulrich von Weizsäcker and Helmuth Schreiber deal with the environment, Horst Schilling with East German agriculture and Rudolf Brauer with East German trade relations.

Finally, Charlotte Höhn investigates demographic and social trends in the united Germany. She comes to the conclusion that demographic ageing is inevitable for advanced societies in Europe, and that Germany is just a forerunner in this respect. She nevertheless argues that the problematic consequences of demographic change will be manageable if an appropriate adaptation policy is launched early enough.

Part IV deals with specific challenges to European integration arising from German unification. Koldo Echevarria and Günther Schäfer explore the factors that could condition an effective application of the Community's Structural Fund Programme to East Germany. They argue that a strict application of the existing management process for the Structural Funds Programme to East Germany would be politically infeasible and could undermine the flexibility and effectiveness of the programme. They therefore propose a flexible interim programme, set up outside the Funds and tailored to the needs of the new German **Länder**.

Gerhard Stahl investigates the implications of German unification for the budget and budgetary policy of the Community. He argues that the ground rules of EC budgetary policy make it difficult to provide adequate funding for new functions, such as the integration of the former GDR, and that this danger is aggravated by the clumsiness of the budget procedures, particularly at the Council level. He therefore advocates a general budget reform.

Lammy Betten studies the possible effects of German unification on the Community labour market, particularly in view of the right of free movement of persons. Although she complains that the handling of these problems demonstrates the superior influence of politics over law, she admits that pragmatism has resulted in sensible solutions. She does not expect major pressures on the EC labour market from migrating East German workers. However, since there is no longer a legal distinction between East and West German workers, there are no conceivable legal ways of avoiding pressures should they occur.

Finally, Albrecht Frohnmeyer deals with the implications of German unification for EC transport policy. He sees German unification as having considerably increased the tasks facing the Community. Among the preconditions for dealing with them, he mentions an adequate level of private and state investment in the transport sector of the former GDR and the retraining of personnel. In addition, he argues in favour of reshaping transport agreements with Central and East European countries, including the Soviet Union, in order to counteract the creation of new transport barriers, and developing the transport infrastructure linking Poland, Czechoslovakia and the new German **Länder**.

Acknowledgments

We are pleased to record our thanks here to the Bundesministerium für inner-deutsche Beziehungen, which provided financial support for the project, and to Dr. Michael Stürmer, Director of the Stiftung Wissenschaft und Politik Eben-hausen, which commissioned it from CEPS.

May 1991

Part I

Negotiating German Unification

The German-German negotiations and the "Two-Plus-Four" talks

Peter Ludlow[*]

1. The German-German negotiations

The reunification of Germany had been an official objective of the Federal Republic since its inception. It figured in the Basic Law, notably the preamble and Articles 23 and 146. It was also acknowledged by Germany's Western partners, including the member states of the European Community, which appended to the Treaty of Rome four relevant documents: a protocol on German internal trade and connected problems; a joint declaration on Berlin; a declaration by the government of the Federal Republic on the definition of a "German national"; and a further declaration by the Bonn government on the application of the Treaties to Berlin. All of these affirmed in one way or another that the division was temporary and that Germany should be seen as one.

Although the Federal Republic's foreign policy was based until the late 1960's on the "Hallstein Doctrine" of non-recognition of the GDR, it had been clear since the early 1950's that reunification was not a realistic prospect in the short term. As a result, the FRG's main political parties contrived to combine rhetorical affirmation of unity as a long-term goal with practical agnosticism about its achievement and an overriding commitment to the Federal Republic's links with the West.

In the second half of the 1960's, as the SPD began to emerge as the most creative force in West German foreign policy, tacit acceptance was transformed into open admission of the existence

* Peter Ludlow wishes to acknowledge the assistance of Gaby Jauernig in assembling material relevant to this essay.

of two Germanies as a central feature of the new **Ostpolitik**. The policy did not, of course, exclude the disapproval of specific actions of the East German régime, but vigorous condemnation was not in any way incitement to revolution. On the contrary, West German leaders from Strauss to Brandt repeatedly affirmed through deeds as well as words their acknowledgement of the Honecker régime as an unavoidable partner in the quest for European security.

When the end came, therefore, it was as much of a surprise to West German leaders as to anyone else. For months after the exodus from East Germany began to assume major proportions in the middle of 1989, they exhibited no grand design, only improvisation and not a little anxiety. Pressure came first on the Federal Republic's official delegations in East Berlin, Prague and above all Budapest. In September, it intensified, as the Hungarian government opened the border to Austria and 50,000 East Germans fled via Hungary to the Federal Republic. Within weeks, the East German authorities themselves began to connive at the exodus. In the first week of November alone, 60,000 East Germans left the GDR via Czechoslovakia with the open permission of the East Berlin authorities.

The exodus was not the only sign of the disintegration of authority in East Germany. As demonstrations occurred on an almost nightly basis in the major cities of the GDR from September onwards, some individuals from the churches and other "apolitical" backgrounds emerged as leaders; for the most part, however, the movement seemed spontaneous rather than contrived, its contagion made all the more effective by television.

Faced by this combination of internal unrest and popular flight, the East German régime crumbled. Honecker resigned as head of state and Secretary-General of the SED on 18 October. Initially the succession went to a member of his own party. Even after 7 November, when the whole cabinet resigned, Communists remained at the head of affairs. The party had, however, manifestly lost not only the ability but also the will to govern. On 9 November, it openly acknowledged the fact by allowing a breach in the Berlin wall, the symbol and instrument of its power and separateness for almost thirty years.

The Federal Republic and more generally the West were spectators rather than actors in this extraordinary drama. German unity was manifestly back at the centre of the Federal Republic's political agenda, but notions of how it could be accomplished were still hazy. The dominant focus of official statements in October and even in the first half of November was not on the timetabling of union. On the contrary, there was open division about intra-German policy, notably but by no means exclusively in the SPD.

This initial phase of hesitation ended on 28 November when Chancellor Kohl presented a ten-point programme to the **Bundestag**.[1] He listed the forces that had led to the present situation and paid tribute once again to the roles played by the European Community, NATO and the new leaderships in the East, particularly in the Soviet Union. Given the popular character of the movement in East Germany, it was impossible, he continued, to produce a neat bureaucratic plan for German unification: "Abstract models may have their use in argument but they are going to be of little practical importance". It was, however, possible to envisage a number of steps by which the eventual goal would be achieved.

There should be immediate action to deal with the social and economic consequences of the emigration of the previous weeks and the normalisation of traffic between the GDR and the Federal Republic. There should be an intensification of economic, scientific and cultural co-operation between the two Germanies. Active help would be given by the Federal Republic in the transformation of the political and economic system of the GDR.

Beyond these practical steps, there would be active co-operation with the GDR authorities in the development of what East German Prime Minister Modrow had described as a **Vertragsgemeinschaft** (a treaty community). Common institutions would have to be strengthened and extended to oversee the increasingly complex network of agreements in all areas and at all levels. Furthermore, Mr. Kohl expressed his government's willingness to proceed still further towards "confederal structures" linking the two Germanies following democratic elections in the GDR.

On the European level, said Mr. Kohl, a firm link should be maintained between the development of intra-German unity and the establishment of a secure political architecture for Europe as a whole. For this to come about, it would be necessary to further strengthen both the European Community and the CSCE, leading to the latter's institutionalisation as well as new moves to reduce armaments. On these bases, Mr Kohl asserted, German reunification could be achieved. Reunification remained, he concluded, "the political objective of the Federal Republic".

The content and scope of the Chancellor's speech surprised observers both inside and outside Germany. It was much more explicit about the medium and long-term goals of German policy than any official statement hitherto. It was, even so, quickly overtaken by events. Two factors were of particular importance: the growing evidence of the complete disintegration of the East German economic and political system and, in March, an overwhelming vote by the East Germans themselves in favour of German unification in their first free elections.

Even before the March election, Chancellor Kohl had offered the Modrow government economic and monetary union, based on the principles of a social market economy. The Modrow government itself still adhered to the idea of a confederation between two sovereign states, but it agreed to explore the possibilities opened up by the Chancellor's February offer, and a joint expert commission began work immediately. With the elections of 18 March, however, neither the Confederation nor economic and monetary union were any longer enough. The East German people voted for what the basic law of the Federal Republic asserted as their right: accession to the Federal Republic itself.

In the months that followed, three major landmarks stand out. First, the conclusion of the **Staatsvertrag** on 18 May establishing a German economic, monetary and social union as of 1 July 1990.[2] Second, agreement on 2 August that there would be all-German elections in December 1990. Third, the signature of the **Einigungsvertrag** on 31 August, paving the way for formal unification on 3 October.[3]

Economic and monetary union was, as already indicated, initially conceived as a medium-term objective in itself, distinct in a strict chronological sense at least from the broader objective of political unification. It was, after all, a very ambitious objective. The **Bundesbank** in particular made no secret of the major consequences it foresaw as a result of such an agreement. The West German government, however, took a different view. Whatever economic discomfort might result from over-hasty and over-generous economic and monetary union, the latter was a political necessity. The **Bundesbank** had to give way both on the principle and on the details. By the same token, however, the **Staatsvertrag** contained the seeds of its own obsolescence. It formally buried the old East Germany and established full union in every sense except the political one.

Political union, therefore, could not long be postponed. The conclusion of the **Staatsvertrag** led inexorably to the drafting of an **Einigungsvertrag**. Even the external constraints (discussed below) could not halt the process. On the contrary, their resolution was hastened by it.

Negotiations for the **Einigungsvertrag** began on 6 July. Shortly afterwards, on 22 July the **Volkskammer** in East Berlin adopted a law reconstituting the five German **Länder** as of 14 October. This unilateral action was followed two weeks later by a joint agreement of both governments to hold pan-German elections on 2 December. The date was not arbitrary. The Federal Republic itself was due to hold elections at that time and it was obviously convenient to link the two processes. It was also, however, assumed at this stage that the December date would be the logical moment for the entry into force of the **Einigungsvertrag** currently under negotiation. Even this calculation was, however, swept aside, when on 23 August the **Volkskammer** voted to accede to the Federal Republic on 3 October. This further acceleration of the process made the conclusion of the **Einigungsvertrag** even more urgent. It also prompted a significant revision of the timetables in the negotiations with the external partners. In the end, the **Einigungsvertrag** itself was formally signed on 31 August to take effect on 3 October. On that day East Germany ceased to exist as a state. The Federal Republic's Basic Law became effective in the five new **Länder**. So did the law of the European Community, subject only to special transitional exemptions to be defined in separate negotiations between the EC and Germany.

2. The "Two-Plus-Four" talks

In the formal sense, the "Two-Plus-Four" negotiations were concerned with the abolition of the wartime allies' residual rights over the two Germanies. At a deeper level, however, they reflected the need of the two Germanies to reconcile their own ambitions and internal necessities with the interests of Europe as a whole. The fears that the prospect of a reunited Germany awakened amongst its neighbours and partners were never far from the surface. For this reason, the external negotiations were never simply a formality that had to be cleared out of the way for the sake of good form. They were a vital part of the unification process itself, which, as the Federal Chancellor and Foreign Minister and indeed all leading German politicians constantly maintained, could only be achieved and sustained if it was seen as a step towards the creation of a new, peaceful European structure rather than a potentially destabilising development.

The dangers - and opportunities - were very much apparent in the first weeks after the fall of the Berlin wall. Public debate both in the Western democracies and in the East mirrored the preoccupations aroused by the prospect of a united Germany.

German political leaders were constantly reminded that they were under observation. Loose formulations - or to take a specific example, the failure of the Chancellor to give explicit assurances that a new, united Germany would not seek to reopen the issue of its Eastern frontiers - were fastened on as evidence of bad faith or potential menace.

It is beyond the scope of this chapter to provide a detailed analysis of external reactions to the events of October and November 1989.[4] There were divisions in every country, and none were entirely positive or entirely negative. It is, however, possible to distinguish certain general trends. Of Germany's major partners, three were initially cautious, if not hostile, towards any speedy movement towards German unification: the Soviet Union, Britain and France.

The clearest statement of the Soviet position in the first few weeks was probably the speech that Foreign Minister Shevardnadze made in Brussels in December. It contained the following:

> We emphasise with the utmost determination... that we shall protect the GDR from any attack. That country is our strategic ally and a member of the Warsaw Treaty Organisation. It is necessary to proceed on the basis of the post-war realities, namely, the existence of two sovereign German states members of the United Nations. A retreat from that would be fraught with destabilisation in Europe.[5]

British and French reservations were also well known, if not quite so overtly displayed. In London, Mrs. Thatcher made no secret of her concern. The French President's views were, on occasion, hardly less negative. Gestures towards the Communist leadership in East Berlin, indiscretions in the course of discussions with Mr. Gorbachev in Kiev at the beginning of December and innumerable instances of "off-the-record" statements of alarm to official and unofficial visitors to Paris, suggested that M. Mitterrand, like many others in France, saw developments in Germany as a threat.

The Bonn government, however, had allies from the very beginning. Two were of particular importance: the Bush administration and the European Community, the latter acting through both the European Commission and the Council machinery. The

Americans were consistently supportive. There was undoubtedly an element of resignation before the inevitable. The strong, positive tone adopted by the President and his senior advisers both in Washington and Bonn itself, was, however, in the final analysis based on calculations of interest.

By November 1989, the "special relationship" between the Bush administration and the Bonn government was an established fact. It had been the theme of several celebrated speeches by the President and the Secretary of State, and it had been consolidated by a number of meetings and still larger number of telephone conversations.[6] In a period in which the United States was having to reassess its own global role, it needed Germany, the single strongest member of the European Community, as a major partner. Nothing happened in November or December 1989 to undermine that perception. Hyperactive diplomacy by the German Chancellor and Foreign Minister further assuaged any temptation that there might have been in the highest ranks of the administration to review its priorities.

The positive evaluation of events in Germany in Washington was more than matched by the response of the European Community institutions. The relationship between the EC and the new Germany will be looked at in a more technical sense in the following chapter. The early reactions of Commission President Delors and his colleagues and, more generally, of the European Council in November and December had, however, a direct bearing on the high political negotiations subsequently carried out within the 'Two-Plus-Four" framework.[7] The EC as a whole proved decidedly more rational and generous than its parts, and in so doing first contained and then overcame whatever damage the negative reactions of individual member states might have done. The lead was undoubtedly given by the Commission. From October onwards, building on strong personal relations with decision-makers in Bonn, M. Delors in particular not only reacted to, but also in important respects anticipated, events in Central Europe with a series of statements which were notable in their warmth and constructiveness. It would, however, be a mistake to personalise the Community's reaction. The Commission President undoubtedly consolidated his position as a leader, but the true victors in the last months of 1989 were the institutions themselves, particularly the European Council, which met twice in the course of four weeks in November and December. Given what was known about the personal feelings of some of the more important members of that body, not least the French President and the British Prime Minister, the conclusions of the two Council meetings were remarkable. The following passage from the conclusions of the Strasbourg Council in December is a case in point:

> We seek the strengthening of the state of peace in Europe in which the German people will regain its unity through free self-determination. This process should take place peacefully and democratically, in full respect of the relevant treaties and agreements and of all the principles defined by the Helsinki Final Act, in a context of dialogue and East-West co-operation. It also has to be placed in the perspective of European integration. The Community is and must remain a point of reference and influence. It remains the cornerstone of a new European architecture and, in its will to openness, a mooring for the future European equilibrium... Construction of the Community must therefore go forward: the building of European union will permit the further development of a range of effective and harmonious relations with the other countries of Europe.[8]

The fact that the French government held the Presidency of the Community at the time only reinforced the importance of the Community dimension in the development of the 'Two-Plus-Four" process. The French leadership was pushed willy-nilly into a constructive frame of mind, at the core of which lay the calculation implied in the Strasbourg conclusions: German unity need not be threatening if the opportunity that it offered to accelerate European union was grasped. By the end of 1989, Paris and Bonn had together begun to move towards a view of what was desirable and feasible which eventually found expression in the joint letter of President Mitterrand and Chancellor Kohl to the Irish Presidency proposing a second intergovernmental conference on political union.[9] Against this background, the French were almost bound to be helpful in the context of the 'Two-Plus-Four" negotiations, and so it proved. The British position remained more ambivalent, since the British Prime Minister viewed European union as negatively as she did German unity. With two of his Western allies firmly behind him, however, Chancellor Kohl's position on the eve of the negotiations with the four allied powers was much stronger than had seemed likely in the immediate aftermath of his Ten-Point Plan at the end of November.

At the beginning of 1990, therefore, the principal priorities for the Bonn government were to establish an acceptable negotiating framework and to win over the Soviet Union to its fundamental objective, which was the renunciation by the Four Powers of their residual rights, and, as a consequence, to a commitment to the phased withdrawal of Soviet forces from the territory of the new Germany.

Both objectives were achieved by the middle of February 1990. The US administration played a decisive role in ironing out remaining differences in the Western camp over whether or how Germany should be represented in the negotiations, while the West German government itself, in the persons of Chancellor Kohl and Foreign Minister Genscher, made the decisive breakthrough with the Soviets. At their meeting on 10 February, President Gorbachev assured Chancellor Kohl that the Soviet government would not oppose German unification as such and that it would be ready to negotiate the agreements that this entailed.[10] This accord paved the way for the agreement in Ottawa on 13 February, at a conference of foreign ministers of NATO and the Warsaw Pact, that negotiations should open on the external aspects of German unification on the basis of the 'Two-Plus-Four" model.[11]

Formal negotiations began in Bonn on 5 May. It was agreed that the agenda should include border questions, the status of Berlin, the final legal settlement of German sovereignty, the political/military questions relating to the new European structure and more particularly the future role of the CSCE process, and the place, if any, of the new Germany within the alliance structures. Negotiations went smoothly on most issues, including the question of the Polish-German frontier, on which both German parliaments issued a reassuring resolution on 21 June.[12] The most controversial issue in the negotiations was, however, the alliance question. The Soviets changed their position several times, but until early July seemed at most ready to concede an associate membership for the unified Germany in both alliances for an interim period, coupled with the reduction of all German forces to 250,000 men. None of the Western allies found this acceptable.

Two developments in July hastened an eventual compromise: the NATO summit in London on 5-6 July which redefined the role of the alliance in European security and called for a new relationship with the members of the Warsaw Pact and, still more important, a bilateral agreement reached at a meeting between Chancellor Kohl and President Gorbachev in the Soviet Union in mid-July.[13] At that meeting, the Soviet President agreed to Germany's obtaining full sovereignty on the day of unification, including the right to NATO membership. Soviet forces would be withdrawn from East Germany by the end of 1994. In return, Mr. Kohl gave a commitment to reduce the total of German military forces during the same period to 370,000. Finally, he agreed to bilateral negotiations on the withdrawal of Soviet troops, cooperation and good neighbourliness. These negotiations took place in the following weeks.

When, therefore, the foreign ministers of the two Germanies and their counterparts from the four wartime allies met in Moscow on 12 September 1990, they had before them a complex set of agreements. The cornerstone was the 'Treaty on the Final Settlement with respect to Germany", which was signed by all six of them.[14] In this document, the four allies accepted German unification and renounced all rights and responsibilities relating to Berlin and Germany as a whole. The main body of the treaty covered five points.

Territorial issues. The external borders of the new Germany were to be those of the Federal Republic and the German Democratic Republic. The definitive nature of these frontiers was confirmed as "an essential element of the peaceful order in Europe". A specific agreement was to be concluded with Poland.

The non-agressive character of a new Germany. "According to the Constitution of the united Germany, acts tending to and undertaken with the intent to disturb the peaceful relations between nations, especially to prepare for aggressive war, are unconstitutional and a punishable offence".

Renunciation by Germany of the manufacture, possession and control of nuclear, biological and chemical weapons. This was coupled in article 3 with a pledge by the two Germanies to reduce the personnel of the armed forces of the united Germany to 370,000 within three to four years.

Bilateral arrangements for the withdrawal of Soviet armed forces from German territory.

Undertakings regarding German troops on the territory of the (former) GDR. Until the completion of the withdrawal of the Soviet armed forces, only German territorial defence units which were not part of NATO would be assigned to the territory of the former GDR. During the same period, moreover, the armed forces of other states would not be stationed there. In the longer term, the two Germanies undertook that, even when German forces linked with NATO were stationed in the former GDR, they would not be armed with nuclear weapons.

This multilateral treaty was linked with a number of bilateral agreements which were initialled by the West German Foreign Minister at the same time.[15] These included a treaty on good neighbourly relations which, it was stated, was intended to "lend a new quality to German-Soviet relations" and envisaged the comprehensive development of co-operation in all fields. There were also more detailed agreements pertaining to transitional measures made necessary by the currency conversion in the GDR in July, the financial situation of the Soviet forces stationed there and the cost of their withdrawal. The total package seemed likely to cost approximately 15bn DM over a period of three to four years.

References

1. **Presse-und Informationsamt der Bundesregierung, Bulletin** Nr. 134/S.1141, Bonn, 29 November 1989.

2. **Presse-und Informationsamt der Bundesregierung, Pressemitteilung** Nr. 206/90, 18 May 1990.

3. **Bundesgesetzblatt Teil II**. Z 1988 A. 1990 Nr. 35, 28 September 1990.

4. For a fuller account of EC reactions, see my introduction to **The Annual Review of European Community Affairs 1990** (London: Brassey's UK for CEPS, 1991), pp. XLVIII - LI.

5. **Financial Times**, 19 December 1990.

6. Cf. especially the speech by President Bush in Mainz, 31 May 1989.

7. Cf. **CEPS Annual Review 1990**, p. XLVIII ff.

8. **Europe**, 10 December 1989.

9. **Europe**, 20 April 1990.

10. **Frankfurter Allgemeine Zeitung**, 11 February 1990.

11. **Atlantic News**, 14 February 1990.

12. **Presse-und Informationsamt der Bundesregierung, Vertrag über die abschliessende Regelung über Deutschland**, Anhang p. 23, September 1990.

13. **Ibid.**, p. 26.

14. **Presse-und Informationsamt der Bundesregierung**, September 1990, documents on German unification.

15. Note 12 above, p. 68.

The European Community's negotiations on German unification

David Spence

1. Germany as a special case[1]

It was clear from the outset that German unification implied integration of the German Democratic Republic into the European Community. The process by which the GDR would join the Community clearly resembled an accession. There was, however, near-unanimity in Germany and abroad that, as with an accession, the integration process would take years. For the Germans, there were two constitutional routes to incorporation of the GDR into a new German state and these influenced the Community path chosen. The GDR could become part of the Federal Republic of Germany by dint of Article 23 of the **Grundgesetz**, whereby new **Länder** may opt for membership of the federation. This would simply enlarge the existing territory of the Federal Republic. Alternatively, under Article 146 of the **Grundgesetz** a new constitution resulting from negotiations between the two states would be necessary. The unified state would be the result of an international treaty. In practice the route chosen was via Article 23, with two inter-state treaties (**Staatsvertrag** and **Einigungsvertrag**[2]) clearing the economic and political path to union before the new **Länder** exercised the Article 23 option.

Article 23 was subsequently repealed, since its original purpose was to allow for reunification of the Federal Republic with the territories within Germany's 1937 borders. The accession of the five new **Länder** and the recognition of the Oder-Neisse line as the eastern frontier of Germany rendered Article 23 void of purpose. Its continued existence would have implied German demands over parts of present-day Poland within the 1937 boundaries of the German state. The counterpart in international law to the repealing of Article 23 is the 'Treaty on the Final Settlement with Respect to Germany" signed by the Four Powers and the two German states in Moscow on 12 September 1990.[3]

There is a parallel between the integration of the two Germanies and the route to integration of the GDR into the European Community. If the Community were to take the view that treaty references to the Federal Republic of Germany assumed no fixed territorial definition for the country as a whole, then the existing member-state would be able to simply redefine its territory without constitutional implications. Under this hypothesis, Article 227 of the EC Treaty defining the territory of the Community would not need revision. There would be no need to invoke Article 237 on new accessions, and no need for assent from the European Parliament, ratification by member states or formal negotiations between the Community and the GDR. While the government of any member state could request treaty amendment under Article 236, there was no legal obligation involved. In fact, none felt the need to do so.

These legal deliberations, though causing some concern at the time, were of a largely formalistic nature. The running was clearly being made by the Germans, and the timetable set by the action of East German citizens. While there were parallels with an accession, Germany was clearly a special case.

Three legal and administrative issues required consideration. First, the effects on the institutions - in particular, the question of revising the voting arrangements in the European Council and the representation of the new **Länder** in the European Parliament. The second issue concerned the implications in international law of merging the two states; whether in practice the Federal Republic as the surviving state would legally inherit international rights and obligations for which competence had already been ceded to the Communities. Third, the transitional arrangements applicable to the new **Länder** had to be agreed by the Council of Ministers.

2. The preparation process: organisational arrangements in the Commission and the Parliament

As the implications of German unification became clear, a co-ordinated response by the institutions was increasingly necessary. The Strasbourg summit had asked the Commission to prepare a paper outlining the essential elements of a Community reponse. Within the Commission, responsibility remained with the President and a small group of Commissioners known internally as the "group of four". These four, Delors, Bangemann, Christophersen and Andriessen, ensured that the Commission's strategy "Europeanised" the process of German unification, thereby enhancing European integration itself.

In January 1990 a special group of Commissioners was set up under the chairmanship of Vice-President Bangemann. Commissioners, senior German politicians and officials were invited to address the Commission on individual policy areas likely to require derogations from secondary legislation. The "Bangemann Group",[4] as it became known, met for the first time on 9 February and then weekly until July 1990. The German Permanent Representative to the European Communities, Dr. Jürgen Trumpf, and his senior officials in Brussels became regular visitors to the thirteenth floor of the Berlaymont building. On 23 March, Chancellor Kohl himself addressed the Commission in a meeting lasting two hours.

The Commission strategy took account of three concerns. First, German unification should not take place to the detriment of European integration, in particular the completion of the internal market by 1992. Second, the advantages to member states of increased trade should be underlined. Finally, this was an opportunity to demonstrate the effectiveness of the Commission in orchestrating a "fast-track" accession.

Meanwhile, on 15 February the Parliament had agreed to set up its own 'Temporary committee to consider the impact of the process of German unification on the European Community". The Committee met for the first time on 1 March under the chairmanship of Gerardo Fernández-Albor, a Spanish Christian Democrat, with the British Socialist Alan Donnelly as rapporteur.[5] The work programme of the Committee was subsequently agreed by the Parliament's enlarged bureau on 13 March 1990. The Committee's brief was to consider the institutional aspects of German unification, the overall political context, both in the Community and within Germany itself, and the impact on sectoral policies.

The Temporary Committee's strategy was to insist that overruling the Parliament's view on the accession question by no means diminished the role the Parliament intended to play. From the outset the Committee adopted a high profile. The Commission's Secretary-General, David Williamson, attended the constituent meeting on 1 March and promised extensive Commission collaboration. Invitations to the two German governments and parliaments to participate in the work were immediately issued. The East German **Volkskammer** began sending representatives on 19 April, but before this the Committee had taken evidence from Commission President Delors, Council President Collins, Frau Adam Schwätzer, FRG Minister of State for Foreign Affairs and Commissioners Andriessen, Bangemann and Christophersen.

The final stage in the preparation process was the meeting of the European Council in Dublin on 28 April 1990. The Commission communication[6] to the Council was based on deliberations in the Bangemann Group and preliminary observations by the Commission's services. The paper gave a brief analysis of the East German economy and of the advantages of German unification for Europe as a whole. It then set out a strategy for the gradual incorporation of the GDR into the European Community.

The East German economy, in the Commission's view, was impressive compared with that of other CMEA countries, and its per capita GNP was certainly higher than in Ireland, Greece and Portugal. However, this seemingly positive state of affairs disguised inefficiencies in both production and distribution. As to how the Community should proceed, the Commission asserted that accession under Article 237 of the Treaty of Rome indeed did not apply. The integration process was in every respect comparable to an accession, with two exceptions. First, much of it would occur before formal integration into the Community by virtue of the projected State Treaty on Economic, Monetary and Social Union between the two parts of Germany (**Staatsvertrag**). From the date of its implementation (1 July 1990), this would provide the basis for harmonising legislation in areas of Community competence. The second difference was that the process of integration would not involve negotiations with the GDR itself, but with the Federal Republic of Germany, the existing member state.

The Commission foresaw three stages of integration. The first, interim, stage would commence with the implementation of the **Staatsvertrag**. The second, transitional, phase would commence with unification itself and the final stage would be determined when the **acquis communautaire** became fully applicable.

During the first phase, the Commission argued, the gradual adoption by the GDR of West German legislation would provide the precondition for membership of the Community - a market economy. The Commission would ensure that the Community's competition and state-aid requirements were being met. At the same time, the Commission saw this phase as the period when the GDR's price, credit and monetary system would be totally overhauled, when VAT would be introduced and the tax and social security system adapted. This was a tall order, but the Commission expressed its intention to safeguard Community interests and to ensure on behalf of Community institutions that the implications for Community competence would be monitored.

On the transitional phase, the Commission's communication pointed to major problems which were the subject of the subsequent negotiations in the Council. Since 1992 was to see the end of intra-Community controls on free movement, 31 December 1992 would clearly have to be the target date for the expiry of transitional measures. This was particularly the case in the field of the internal market, the environment and transport. There would also be important implications for the Commission's proposals on relations with the GDR's main trading partners in the East. The Commission declared its intention to ensure that the problems likely in the transition period would not affect Community policy on free movement and free competition. The various policy areas affected included transport, fisheries, structural funds, the environment, social affairs, and trade policy - in short, the whole gamut of Community policy.[7]

The Commission's paper on the economic situation likely to result from unification identified the potential short-term difficulties. But the Commission also argued that "in general terms, we are likely to see vigorous economic growth in the German Democratic Republic, generating high demand throughout the Community, and an increase in imports from the other member states. This additional growth will be reflected in additional (Community) revenue."

In retrospect, these views were over-optimistic. Political circumspection and the need to provide positive leadership within the Community may have led the drafters of the various papers and proposals to emphasise the hopes for the future rather than the handicaps of the present.

3. The Community, German EMU and preparatory work for the package of transitional measures

The Dublin Council of April 1990 accepted the Commission's views on the route to integration of the GDR into the Community and the phasing proposed. It required the Federal Republic to keep the Community informed of developments between the two Germanies and the Commission to be fully involved with these discussions. This marked a considerable success for the Commission in raising its profile, since it was now guaranteed a role in the intra-German negotiations on the **Staatsvertrag** and **Einigungsvertrag.** The fact that the Commission thus became a prime source of information for member states did not remove from the Germans the obligation to keep the Parliament and the

Council informed. But it did obviate the need for a continuous German defence of what were to become Commission proposals.

The Summit granted the GDR full access to the European Investment Bank, EURATOM and the loan facilities of the European Coal and Steel Community. This accompanied continued support from the Community within the G-24 framework and participation in EUREKA.

The European Council confirmed that the transitional measures would recognise "all the interests involved, including those resulting from the **acquis communautaire**" and that the measures should be "confined to what is strictly necessary and aim at full integration as rapidly and as harmoniously as possible." This went some way towards allaying fears that German unification would jeopardise aid and investment in the less prosperous member states. The Commission now began work on a paper to the Council on the coming **Staatsvertrag**.

The Dublin Summit conclusions allowed the Commission to formalise co-ordination arrangements at service level. Previously, arrangements had featured German unification on the weekly agenda of the Commission, the Group of Four and the Bangemann Group meetings. In addition, a high-level steering group was now created. Composed of all directors-general, this "inter-service group" was chaired by the Secretary-General himself.[8] The operational level was handled by the Task Force for German Unification (TFGU) under the chairmanship of the Deputy Secretary-General, Carlo Trojan. It met for the first time on 8 May 1990.

The TFGU was not a task force in the strict sense. It did not involve permanent secondment from directorates-general and, unlike previous Commission task forces which became directorates or divisions in their own right, it had a short-term remit. The only supernumerary staff member was the secretary, recruited from a national administration specifically for the purpose. Otherwise, the members of the TFGU were officials delegated by their directors-general.

Earlier discussions in the Bangemann Group had shown several obvious areas of concern. The appropriate directorates, DGs I, II, III, XIX and XXI and the Legal Service became the permanent members of the TFGU and were required to attend all its meetings. All other directorates nominated one official to analyse the implications of adaptation to secondary legislation in specific sectors. Periodic reports to the Task Force were required. These covered the ongoing situation in the GDR, the intra-German discussions and the preparation of the transitional measures.

With negotiations on the **Staatsvertrag** now under way, the first priority of the task force was to analyse the areas of Community competence affected by the German economic, monetary and social union to be implemented on 1 July 1990. It was important for the Commission to be seen to be controlling the interim stage in which the GDR would come into the Community. This was the point of the position paper presented by the Commission on the implications of the **Staatsvertrag**.[9] The Secretary-General of the Commission, David Williamson, and his deputy, Carlo Trojan, formed a Commission delegation to Bonn where discussions with Hans Tietmeyer (Head of the West German negotiation team) on the fringes of the 'Two-Plus-Four' talks on 5 May led to several adaptations of the draft **Staatsvertrag**. It was one of several such meetings.

The Commission's communication on the **Staatsvertrag** provided an economic analysis of German economic, monetary and social union. It assessed the **Staatsvertrag**'s compatibility with Community law, highlighting immediate implications for the interim period and setting out the constraints on rapid action (such as the lack of data and the enormous workload involved). It stressed that co-operation with the Parliament would continue unabated in a new time-frame, since unification now seemed on the cards for early 1991. Proposals for transitional measures would therefore be necessary by September at the latest.

The Community legislative requirements resulting from German economic, monetary and social union were threefold.

The Commission proposed setting up a de facto customs union between the GDR and the Community with special provisions for agriculture,[10] industrial products[11] and ECSC products.[12] These proposals were made on 20 June 1990 with the intention of aligning the Community legal framework immediately after the implementation of the **Staatsvertrag** on 1 July. A further legislative proposal empowered the Commission to issue EURATOM loans for projects in the GDR.[13] The GDR was thus becoming a de facto member of the Community before unification and certainly before the Community would have time to consider all the implications and settle the transitional measures.

4. The foreshortened timescale and the need for interim measures

The Task Force continued its work until the end of July, then drafted a major submission to the Council and the Parliament.[14] It was now assumed that a "fast track" to unification would mean the Commission making its proposals by September and the inter-institutional negotiations being completed in the minimum of three months necessary for the co-operation procedure to function. Since all-German elections were foreseen for 2 December, unification and general elections would probably take place on the same day.

The Commission was asked by its President to attend a meeting on 21 August to begin consideration of the draft proposals. However, events in Germany continued to accelerate unification. In early August, the German government informed the Commission that the link between the election and unification no longer held. The 'Two-Plus-Four' talks were due to end formally on 12 September and there would thus be no legal hindrance to implementation of the **Einigungsvertrag**. Unification would therefore take place on 3 October. Consideration and ratification of the transitional measures in the new time frame was now totally excluded. Only one plenary session of the Parliament was due to be held between the presentation of the Commission package and the new unification date. The Commission therefore included in the proposals for the transitional period a set of emergency interim measures allowing it to authorise temporary implementation of the proposed transitional measures before member-state governments had had time to debate the contents.[15]

Member-state governments and the European Parliament had been presented with a fait accompli by the German government. Pressures for unification could not be held back without enormous political cost to Germany. Collapsing confidence was leading to a haemorrage of East German citizens moving to the West in search of work. Either the Community institutions accepted the Commission's proposals or the new Germany would be in immediate breach of its obligations under the treaties. There would then be a legal vacuum during the period of negotiation of the transitional measures.

Before turning to the transitional measures and the autumn negotiations, it is worth considering the unorthodox yet highly efficient process by which the Community agreed to the Commission's proposals for emergency interim measures. The European Parliament's temporary committee had begun its work long before the Commission embarked on formal preparations, and the Commission had often declared the need for collaboration. Drawing on these declarations, the Parliament requested an inter-institutional agreement to be decided by a "trialogue" between the Community's presidents. The Parliament's President, Enrique Barón Crespo, President Delors and Italian Foreign Minister Gianni De Michelis, for the Presidency in Office of the Council, met on 6 September.

The resulting inter-institutional agreement limited the validity of the emergency interim measures to the end of 1990. The Parliament agreed to hold two readings in the September plenary, on 11 and 13 September respectively. The Council agreed, in turn, to consider the Parliament's amendments and reach its common position on 12 September. The Commission's re-examined proposal would then be presented to the General Affairs Council scheduled for 17 September. This implied a 27-day period between Commission proposal and Council acceptance and left the Federal Republic and the Commission 15 days to implement the interim measures before unification on 3 October.

The agreement also covered arrangements for consideration of the transitional measures. It was settled that the Parliament's view would be both on the "whole" of the package and on the detailed proposals. This was a political agreement, which the Parliament clearly intended to replace the assent procedure valid for an accession. The Council agreed not to take a final decision on the legislative proposals until after the Parliament's second reading and committed itself to completing the first reading in time for a second parliamentary reading in November.

Three issues were of fundamental importance in institutional terms. First, the principle was established that the Parliament could consider a matter in two readings, despite a legal basis allowing only one consultative reading. Thus, it was agreed that the Parliament would have the right to examine both the parts and the whole of the package in two readings. This gave the Parliament a political view of the whole process as opposed to scrutiny of only the separate pieces of legislation. It meant that the Parliament had succeeded in approaching the question as if it were an accession.

Second, the Parliament doubted the wisdom of reserving the Council far-reaching powers. It proposed a change to the committee structure foreseen to monitor Commission execution of the policies decided. The Parliament was successful in persuading the Council to accept committee IIa as opposed to the proposed IIIa procedure (see below),[16] though it was to prove less fortunate in its attempts to repeat the exercise in the negotiations on the transitional measures.

Lastly, the Delors-Plumb procedure on information to the Parliament on Commission proposals submitted to management committees was extended. Hitherto, the practice had been for the Commission not to pass on information deemed "sensitive". The new agreement obliged the Commission to pass on all relevant information. This established a precedent allowing the Parliament later to quote the exercise as a demonstration of its responsibility and efficiency.

5. The Commission proposals and the negotiations with the Parliament and the Council

The parallels between the integration of the GDR into the Community and a "normal" accession have already been pointed out. However, a major difference was the speed of the process. The Commission's preparatory work was accomplished with only fifteen co-ordinating task force meetings. The Council negotiations were completed with the same number of meetings of the ad hoc working group set up by COREPER on 4 September. The Council of Ministers finalised the legislation on 4 December 1990. The whole negotiation process took exactly three months.

The Commission's proposals for transitional measures amounted to more than 350 pages, of which half was made up of 23 legislative proposals. The remainder was an explanatory memorandum, providing what German officials described as the best analysis of the GDR economy available.

The **Staatsvertrag** and the immediate Community measures had provided the basis for incorporating the GDR into the Community by ensuring equal treatment of Community and German firms in the GDR, establishing reciprocal free trade, the applicability of the Common Agricultural Policy, Community rules on company law, freedom of establishment, competition, VAT and customs and excise. Nevertheless, a good deal of secondary legislation still required amendment.

With the exception of the environmental legislation and certain pharmaceutical directives, where derogations were permitted until 1995, the transition period was set to end on 31 December 1992. The Commission's policy was based on three premises. First, the **acquis communautaire** should be the base line to be achieved by 1992. Second, transitional measures should only be proposed where objective legal, social or economic reasons left no alternative. Last, the derogations would be temporary and cause minimum disturbance to the functioning of the common market.

In the following analysis of the negotiations between Community institutions and member states, the essential areas of disagreement over the derogations are highlighted. The Commission's explanatory memorandum gives a succinct overall appraisal of the reasons for the derogations themselves, so further commentary is superfluous.[17]

Three questions led to extensive discussion in the Council working group. They concerned the "flexibility clause", "comitology" and the problem of "control". The same questions exercised the Parliament and were the subject of numerous amendments.

The flexibility clause

The Commission's proposals included the caveat that information was insufficient to establish the full extent of indispensable derogations. A simplified procedure was therefore proposed for two conceivable situations: adopting further derogations and adapting derogations for technical reasons. This was the so-called "flexibility clause". There was much debate in the Council working group over how much the flexibility clause might be used in the following two years to allow **additions** to the derogations or to **adapt** existing derogations.

The Commission's ideal position was to keep maximum flexibility and to be as little dependent as possible on administrative procedures and committees. The Council, naturally enough, was keen to limit the Commission's power. The Germans supported the Commission, since any resulting practical decision would clearly be taken in the German interest. However, there was a general principle at stake and the Germans would obviously toe the Council line on the question of principle.

Comitology

The question of changes to the scope of the flexibility clauses was compounded by the question of "comitology". The choice of monitoring committee in any delegation of powers to the Commission is crucial. It affects the voting procedure and even the ability of the Commission to act regardless of member-state governments' views, provided the Council of Ministers itself does not override decisions taken in committee.

The Commission had played safe in the proposals by foreseeing a committee structure conforming to model IIIa of the decision on Comitology of 1987,[18] the so-called regulatory committee. Such an arrangement maximises the opportunities for the Council to control the Commission's use of delegated powers. However, in policy areas where committees of a different kind (e.g. Committee IIa under the "Comitology Decision" or management committees) already existed, the Commission opted to use these.[19]

Thus, while the flexibility clause in the transitional measures may have been based on a **principle** of great flexibility, the choice of Committee IIIa allowed the Council tight practical control of the Commission. The Commission argued that the more stringent form had been chosen to allay the fears of member-state governments that administrative shortcuts might be taken, with potentially-negative consequences for their national interests.

When the General Affairs Council met on 22 October to discuss preliminary agreement on the Council's Common Position, the Commission and all delegations but the Spanish reached agreement on a more restrictive flexibility clause. The clause was to be limited to technical adaptations and to the addition of legislation closely connected to derogations already agreed. Several member states would only agree on condition that Committee IIIa procedures were retained in the final texts. The Spanish remained worried about the possibility of extension of the time-limits in certain cases and required an even stricter text. The Germans were willing to go along with any solution acceptable to the Commission. By this stage there was, indeed, a tacit al-

liance between the Germans and the Commission. Both were
concerned to see the measures agreed as swiftly as possible.
However, the Germans repeatedly stressed that environmental
legislation would clearly be likely to cause problems. If the time
limits could remain flexible in that one area, the German government could accept stringency elsewhere.

The comitology question had already arisen in the negotiations over the interim measures in September. For the interim
measures, the Parliament had insisted on a compromise solution
between its own preference for the advisory committee and the
Commission proposal for the regulatory committee. In fact, the
Parliament's rules of procedure made insistence on the advisory
committee for all internal-market legislation mandatory. The Parliament's view was therefore consistent with its usual policies.
This view was shared by the Commission.[20] Hence, in the negotiations over the interim measures the Commission had been obliged to backtrack under parliamentary pressure. Despite the
initial self-denying ordinance, it had been difficult for the
Commission not to support the Parliament's view. The Council
had agreed reluctantly to the compromise formula of the management committee (IIa) on condition that it set no precedent for
the transitional measures. The same proposal for compromise
reappeared in the Parliamentary amendments to the Council's
common position in November. The Commission again supported the amendment, but this time it was rejected by the Council.

At a special session of the Parliament's "enlarged bureau"
Commission Vice-President Bangemann argued cogently, as Deputy Secretary Trojan was later to argue in COREPER, that the
general public would hardly sympathise with the Community
institutions if an issue as historic as German unification were
hindered by a quarrel about committees. But whereas the compromise of a IIa committee had been possible for the interim
measures, neither the Parliament nor the Council would compromise over the transitional measures.

The Council reached a Common Position on the package on 6 November 1990. This was transmitted to the Parliament next day.[21] The package would come under review at the second November session of the Parliament between 19 and 24 November. In the meantime, the Parliament's Temporary Committee had considered a series of further amendments and voted on 12 November to propose certain of them for vote in plenary. The major sticking point was comitology and the flexibility clause.

COREPER examined the Parliament's likely amendments to the Council's Common Position on 14 November. The Parliament was suggesting a compromise proposal of Committee IIa in the areas where Committee IIIa had been proposed, namely the internal market, the environment, statistics and transport. This was flanked with an amendment, to be added throughout the legislative proposals, providing for any use of the flexibility clause raising an important question of principle to be the subject of a separate, full Commission proposal. The Parliament had made it clear that it considered the issue so crucial that the completion of the legislative process would be delayed until a satisfactory compromise were found. Since the interim measures expired on 31 December 1990, this would imply a new proposal to extend them. The Community's blessing for German unification, which had already taken place on 3 October, would thus come embarrassingly late.

However, as it had repeatedly warned, the Council intended to reject the Parliament's amendment. Last-minute negotiations now took place, aimed at avoiding a major confrontation with the Parliament and the risk of delaying the final decision. Some ground had to be given if the time-scale agreed in the inter-institutional agreement were to hold.

The Parliament voted on 21 November. As customary, the Commission then presented "re-examined" and "modified" proposals consequent to Parliamentary amendments under the co-operation and consultation procedures.[22] The Commission officially supported the Parliament's amendment providing for IIa Committees throughout the package, in the knowledge that the Council would unanimously reject the amendment. In the Parliamentary plenary Vice-President Bangemann had also declared the Commission's readiness to support the view that new derogations should fall outside the scope of the flexibility clause and be subject to completely new proposals.

The formula finally agreed between the Commission and the Parliament and endorsed by the Council allowed the flexibility clause to **amend** derogations where they had proved incomplete, but not to add new ones. If additional derogations were required, a new Commission proposal would be necessary. This would necessitate the agreement of the Council and the Parliament and remove the flexibility of a decision by committee. Thus, to sum up, there was a compromise restricting, but retaining, the flexibility clause, while there was no compromise on comitology. Committee IIIa would remain, and the Council accordingly rejected the Parliament's amendment. The flexibility clause was now considerably reduced in scope.

This seemingly-simple solution was the result of extensive bargaining between the Parliament and the Council, with the Commission acting as mediator between the two. As extraordinary as it may seem to the uninitiated, it was the one issue over which the process of integrating the former GDR into the Community might have come unstuck.

The problem of control

The third major issue was the question of how the Commission and the Germans would supervise the correct application of the transitional measures. The issue arose soon after the implementation of the interim measures in September 1990 as the detail of what member states had agreed to on a provisional basis became clear. The interim measures had consisted of a Council directive and a Council regulation.[23] These authorised the Commission to apply the transitional measures proposed in advance of the completion of the legislative process.[24]

Both measures obliged the Commission to report to the Parliament and the Council on how it intended to verify the application of EC law and ensure the proper management of EC income and expenditure. There were legitimate concerns about how the Commission and the German authorities would police an area of German territory with no physical frontiers. The run-up to the deadline on the derogations coincided with a period when the frontiers between member states themselves were destined to disappear. It would be ironic if precisely at a time of relaxation of border controls, the Community was obliged to enhance them to ensure application of EC law in the ex-GDR.

The German authorities were reluctant to introduce measures requiring stricter control procedures in Germany than in other member states. The Commission, too, was keen for specific controls not to provide precedents leading to a dilution of the progress towards a frontier-free Europe. In addition, there was a clear risk of incompatibility with Articles 30 and 34 of the EEC Treaty. The Commission set out its position on 16 October in a report to the Council and the Parliament on the measures envisaged to control the risks identified.[25] Naturally, goods conforming to Community standards were to be allowed full circulation within the Community. There were three broad categories of product liable to escape the territory of the former GDR: goods produced within the framework of the derogations, goods imported from third countries to which the same derogations on standards would apply, and goods on which Community duties would not be paid. In addition there were specific problems for agricultural products.

Member-state governments and MEPs were particularly exercised by the risk that the derogations would allow abuse. Non-standard goods might find their way to Community markets. In addition, since the derogations included the lifting of quantitative restrictions and external tariff constraints, a flood of East European goods transiting through East Germany was conceivable. The effects on markets of cheap sub-standard products either from the GDR or from CMEA countries were potentially serious.

The Commission argued that current methods of control would suffice. Technical controls at the place of production for foodstuffs or authorisation for pharmaceuticals would be the logical (and usual) complement to identification by labelling. As for imports, the "End-Use Relief Scheme" provided the framework.[26] The End-Use Regulation ensures that final consumption, or the incorporation of goods into other products acquiring Community origin, are subject to authorisation, the obligation to keep precise records, inspection and, finally, stiff penalties in the event of infringement. By requiring the German government to enhance controls already applied in the Federal Republic and reiterating member states' rights to control goods in transit and at the final point of importation, the Commission was able to satisfy the concerns of the Council and the Parliament. The Commission's acceptance of a complaints procedure allowing rapid action in cases of infringement completed the framework of controls.

The German government was therefore obliged to report to the Council and the Parliament on the implementation of the transitional measures. The question of control was to be the subject of a special session of the Parliament's Budget Committee in Potsdam on 24 June 1991. The Parliament's Temporary Committee concluded its formal work in December 1990, but was revived specifically for the purpose of following up the transitional measures.

The Commission's package of 21 August 1990 contained twenty-one specific legislative proposals. For many issues of apparent relevance at first sight, there were no negotiations since there was no question of derogating from Community legislation. Thus, for example, Community legislation was already applicable in the field of competition policy, free movement of persons and capital, financial services and public procurement.

On state aid, flexibility in the area of shipbuilding and the steel industry was proposed, but the issues were hardly contentious. Legitimate concerns of member-state governments regarding the continuation of aid to Berlin and the former frontier area between the two Germanies (**Zonenrandgebiete**) had surfaced early on in the process, and been answered by the commitment of Vice-President Sir Leon Brittan to ensure that the Germans phased out this aid in due course. In fact it took until May 1991 for negotiations with Germany on completion of the phasing-out process. Under the circumstances there has been general sympathy for the dilemma of the all-German government in a field where the business plans of large numbers of small and medium-sized firms are totally dependent on tax concessions which have been in existence for decades. The special aid schemes are now to be phased out by the end of 1993.

In most areas of Community policy, however, there was a remarkable lack of contentious issues, with the following exceptions.

Environmental policy was an area of great concern. Negotiations on environmental issues took up a good deal of time in the Council working group. The Commission argued that even the relatively-long derogation period till the end of 1995 would probably be insufficient to remedy the catastrophic environmental situation in the GDR. Nevertheless, the German authorities took the view that they would be able to fulfil their obligations under the transition arrangements and meet the timetable. Member-state governments were particularly exercised by the risk that the exclusion of new installations from the derogations would lead to abuses, owing to a lack of clarity concerning the definition of "old" and "new" plant.

The Structural Fund provisions also caused a good deal of internal debate within the Commission. It was generally agreed that the necessary data for the correct application of the structural fund principles in assessing eligibility was not available. But there was reluctance to accept blanket solutions dispensing with tight rules on the definition of eligible areas according to the objectives set out in the structural fund regulation.[27] In practice, however, the alternatives were very limited. The fears of member-state governments that sloppy application of the rules would lead to precedents were countered by the German and Commission delegations. The point was that these were extraordinary, never-to-be-repeated arrangements. There could be no question of precedent-setting. Nor was there a risk, as was feared by certain southern European Community members, that the distribution of the structural funds was a zero-sum game. The German funds voted were "additional".

The major area of negotiation concerned the former GDR's external relations. No exemptions were proposed from existing Community treaties, which therefore applied immediately upon unification. Reference was made above to the principle of **Vertrauensschutz**, or respect of legitimate expectations, in the field of trade with European CMEA countries and Yugoslavia. Using this principle, the Commission proposed the suspension of customs and anti-dumping duties on goods imported from European CMEA countries and Yugoslavia. The suspension would be valid in the first instance until the end of 1991, with a possible one-year renewal to be decided.

The principle was acceptable to member-state governments, though the question of monitoring the correct application of the derogation, as we have seen, was difficult for delegations to resolve. A practical question concerned the inclusion of anti-dumping duties in the suspension of import duties. It was argued that special conditions in this particular case could be considered a precedent by CMEA countries in other negotiations with the Community. The Commission made it clear that the suspension of anti-dumping provisions would be limited to existing anti-dumping duties. It would apply only to fixed quantities of goods listed in the proposals as being subject to trade agreements.

The details of this thorny problem were thus debated in the Council. The Commission was under pressure to give precise lists of the products concerned and the quantities likely to be involved. The matter then became further complicated by the realisation that agricultural products had accounted for a considerable proportion of the total trade between the CMEA and the GDR. Did **Vertrauensschutz** and the suspension of import duties now mean that the instruments of the Common Agricultural Policy were not to apply? In particular, would agricultural imports now be possible outside the regime of levies and price-fixing current in the Community? On the one hand the Commission had been making positive noises to successive delegations from CMEA countries expressing their concern at the possible effects on their export market in the GDR. On the other hand, it now became clear that such positive noises had not taken full account of the agricultural implications.

This was a classic case of the need for closer co-ordination at Commissioner level. The Commission was able to complete the process in a matter of days. It hurried through a modified proposal including a disclaimer on agricultural goods subject to levies, reference prices and minimum prices, where the existing rules would be maintained. The new proposal seemed to meet the concerns of the governments of member-states, though those from Mediterranean countries were keen to discover from the Commission whether there was a balance between "southern" and "northern" goods benefitting (or suffering) from new conditions of competition in the former GDR. It was at this point, however, that the Spanish delegation produced the legendary rabbit from the hat.

The Spanish were justifiably concerned at the implications for their access to the new Community market, open now to traditional imports from former East European trading partners and to all EC member states - with the exception of Spain and Portugal. Their access to Community markets in general was still subject to the limitations of a transition period applicable until the end of 1995. Until German unification Spain was able to export goods to the GDR, a non-EC country, without the imposition of import duties. Henceforth Spanish exports to the ex-GDR would attract part of the Community External Tariff (CET) and partial levies. They would be in competition with goods from CMEA countries, for which the principle of **Vertrauensschutz** was to lead to a suspension of the CET. Spain could thus plead a loss of Community preference. Under these circumstances it was unlikely that the package of transitional measures would prove acceptable.

The European Parliament, too, had spotted the inconsistency and was proposing a corresponding amendment. The Parliament had also concluded that offering a mere year's suspension of import duties would not assist the beleaguered East and Central European countries. It proposed extending the dispensation from one to two years. December 1992 rather than 1991 would thus become the cut-off date for tariff-free access.

These two issues now threatened to block the legislative process by compromising the timetable settled in the inter-institutional agreement. The Council was faced with two alternatives. Either there could be an amendment to the Treaties of Spanish and Portuguese Accession or the Council could decide to split the package by removing the external and agricultural elements and letting the Parliament consider the remainder of the package in second reading.

Two procedural commitments in the inter-institutional agreement were of relevance here: first, the agreement on timing and second, the granting to the Parliament of the right to an opinion on the whole and the parts of the package in one second reading.

The inter-institutional agreement had foreseen the completion of the Council's deliberations in time for a second reading to be completed by the second Parliamentary sitting in November 1990 at the latest. It was now the end of October. The Council could, at the earliest, settle outstanding agricultural issues at the Agricultural Council due on 5 and 6 November 1990 and give simultaneous agreement to the outstanding trade policy issues. The time was already unreasonably short for the Parliament's committees to deliberate on amendments for second reading. In addition, there was no certainty that the Agricultural Council would be able to settle these outstanding issues of German unification.

The second procedural commitment concerned splitting the package. The Commission was unwilling to envisage this and it would in any case have contradicted the "whole and the parts" commitment made to the Parliament. Once again, agriculture was proving the major difficulty in reaching Community consensus, and it would be unwise for the impression to be given that the only hindrance to the integration of the five new **Länder** into the Community was agriculture. This was all the more true since the interim period had seen upheavals in the former GDR's agriculture and there had been some abuse of the situation by Community traders anxious to benefit from cheap beef prices there.

The way out of the dilemma lay in a new proposal from the Commission under the terms of Articles 89(2) and 234(3) of the Membership Treaties for Spain and Portugal. The proposal allowed Spain and Portugal equal access to the former GDR market for the period of validity of the derogation from the CET. The General Affairs Council was thus able to settle almost all the outstanding issues, but not without a further last-minute request from the Portuguese delegation for the Community to consider anew the question of free movement of workers and the transitional period applicable to Portugal under its accession arrangements. Again, such considerations would not apply to the former GDR and justice demanded that the Community take account of this. A corresponding commitment was made for analysis in 1991.

The Council of 22 October was not in a position to finalise the Common Position on the package, since the Parliament was to vote on amendments on first reading on 24 October 1990. COREPER therefore considered the parliamentary amendments and the Commission's corresponding "modified proposal" on 25 October, and the common position was agreed in principle at the Transport Ministers' Council on 29 October. The Parliament's amendment extending the suspension of tariff measures to the end of 1992 as opposed to the end of 1991 was now accepted.

It only remained for the Agricultural Ministers on 5/6 November to settle the outstanding problems of Spanish accession and other remaining agricultural issues and the agreed timetable could be respected.

The Spanish and Portuguese governments had expressed their readiness to agree to the new Commission proposal covering their specific concerns and thus to accept the whole package of measures. However, once again, just as agreement seemed complete, a further request arrived from the Spanish and Portuguese delegations. The new Commission proposal had provided for extension of the terms offered to the CMEA countries to Spain and Portugal, i.e. continuation of tariff-free exports to the former GDR within the quantities of traditional trade flows. The Spanish now required that all products allowed duty-free entry from CMEA countries should form part of the new Spanish and Portuguese duty-free arrangements. This appeared to be more a question of principle than of real concerns about market access in specific areas. By this late stage it was in any case clear that trade flows between CMEA countries and the five new **Länder** were in steep decline, as West European products replaced those exported from the GDR's traditional trading partners. Hence, this further modification met with little resistance, and the final package was approved at the Council of Agriculture Ministers on 5/6 November.

References

1. This essay is written in a personal capacity and does not necessarily conform to the views of the Commission of the European Communities.

2. **Staatsvertrag**: State Treaty on Economic, Monetary and Social Union; **Einigungsvertrag**: Treaty of Union.

3. Article 1 of the "Treaty on the Final Settlement with Respect to Germany" requires the Federal Republic and Poland to confirm the border by treaty. Article 7 terminates the reponsibilities of the Four Powers for Berlin.

4. Or "groupe ouvert des membres de la Commission consacré à l'examen des conséquences des relations inter-allemandes pour les compétences communautaires."

5. Amongst the distinguished politicians appearing as committee members were Simone Veil, Claude Cheysson and Leo Tindemans.

6. "The Community and German unification: communication from the Commission to the Special Session of the European Council in Dublin on 28 April 1990" (SEC/90/751).

7. Analysis of the various policy areas involved can be found in the subsequent section dealing with the Council negotiations.

8. In fact, the group met on only two occasions and functioned more as a forum for a high-level exchange of information than as a steering group in the strict sense of the word. This was partly due to the rapidity with which the unification process took place and partly to the assiduous and comprehensive work undertaken by the Deputy Secretary-General in the Task Force.

9. "The Community and German unification: implications of the Staatsvertrag" (SEC 90/1138).

10. COM (90) 282.

11. COM (90) 265.

12. SEC (90) 1229.

13. SEC (90) 1076.

14. "The Community and German unification", COM (90) 400, consisted of three volumes - an explanatory memorandum, a raft of legislation and comments on financial implications.

15. A regulation and a directive were proposed. Two legal instruments were necessary, since some of the areas covered required the co-operation procedure for which only directives are applicable. The legislation was adopted by Council on 17 September 1990: Regulation 2684/90 and Directive 90/476.

16. Council Decision no 87/373 of 13 July 1987. (OJ L 197, 18.7.1987, p. 33). This has become known as the "Comitology Decision".

17. "The Community and German unification", (COM (90) 400, **op. cit.**).

18. See note 15 above.

19. "IIa" Committees are used for agriculture, fisheries, and commercial policy.

20. See, for example, the Commission's opinion of 21 October 1990 on amendments to the Treaty: "As far as delegation of powers to the Commission is concerned, efficiency demands that both the letter and the spirit of the Single European Act be fully applied in practice... The Commission takes the view that only two formulas should be allowed under the Treaty: the advisory committee and the management committee." (COM (90) 600 Final).

21. The fact that the Parliament had insisted on being allowed both a general political view on the package as a whole and a view on the specific detail of

the proposals meant that a formula had to be found for its second reading of both co-operation and consultation proposals. It was therefore agreed to refer to the two sections of the Council's first reading as a "common position" (co-operation procedure) and a "favourable view" (consultation procedure). In essence, this meant that the consultation measures were not yet decided by the Council, so that Parliamentary amendments on the second reading could still be accepted as technically first reading amendments. While there would be no obligation on the Council to seriously consider amendments on a second reading from the Parliament in the area of consultation, this meant the inter-institutional agreement could be honoured. Naturally enough, and despite warnings about the precedent-setting involved, the Parliament was to consider these extraordinary procedures as the purest of precedents. (For the Council's "common position", ref. 9532/90; for its "favourable view" - also referred to as its "sympathetic consideration" - 9533/90).

22. COM (90) 569 final dated 24 November 1990. Re-examined proposals concern the co-operation procedure (Art. 149 para 2d EEC), while modified proposals concern the consultation procedure (Art. 149 para 3 EEC).

23. Council Regulation (EEC) no. 2684/90 of 17.9.1990 (OJ L 263) and Council Directive of 17.9.1990 (OJ L 266).

24. See above, note 15.

25. Communication from the Commission, "German unification - control measures." SEC (90) 1983 Final.

26. The End-Use Regulation applies to imports of all goods under the End-Use Relief Scheme. Commission Regulation (EEC) 4142/87.

27. Council Regulation 2052 of 1988.

Part II

Political Issues

Like fire and water? Two Germanies in one

Anne-Marie Le Gloannec

On 3 October 1990, the German Democratic Republic disappeared as a state with the decision to merge it into the Federal Republic of Germany under article 23 of the latter's constitution. Demonstrators calling for reunification in the streets of East German cities, and immigrants escaping oppression to seek a better life in the West, had imposed this decision on both German governments in the previous autumn. Not only had the East German régime failed to fulfil its promises, but the state itself proved to be a fiction, a Potemkin state, long sustained by enclosure, Soviet will and Western compliance. The GDR's ruling Communist party, the SED, had claimed to create a new state, at the cost of insulating it from the rest of the world by a wall, yet the GDR never ceased to import goods, news and values from the West and to rely upon the political and financial credits bestowed by the FRG. The more insulated the East German state and society became, the more they depended on the West German state and society. The West Germans alone would provide them with goods and news from abroad; in short, they brought the world, their view of the world, to the East Germans.

As President Gorbachev decided to dismantle the Soviet empire in Europe, and as the East German authorities opened their borders, on 9 November 1989 most East Berliners and East Germans discovered the Western part of their city and their country for the first time in their life. They were struck by both similarities and differences - similarities in background and behaviour, and differences in the abundance of goods and variety of life-styles. The GDR proved to be no alternative. Soon after 9 November, East Germans started to call for unification. The **Befreiungsrevolution** turned into a **nachholende Revolution**: "Nachholen will man, was den westlichen Teil Deutschlands vom östlichen vier Jahrzehnte getrennt hat - die politisch glücklichere und ökonomisch erfolgreichere Entwicklung".[1]

The first democratic election on East German soil (18 March 1990) gave a majority to an alliance of conservative forces. This victory was interpreted as a plebiscite in favour of Chancellor Kohl and his offer of a "quick fix", i.e., an economic and monetary union (spelt out in February 1990), and a promise of unity through the incorporation of the GDR in the **Bund**, under article 23 (publicly discussed in the spring). After the opening of the borders, the Deutsche Mark rapidly became the most widely-used tender in Eastern Germany; to legalise it, however, required the establishment of a single economic system throughout Germany which, in turn, required a unification of decision-making structures and processes and the constitution of a single parliament.

Article 23 therefore provided the shortest conceivable way to political unity. While the reunification of the two German states under Article 146 of the West German constitution would have led to the creation of a new state endowed with a new constitution, incorporation meant the inclusion of the GDR in the Federal Republic, as happened with the Saarland in 1957. The East German authorities thus merely legalised the demise of their state, which effectively ceased to exist on 9 November 1989. No new successor state, therefore, to the two Germanies will be created. There will be no negotiation on a new constitution, which might have preoccupied the Germans for months, if not years to come. Nor will there be any uncertainty as to the international commitments of the new Germany. Finally, there will be no time-lag to hamper the creation of a new European architecture. Yet the new Germany will not just be a Federal Republic writ large. Indeed, the West has politically triumphed over the East, and the dream of Western Europe's founding fathers has come true: the **Kernstaat** has been enlarged to encompass the "lost" Eastern territories.

Yet as the new Germany moves eastward, it will have to absorb 16 million new citizens with a different political culture and, for a while, to grapple with the economic, political and social reconstruction of Eastern Germany and the delicate and difficult task of bringing together again what forty years of partition and estrangement have torn apart. The political and legal process of uniting the two German states has been introduced very swiftly in order to harmonise different structures and synchronise different economic, political and legal rhythms. Political unity, however, is a necessary, but not sufficient, condition to draw the two Germanies closer together. Transitions will take either more or less time - less to bring legal or administrative structures into line, and more before standards of living, ways of life and modes of thinking become similar. While this is the principal argument for a swift unification process, it is also a source of difficulties. The unification process has merely begun with the GDR's incorporation into the Federal Republic.

Who are the East Germans?

In the 1960's, after the SED had finally given up its claim to unify Germany, the first Secretary-General, Walter Ulbricht, compare the two Germanies to fire and water. Have the Germans in fact grown apart, as members of differing societies? Twenty years ago, that is, after about twenty years of Communist leadership, one of the most astute observers of East German political culture wrote:

> Man kann wohl mutmassen, die DDR-Gesellschaft würde sich für den Fall, daß die politische Verfassung und die soziale Ordnung, die ihr von ihrer politischen Führung aufgelegt worden sind, von ihr abgenommen würden, zum überwiegenden Teil und vielleicht sogar ziemlich rasch dem Lebensstil einer liberalen Industriegesellschaft annähern; es gibt genügend Anzeichen dafür, daß Leistungswille und Konsumeifer, mit dem sie sich in das Räderwerk einer solchen Gesellschaft stemmen würde, denen vergleichbar wären, die die Bundesrepublik seinerzeit zur Bestürzung ihrer Nachbarn entwickelte. Doch schiene auch für diesen Fall sicher, daß sie nicht ohne weiteres und ohne deutlich spürbaren Rest in die Geleise einer Gesellschaft diesen Typs zurückspringen würde. Was sie daran hinderte, was ihr auch ohne die Gegenwart des politischen Systems bliebe, wäre wohl ein Bodensatz von Erfahrungen und Fixierungen, von Animositäten, Vorlieben und Physiognomischem, zu-

sammengesintert in den vergangenen zwei Dezennien aus den verschie-
densten Elementen und nur mittelbar vom politischen System geprägt.[2]

In other words, the post-war generations of East Germany have
been moulded not only by the political system as they absorbed,
resisted or distorted the official and the dominant political
cultures;[3] they have also been moulded by living conditions, by
limited horizons, by the slow decay of ageing industries, and by
the continuities and discontinuities between the pre-war and
post-war eras.   While the Federal Republic turned to Western
values and culture, the GDR proved, in a sense, to be the more
conservative régime and society.   Though the SED argued that a
revolution had taken place, conservatism prevailed.   This was
nurtured by a certain isolation from international events, the slow
pace of modernisation, a marked respect for traditions inherited
from the labour movement, a paternalistic, if not authoritarian
system, and the preservation or the re-emergence of pre-modern
structures such as the **Nischen** ("niches" of entrenched authority)
described by Günter Gaus.[4]   Last but not least, conservatism was
maintained by the survival of a partly unbroken national
consciousness, exculpated by an explanation of Nazism in terms of
fascism, and fortified by the Wall as it sealed off an ethnically and
socially homogeneous group of workers and bourgeoisie.[5]
Whereas the Federal Republic's integration into the West resulted
in the overhaul of its older structures, the closing of the East
German borders solidified its geographical, economic and social
landscape.

A sense of identity may have ensued, some kind of speci-
ficity, a feeling of being different, though German, whether or not
those Germans actually supported a separate East German state.
Observers travelling to the GDR in the 1960's recalled the emer-
gence of an East German identity, which showed itself as a pride
in rebuilding this part of the country in spite of adversity. Decades of togetherness within closed borders have shaped the East
Germans of today.   Indeed, in the first weeks of the revolution of
autumn 1989, a number of East Germans recoiled from adopting
the Western system.   According to the West German weekly

Quick, 67% of East Germans favoured "socialism with a human face" while only 33% advocated the adoption of West German economic and social systems. The **Frankfurter Allgemeine Zeitung** published similar results: 25% wished to see a reformed socialist system, 32% a mixed type of system and 41% a market economy. While a partial lack of information may have accounted for these preferences, fear of novelty, freedom and competition has certainly played a role. Used to being taken care of from the cradle to the grave, a number of East Germans are not prepared to face new rules for living. While East German psychiatrists formerly reported that their patients suffered from being imprisoned in a closed state, they have recently begun to diagnose depression due to the new freedom.[6]

Yet some of those East Germans consulted in the opinion surveys may have spoken in favour of socialism for other - i.e., idealistic - reasons. Writers and artists, members of the Protestant Church and technocrats have supported a form of socialism cleansed of Stalinist distortions. In 1978, for instance, the Protestant Church concluded a kind of **compromesso storico** with the SED. Thereafter, it defined itself as a "church in socialism" (**Kirche im Sozialismus**), ready to transform the régime rather than seek its overthrow. The Church thus became the sole institution enjoying material and spiritual autonomy in the GDR. In the early 1980's, the pacifist movement could not have blossomed without the facilities provided by the Church, just as, later, the promoters of democracy resorted to its protection. Writers, too, like Stephan Hermlin, Stefan Heym, Christoph Hein, Christa Wolf and Heiner Müller expressed a desire to transform the régime into one of democratic socialism. In a country deprived of a free press and public opinion, they acted as intermediaries between East German society and its unelected government.

For all of these groups, socialism may have been the only acceptable choice, for a number of reasons. Conceived as an alternative to the FRG, the GDR was thought, above all, to have no **raison d'état** beyond socialism. As an alternative to the FRG, the GDR was also thought of as a corrective to Germany's Nazi past.

One of the more radical East German writers, Günter Kunert, who was forced to leave for the Federal Republic in 1979 because he would not strike a compromise with the SED, nevertheless explained recently that "anti-fascism", on which the SED was attempting to build the foundations of the new state, seemed "als die einzige Möglichkeit, in Deutschland einen neuen Weg zu gehen, also zu einer neuen Welt - pathetisch gesagt - zu kommen."[7]

The idea - or dream - of socialism may also have fallen on fertile political ground, enriched by Protestantism. In a pamphlet entitled **Sozialismus und Preussentum**, Oswald Spengler drew a line between Anglo-Saxon and Prussian Protestants: while the former, he said, found the value of work in the profit it brought, the latter cherished work for its own sake. This apology for austerity finds echoes in other German, sometimes illiberal, traditions: the advocacy of German **Kultur**, for example, as opposed to Western **Zivilisation**, that is, true values as opposed to technocracy. It also echoes the myth of a third way between capitalism and socialism which a few Protestants and intellectuals sought in post-war Germany. In the years preceding the 1989 revolution, Christa Wolf, Volker Braun and Heiner Müller, amongst others, nurtured a "Vision von sozialer Gerechtigkeit und Trotz gegen den reichen, zum Bevormunden neigenden Verwandten im Westen", as Günter De Bruyn, a fellow writer and one of their critics, put it.[8] Calling for an alternative to West German society, advocating softer technologies and milder markets, Volker Braun emphasised that

> wir müssen nicht die absolute Schneelinie der kapitalistischen Großproduktion erreichen... Wir sind die politische Kette los; halten wir uns nicht ans Gängelband eines falschen gesellschaftlichen Interesses, das im Kaufhaus des Westens zu haben ist. Wir kannten den Opportunismus der Macht: fürchten wir jetzt den Opportunismus der Freiheit.[9]

Yet if most East Germans yearned for some kind of socialism in the first weeks of the revolution, the opening of the GDR's borders (showing the blatant superiority of economic liberalism) and the necessity of drawing up reforms and political programmes brought a split between most of the intellectuals, writers or technocrats who had set the revolution in motion, and the bulk of the population, that is, members of the working class or bourgeoisie. Soon after 9 November 1989, demonstrators started chanting "Deutschland, einig Vaterland", and calling for reunification in the streets of Leipzig. In the 18 March 1990 elections, a majority voted for an alliance of conservative forces. A comparison of voting patterns across the century shows that those provinces of Saxony and Thuringia which had returned the highest number of Communist Party members to Parliament at the last free elections of 5 March 1933 cast their ballots in favour of the Conservatives.[10]

In other words, the working class chose reunification under the banner of Chancellor Kohl, motivated by the wish for rapid but safe change. However, as shown by the votes in favour of the Social Democrats and the PDS, the heir to the SED, not all East Germans are conservative or have discarded the dream of a socialist way. The PDS in particular obtained 16.33% of the ballots cast, a much better result than former Communist parties achieved in other Central European countries. Certainly, the party received all of the votes of its members; but in other countries, former Communists have swiftly turned to other parties or become new-born entrepreneurs. The relative popularity of the PDS may also symbolise a lingering nostalgia for a lost East German identity. At all events, it did better in areas where Protestant culture prevails, as opposed to predominantly Catholic areas, of which there are few in the former GDR.

Consistent with their conservatism, East Germans may display national - sometimes nationalistic, or even xenophobic - feelings more readily than West Germans. According to one survey, 79% of the East German population and 70% of West Germans voice their pride in being German, while one young East German out of four harbours xenophobic feelings. Fewer East Germans than West Germans appear to consider themselves European citizens.[11] The undemocratic past; the explanation of Nazism in terms of fascism, thus exculpating Germany from crimes committed in its name; the withdrawal behind borders in an ethnically-homogeneous state; the limitations imposed on travel - all these account for the "Germanness", willed or real, of East German society. Economic disruption and social turmoil might nurture these feelings for some time to come. According to recent statistics, the authorities have registered a rise in crime as well as an increase in the popularity of extremist political groups.[12] This is one of the reasons why no German government can afford to let investors ignore the Eastern part of Germany. For the years to come, the coalition in power in Bonn will have to promote the economic development of this area to counter social disorder and political disruption.

What will the new Germany look like?

With the addition of 16 million East Germans and with the excruciating task of bringing the two Germanies closer together, first and foremost economically, the new Germany will probably be more conservative than the Federal Republic has been in recent years. If present trends persist, one may even safely predict that Conservatives, Protestants, and entrepreneurs will dominate the political scene, rather than Social Democrats, Greens, Catholics, or white-collar workers. Large corporations, rather than smaller firms or trade-unions, will get the upper hand; men rather than women will shape the new Germany.

In spite of the reservations of the **Bundeskartellamt**, therefore (felt in Brussels as well), big corporations will rebuild Eastern Germany because the costs entailed, involving de-pollution and reconstruction, are enormous. Three major energy-producing and distributing companies, RWE, PreussenElektra and Bayernwerk, will rebuild the East German energy sector - though not to the exclusion of other companies. Deregulation, which has moved at a much slower pace than in Great Britain or the United States, will proceed more quickly as a result of competition over East German spoils. The three main German banks, Deutsche Bank, Dresdner Bank and Commerzbank, have already begun a fierce battle. Trade unions will have some difficulty in restoring their authority over a single country with two labour markets. As hundreds of thousands of Germans have moved from the former GDR and from Central and Eastern Europe in the past years, and as new generations have reached adulthood, the labour population has become more adaptable and more mobile, like the immigrants and upwardly-mobile Germans who, in the post-war era, helped rebuild the Federal Republic. Some analysts, like Norbert Walter from Deutsche Bank, even predict a renewed interest in new technologies. Conservatism, in short, will bring modernisation in its train. It will be akin to the kind of conservative modernisation which, in the fifties, brought about the German economic miracle. As **The Economist** recently put it: "This unification is the sort of shake-up that any prosperous 40-year-old needs to fight off middle-aged spread".[13]

The social and political turmoil will, however, be rougher than at the time of the **Kanzlerdemokratie**. West German democracy then was still partly in its infancy. Though West Germans demonstrated, sometimes loudly, against re-armament or nuclear weapons, they had not yet fully taken possession of the democratic institutions that the founding fathers had bestowed upon them. It took some years before they learnt to use extensively the Constitutional Tribunal of Karlsruhe or before they founded citizens' initiatives. As for East Germans, it took decades before they learnt democratic habits. One might add that the immigrants of the 1950's were probably more eager to integrate themselves into West German society than present-day East Germans, some of whom want to maintain some of the **Errungenschaften** of the defunct régime.

In short, socialism - or Protestantism - has tainted East German conservatism with tinges different from those of Western conservatism. The East German approach to abortion, for instance, is more liberal than the Western one, due to more liberal laws and practice and to a greater permissiveness on the part of the Protestant Churches. The debate on the abortion law, put onto the back burner by a political compromise, will probably turn out to be one of the most violent of the coming years, revealing different approaches to the role of women in German society.

Another debate, already flaring up, pertains to the status and role of Berlin versus that of Bonn. Enormous interests are at stake, public and private, economic and financial, political and ideological, practical and symbolic. On the one hand, those who plead in favour of the **Westdeutsche Lösung** - that is, of maintaining governmental institutions in Bonn - argue that Bonn will demonstrate the continued anchorage of the New Federal Republic in the West and the preservation of the federal character of the state: a small capital city, bourgeois and western, a symbol of the post-war renewal, will be the best insurance policy for all, Germans and non-Germans, who are wary of past symbols or eastern temptations. The advocates of Berlin, meanwhile, plead for a reconciliation of East and West Germans in the city which for forty years has been the **Hauptstadt im Wartestand**. Beyond economic arguments - whether one puts forward the costs of moving governments, institutions, embassies and private homes from Bonn to Berlin, or whether one hopes that Berlin will turn into a development area, promoting the economic take-off of Eastern Germany - it certainly seems necessary for the West Germans to make a step towards the East Germans and at least install the Presidency in Berlin as a link between East and West. Another solution might lend credence to one of these legends German history is rich in, in this case the legend of the **Anschluss** which some, East and West, are already propagating.[14]

The debate on the future capital city of the new state brings forth two crucial sets of issues which will be at the centre of political discussion and negotiation. The first pertains to the internal balance of the future state. Obviously, the **Länder** wish to lose as little as possible, and to gain as much as desirable, from German unity. On the face of things, moreover, federalism should increase in importance and centralism dwindle (a trend which would plead against Berlin as a capital city). Yet the game is much more intricate than it sounds at first. The addition of five more **Länder** to the existing eleven will certainly increase the might of all against central government and institutions - a reason why the **Bundesbank**, for instance, rejects an increase in the number of seats allocated to the **Länder** lest the decision-making process become more difficult. Conversely, an increase in the number of **Länder** diminishes the relative importance of each **Land**, a reason for the Bavarian CSU to worry. At the same time, Western and Eastern **Länder** do not necessarily share all interests. The Western **Länder** in particular have successfully prevented their Eastern counterparts from immediately benefiting from the redistribution of the **Umsatzsteuer**, according to the rules so far applied in the West, whereby redistribution is intended to benefit poorer **Länder**. Fierce battles over redistribution will thus take place, between **Länder** as well as between **Länder** and **Bund**, between East and West as well as between purveyors and beneficiaries of funds. The central government will have to arbitrate between these various interests. If it does so successfully, it might eventually consolidate its power; thus federalism will, paradoxically enough, further centralisation.

The second set of issues that the debate on the capital city raises pertains to the **raison d'état** and international role of the New Germany. Berlin as a capital may signal a new departure, a new understanding for the role of the new state. The new Germany, however, is both a continuation of the Federal Republic and somewhat different from it. It is not a **Provisorium** any more, a mere **Transitorium** heading towards European unity or German unification. Unified, though endowed with federal institutions, the New Germany will be a "nation-state". Moving eastwards while at the same time embedded in the European Community, will its **raison d'état** be redefined? Jürgen Habermas has expressed fears that "ein DM-Nationalismus", "eine Art wirtschaftsnationale Gesinnung das republikanische Bewusstsein überwältigt".[15]

Though nationalism has certainly overwhelmed Germany in the months following the 1989 revolution, economic reconstruction may yet absorb all energies and prevent Germans from pondering the **raison d'état** of their Republic. A number of politicians and intellectuals argue that being federal, the new Germany will not in fact be a nation-state. This, however, amounts to interpreting the concept of the nation in terms of institutions. This is not enough. Not only do institutions matter, so do values. It will therefore be necessary to think in due time about national and republican values and to endow the new national state with a republican **raison d'état**. Otherwise, as Habermas puts it, "[könnte] die nationale Frage wieder einmal in Gegensatz... zu Fragen republikanischer Geslichheit und sozialer Gerechtigkeit (geraten)".[16]

References

1. Jürgen Habermas, "Nachholende Revolution und linker Revisionsbedarf. Was heißt Sozialismus heute?" in Jürgen Habermas, **Die nachholende Revolution** (Frankfurt: Suhrkamp, 1990), p. 181.

2. Hermann Rudolph, **Die Gesellschaft der DDR - eine deutsche Möglichkeit? Anmerkungen zum Leben im anderen Deutschland** (Munich: Piper Verlag, 1972), p. 24.

3. Students of political culture generally distinguish between an official political culture, a dominant one and counter-values.

4. Günter Gaus, **Wo Deutschland liegt: eine Ortsbestimmung** (Hamburg: Hoffmann und Campe, 1983).

5. For more details, see Anne-Marie Le Gloannec, **La Nation Orpheline: Les Allemagnes en Europe** (Paris: Calmann-Lévy, 1989), chapter 1 in particular.

6. See Annegret Hofmann, "Macht die neue Freiheit krank? Wie DDR-Bürger die Wende seelisch verkraften", **Süddeutsche Zeitung,** 27 March 1990.

7. "Der ausgeträumte DDR-Traum von Antifaschismus und Solidarität. Interview mit Günter Kunert" in **Deutschland-Archiv,** 23 (2), 1990.

8. Günter de Bruyn, "Fromme Wünsche, offene Fragen", in Michael Naumann (ed.), **Die Geschichte ist offen: Hoffnung auf eine neue Republik** (Reinbek bei Hamburg: Rowohlt Verlag, 1990), p. 28.

9. Volker Braun, "Kommt Zeit, kommen Räte", in Michael Naumann (ed.), p. 18. A first version of this article was also published in **Neues Deutschland,** 8 December 1989.

10. 16,49% of the voters of the Free State of Saxony, 15,88% of the Province of Saxony and 15,28% of Thuringia cast their votes in favour of the KPD, in

Brandeburg 11,93% and 7,3% in Mecklenburg-Schwerin. On the other hand, Thuringia and Saxony were those which most decisively rejected the SED in the elections of 1, 8 and 15 September 1946: respectively only 50,50% and 53,69% as compared with 69,57% in Mecklenburg for instance. 60,2% in Thuringia and 57,7% in Saxony voted for the Alliance at the 18 March 1990 elections while only 39,3% in Mecklenburg chose the Alliance. For an interpretation of the 18 March 1990 elections, see Manfred Berger, Wolfgang G. Gibowski and Dieter Roth, "Ein Votum für die Einheit. Die Arbeiterschaft entschied sich für die Allianz", in **Die Zeit**, 23 March 1990.

11. See Günter Bannas, " **Erstaunlicher Gleichklang** bei Deutschen aus Ost und West. Umfrage des Innenministeriums in der DDR", **Frankfurter Allgemeine Zeitung,** 18 August 1990; Bernd Hannemann and Helmut Francke, "Nur vier Prozent der Bürger sind gegen die deutsche Einheit. Vor allem Bauern und Arbeiter befürchten soziale Härten - Mehr Frauen als Männer betonen die nationale Eigenseständigkeit", **Süddeutsche Zeitung,** 18/19 August 1990, and "Jeder vierte ist gegen Ausländer. Labilität des Landes als eine Ursache bezeichnet", **Süddeutsche Zeitung,** 4 April 1990.

12. As well as in motor car accidents: in the first half of 1990, an increase of 60% in motor car accidents was recorded. A number of reasons may account for this: the increase in the number of cars, the state of these cars, the lack of familiarity of the drivers with traffic, but also pressure, competition, and aggressiveness.

13. See "The spontaneous union: a survey of the new Germany", **The Economist**, 30 June 1990, p. 22.

14. See for instance Hermann Rudolph, "Abschied vom Gestern. Die Einheit verlangt den Westdeutschen auch ein neues Selbstverständnis ab", **Süddeutsche Zeitung** (Feuilleton-Beilage), 16-17 June 1990.

15. Jürgen Habermas, "Der DM-Nationalismus", **Die Zeit**, 30 March 1990, and "Nochmals: Zur Identität der Deutschen. Ein einig Volk von aufgebrachten Wirtschaftsbürgern?", in **Die nachholende Revolution, op. cit.**, pp. 205-224.

16. Jürgen Habermas, "Nochmals: zur Identität der Deutschen", p. 215.

German unification: views from Germany's neighbours

Renata Fritsch-Bournazel

For more than four decades after the Second World War, the "German question" hung in a suspended state. It signified not only the division of Germany but also that of Europe. Like all other Europeans, the Germans were directly affected by the East-West confrontation of the immediate post-war period and by the formation of the political blocs which, in the mid-1950's, led to their participation in the military alliances on either side. The clash of two politically and ideologically opposed systems on German soil, which led in 1949 to a divided Germany, accelerated the divergent development of political forces in the Eastern and Western sub-states.

On the other hand, up to the end of the 1980's, the two states in Germany were the only ones in Europe still living under the unstable system of co-operation that had arisen out of the wartime alliance against Hitler's Germany. It must be historically unique for four great powers to have jointly occupied the capital of the former aggressor, then fallen into dispute, but nevertheless kept unswervingly to their common rights as victors.

This very peculiarity of the German situation points to the continuing interest of the outside world in German affairs, illustrating the political maxim that the German question never belonged to the Germans alone. The state of the question, however, in the larger historical consciousness of Germany's neighbours and near-neighbours, has not been a new feature of the period after the Second World War. It reflects the experience of all the Central European peoples since the 19th century. The division after 1945 and the restoration of unity in the last decade of the 20th century can thus be seen in historical perspective as variants of Germany's historical link with the overall European state system embodied in German history. To that extent, the German key role in and for Europe is nothing new, and Germany's neighbours have never ceased to see their own future as indissolubly linked with that of the Germans.

Since the basic structures of post-war Europe, which seemed so firmly established, began to crumble in 1989, the question of the connection between the German question and European order has been posed in an entirely new form. At a stroke, everything that previously seemed defined, decided or devoid of prospects, now seems open and mutable again. For many years the basic presumption had been that the overcoming of the division of Germany would be realised only after the gradual growing-together of the European continent. Revolutionary change in the former GDR has reversed this temporal sequence, and, as several times previously in its history, Germany has become a catalyst for a new order in Europe. There is thus a special duty for Germans not to lose sight of European challenges because of the immense tasks presented by national unity.

New framework conditions

The restoration of German unity presupposes accord in Europe as to the political location of the Germans. As long as this was lacking, the common responsibility of the four victorious powers pursued a shadow existence. It has come alive again at a moment when the objectives stated in the Yalta "Declaration on Liberated Europe" - peace, free elections and democratic conditions - finally have a chance of being realised by all Europeans and powers involved in Europe. Accordingly, the replacement of the reserved Allied rights over "Germany as a whole" also have direct implications for the fate of Europe "as a whole".

On the eve of the anniversary of the day on which, forty-five years ago, the Potsdam Conference began, the Soviet Union definitively wrote off the Yalta system. While the first half of 1990

had still been overshadowed by Moscow's reluctance to grant
united Germany a free, autonomous decision as to its future alliance membership, the Kohl-Gorbachev meeting of 15-16 July
1990 brought clarity. It removed the last obstacle in the way of
an unambiguous tie to the West for united Germany; a tie which
the three Western powers, like the Federal Republic itself, had
previously seen as the best precondition for the establishment of
a new security architecture for Europe.

It was therefore a fundamental interest of the FRG's Western
allies not to impede the Federal Chancellor in his offer of economic assistance to the Soviet Union in exchange for Soviet acceptance of NATO membership for a united Germany. With this
insight, however, there has come a growing recognition among
neighbours and allies alike that the rapid accord between Bonn
and Moscow, which pre-empted the outcome of the Two-plus-
Four talks on external aspects of German unification, also
pointed to the growing specific weight that will accrue both to
united Germany and German-Soviet relationships in the future
Europe.

This is also the starting-point for a certain unease as to the
medium and long-term consequences of the restoration of
German unity. On the one hand, there is relief that the "German
question", so long a burden for Germany's European neighbours,
and an element of uncertainty in Europe generally, can now
largely be regarded as closed. On the other hand, the present
weakness of the Soviet Union and the resulting "Russian question" has faced Western policy-makers with a new challenge, and
one which still requires an appropriate answer.

This redistribution of political weight in Europe embodies,
in the view of French left-wing socialist (and former Defence
Minister) Jean-Pierre Chevènement, the danger of German-Soviet
collusion:

> It is henceforth certain that the Soviet Union will play a less important
> role in Central Europe than was the case in the previous half century,
> while Germany's role, in one of the seesaw movements to which Ger-
> mans and Slavs have for centuries been accustomed, will grow strongly.
> As might frequently be observed in the past, the balance of forces

between these two powers, which act expansionistically towards each other when their individual strength is too divergent, may in the next stage lead to a sort of accord.[1]

While M. Chevènement sees this as the resumption of a practice initiated at Rapallo in 1922,[2] and continuing through the Nazi-Soviet pact of 1939, and even Adenauer's trip to Moscow in 1955, other observers do not see the new conditions for German influence after the achievement of unity as a cause for concern. Thus, for instance, while the British **Economist** headed its commentary on the German-Soviet accord at Stavropol with the rather ambiguous headline "Encounter at Stavrapallo", the analysis presented was aimed more at refuting the thesis of a return to a special relationship of a Rapallo type.[3]

The overcoming of German division at a time when Moscow has ceased to be the centre of the world for its Eastern and Central European neighbours affects not only Germany's weight in Europe but the overall East-West relationship too. The post-war system in Europe may have been appropriate both for containment of the Soviet Union and for freezing the German question; the challenge now is to cope with the risks of instability arising from change in Eastern Europe, particularly in the Soviet Union. This assigns to a united Germany, as a country irreversibly tied in with the West, the task of supporting the processes of change in the whole of Europe and underpinning them economically. One American observer, R. Gerald Livingston, describes this task as follows:

> Germany's **Mittelage**, its central location in Europe, has always determined its foreign and much of its domestic policy. It becomes a huge economic and political advantage in a Europe that is no longer divided... Sharing Western liberal democratic values, irrevocably incorporated into Western institutions and possessing a dynamic economy, Germany is best equipped to win and keep Eastern Europe and Russia for the West.[4]

On the day of unity, one Berlin daily published an article by Soviet poet Yevgeny Yevtushenko, who had already made a name for himself in the Khrushchev period as a maverick and had three years earlier, in readings in the Renaissance Theatre in Berlin, provided the occasion, in a poem against the Berlin Wall, for Honecker to make a formal protest to the Soviet ambassador. In his subsequent considerations on the future of German-Soviet relationships, Yevtushenko took a position quite close to Livingston's analysis:

> The next stage will be about united Germany's spiritual reunification with the renewed Soviet Union... No-one knows better than Germans and Russians how dreadful totalitarianism is. That is why we can be prime allies in the fight against the rebirth of totalitarianism, among us and wherever it may show its face... No-one knows better than Germans and Russians that walls erected between people ultimately fall back upon those that built them.[5]

The burden of history

The West's victory in the Cold War, described by Francis Fukuyama as the "end of history",[6] could in the opinion of long-term observers of change in the international system like Pierre Hassner[7] mean more of a return to history. The possibility of the failure, in Eastern Europe, of the Western model of pluralist democracy and the capitalist economic system, and of a collapse back into military power politics, cannot for the moment be ruled out. French philosopher Bernard-Henri Lévy, for instance, warns in his "Backward Look at Socialism" against the fatal step from history to the revision of history - a warning he addresses above all to the Germans, but also to their Central and Eastern European neighbours:

> These nations have something of the Messianic. They have been assigned a mission the legitimacy of which is to be read off in the history books, that new Holy Writ... That is where you will find the German just mentioned, the reader of Fichte, who presented me as the latest product of his sleepless nights with a recounting of the historical rights of the minority in Silesia and Pomerania. And there is our little priest from Warsaw who jabbered out the theory to me, seeking, against the claims of a greater Germany, to justify a greater Poland.[8]

A return to history can also lead to the revival of clichés from an area of national psychology long regarded as outdated. An outstanding example of hackneyed conceptions of a specifically German national character was demonstrated in spring 1990 at a seminar of British and American experts on Germany, who spent a day at the British Prime Minister's country seat discussing such themes as "Who are the Germans?", "Have they changed?" and "What consequences will unification have for Europe?". The minutes of this meeting, written by Charles Powell, Mrs Thatcher's chief foreign-policy adviser, amount to a national stereotype, indeed, a caricature. There the Germans are seen as unconcerned with others' feelings, plagued by anxiety, overbearing and pushy but wanting to be loved, suffering simultaneously from inferiority and superiority complexes, wallowing in self-pity while rebelling against constraints. The Germans, the account goes on, no longer believe that Germanness will heal the world. They have no territorial claims and are no longer militaristic.

Before the Chequers talks got round to the political recommendation to be "nice to the Germans", the possibility of a repetition of history was also discussed:

> It still has to be asked how a cultured and cultivated nation has allowed itself to be brainwashed into barbarism. If it happened once, could it not happen again?... Apprehensions about Germany did not relate just to the Nazi period but to the whole post-Bismarckian era, and inevitably caused deep distrust. The way in which the Germans currently used their elbows and threw their weight about in the European Community suggested that a lot has still not changed.[9]

Presumably the publication of these minutes in July 1990 would have had less serious effects had not the then British Trade Secretary Nicholas Ridley, a few days earlier, made headlines in Europe in an interview with the Conservative weekly **The Spectator**, in which he made thoroughly provocative statements about the danger of German ascendancy in Europe. The magazine's front page, announcing "The Unsayable About the Germans", illustrated the feature with a caricature of Federal

Chancellor Kohl with a lank Hitler forelock and toothbrush moustache.[10]

Even today, neighbours' attitudes are to some extent influenced by the recollection of everything that an overweening Germany once did to them. This concern was clarified in late January 1990 by the title picture of the moderate **Economist**, publishing opinion surveys from five countries about German unification. It shows a two-headed German, with a Bavarian peasant smiling contentedly on top, but below, if you turn the picture round, a glaring, armoured Prussian militarist, with features recalling Bismarck's. The ambivalence of attitudes is emphasised by the question: "Germany Benign? Or Malign?".[11]

Yet the findings published there showed an entirely positive picture of opinion among the Federal Republic's West European allies. About three-quarters of those questioned in Britain, France and Italy were in favour of German unity. In Poland, by contrast, the only East European country in the list, the majority was exactly the opposite: three-quarters expressed concern about the prospect of the reunification of Germany.

The positive attitude of the West Europeans who have in the last forty years become partners of the Bonn democracy has also been confirmed by the latest **Eurobarometer** surveys, done twice yearly on behalf of the European Commission. In spring 1990, a clear majority of 71% in all Community member states continued to be in favour of German unification. The lowest assent rate was among Luxemburgers (52%) and Danes (56%), and the highest among Spaniards (81%) and Italians (77%), while the values for the French (66%) and the British (64%) were somewhat below the weighted average.[12]

Conceptions of an "eternal Germany" that has not changed in half a century were also firmly refuted by Czechoslovak President Václav Havel when he invited Federal President Richard von Weizsäcker to a meeting at Prague Castle on 15 March 1990, fifty-one years to the day after Hitler's invasion. In a carefully-worded speech, Havel drew a clear dividing line between the totalitarian German régime of the past and the democratic, peaceful country of the present, destined, in his conviction, to be the motor for the unity of Europe. "Despising Germans as such," said Havel, "condemning them only because they are Germans or fearing them for that alone is the same thing as being anti-Semitic."[13]

A critical mass?

Nonetheless, alongside the sporadic revival of old prejudices about a sort of permanent misconduct by Germans, there are clearly-articulated fears that a united Germany with the economic power of well-nigh 80 million people will take on an even stronger position in Europe than the Federal Republic has held in the European Community. Without this being clearly stated, there is a clear allusion here to the political weight that the economically-largest partner in integration could bring to bear on Community decisions, especially since the ultimate goal of European integration is political union.

One committed supporter of West European unification, former French Ambassador in Bonn and Moscow Henri Froment-Meurice, simply turns the argument from Germany's strength around by seeing a greater danger in a power vacuum in Central Europe: "I regard a weak Germany as more dangerous than a strong Germany. Germany must be an essential component of European strength. If it grows weak, it will at the same time become unstable. Neither a Fourth Reich nor a second Weimar Republic must be allowed to grow from the enlarged Federal Republic of Germany."[14]

The question of the acceptable size of Germany for its neighbours and near-neighbours runs like a thread through the debate on the role of Germans in Europe. This is a question put not only by others to the Germans but also by Germans to themselves. A classic formulation of the question can be found in a speech by Chancellor Kiesinger to the Bundestag on the "Day of German Unity" on 17 June 1967: "Germany, a reunited Germany, has a critical size.   It is too big to play no part in the balance of forces, and too small to keep the forces around it in balance by itself".[15]

This statement by a German politician has been cited repeatedly in recent international debate, as a sort of verdict against unity; yet it was always overlooked that Kiesinger was assuming the continuation of political structures then in place in Europe, and regarded a "growing-together of the separated parts of Germany", as part of the process of overcoming the East-West conflict, as entirely possible and desirable.   The problem of the numerical preponderance of Germany in Europe is, moreover, in the view of one French diplomat and German expert, merely a pseudo-argument intended to draw attention away from one's own weaknesses:

> As if one did not know that it has for long, in the Community and in the world, had economic preponderance; as if one were refusing to see that its political weight has steadily increased over the last decade as a consequence of its economic power but also of our own failure; as if it was to be only the newly arriving 16 million East Germans that would attain what 60 million West Germans have already done. Does this not show quite clearly that the reasons and arguments of a good part of our intelligentsia are based not on rational but on emotional logic, and on processes that are more like Freudian repression?[16]

This last remark refers to the obvious divergences between parts of the French **classe politique** and public opinion as a whole.   In a Franco-German opinion survey of mid-September 1989,[17] when television pictures from the embassies in Prague and Warsaw were making the whole anomaly of the German situation clear, almost four-fifths (79%) of Frenchmen regarded German reunification as legitimate, whereas German opinion itself, at 68% assent, lagged behind this figure.   Moreover, a telephone survey for the conservative Paris daily **Le Figaro** on 9 and 10 November 1989 showed that for 70% of Frenchmen unification of the two German states represented no obstacle to European unification, while 60% were of the opinion that German unity was a good thing for France too.

Barely a year later - more exactly two weeks before completion of unification - not much of this relaxed attitude could any longer be felt. Fear of the excessive economic power of a united Germany (62%) and, causally connected, concern at the negative effects of the European internal market on their own country (57%) seem to have gained the upper hand. Ultimately, the approaching end of Germany's division delighted only 37% of the French, while 27% of those surveyed feared disadvantages for their country; and a noteworthy 32% of the population on the other side of the Rhine greeted the unification of the two German sub-states with indifference.[18]

Domestic policy considerations and the question of their own self-image in a period of upheaval no doubt also played a part in many negative or warning opinions from the Eastern and Central European countries. The unstable economic, social and political situation in Poland, in its transition from real socialism and central economic planning to parliamentary democracy and a market economy, have certainly contributed not inconsiderably to the revival of national fears vis-à-vis the Germans, manifested, for instance, in the **Economist** opinion poll of early 1990.

In a finely-wrought speech at the congress on the Weimar constitution in September 1990, Adam Krzeminski, the cultural editor and German expert of the Polish journal **Polityka**, summarised the reactions of many of his countrymen to German unity and the resulting restriction on their freedom of movement to and from the former GDR:

> Poles' relaxed attitude does not go so far as to stop them feeling the travel restrictions on them as discriminatory. The Wall is still there in Europe - not in Berlin, but around the German Embassy in Warsaw and along the Oder and Neise... One might imagine that after 3rd October the Germans will realize that a considerable part of their problems cannot be solved by them alone, but only together with their Eastern neighbours. We need you, but you need us too, if this co-existence as neighbours is not to cause friction.[19]

Similar feelings appear to prevail in Czechoslovakia. The new Foreign Minister (former spokesman for the Charter 77 civil rights movement) warned, in an address at Harvard University in May 1990, of a shift in the European balance in favour of Germany:

> Politically, and to a certain extent in the spheres of defence and certainly in the economy too, there is an area of uncertainty, a vacuum as it is often called, opening up eastward of Germany. It will perhaps soon be filled economically by a strong, united Germany, and in view of the glaring inequalities to the disfavour of the East European countries economically, that filling could display undeniably neo-colonialist features.[20]

Mr. Dienstbier's address ended with an urgent appeal to the US to support the creation of an all-European security system, as the only way to fill the defence vacuum created by the disintegration of the existing defence system in Central and Eastern Europe. Moreover, according to the Czech Foreign Minister, only with the aid of such a system could the fears of the neighbours of a future Greater Germany be assuaged, "which they might perhaps nurture as regards the possibility of catastrophic development of that state".[21]

This position also shows the connection between the German and the Russian questions, mentioned in M. Chevènement's evocation of a possible German-Soviet agreement at the expense of their neighbours. Whether the future function of a united Germany is seen positively as that of a partner in modernisation for Eastern Europe and the Soviet Union, acting in the interest of the European Community and the Western Alliance, or negatively, as the expression of neo-colonialism and old-style power politics, it is invariably coupled with the question of the future European order.

European ties

With German unification, essential parameters of the political landscape of Europe, hitherto based on division, the status quo and opposing alliance systems, are changed. The future all-German polity must fit into the newly-emerging configuration of the Old Continent in such a way that it can be felt by its neighbours and the powers involved with Europe as a factor for stability and not for insecurity.

The geographical centre of Europe, still the heart of the military confrontation, and Germany in particular, is where the central pillars of the new security architecture will have to be erected if the whole is to stand up. This necessity at the same time assigns the European Community a central role, as the cornerstone and co-ordinating agency in the structure of relationships between European states and nations. Certainly, there are other diplomatic fora in which Germany is also represented; but no other organisation has the same degree of cohesion in structure, ambition and action.

In recent months, a clear consensus has formed that the process of regaining German unity has also to be understood as a European issue, and therefore seen in connection with European integration. Here it is important to bear in mind that it is not just since the end of the Second World War that the "German question" has become a cardinal problem for intra-European relations. For more than three centuries, there has been no period in which the condition of Germany was not formally, through treaties, or indirectly, through projection of power, a component and a precondition for the European state system. Yet it is only at the end of our century that there is a real chance for giving an answer to this question in the interests both of the Germans and of Europe.

Western Europe, in the organisational form of the European Community, is faced in the 1990's with a dual creative task for which it is only partially prepared: inclusion of the former GDR in the EC treaty system and the reshaping of its relationships with the newly-democratic states of Central and Eastern Europe. The common internal market planned for January 1993, and the management of assistance to CMEA states on the road to democratisation, assigned to the European Commission at the Paris summit of leading Western industrial nations in July 1989, continue to be important milestones in accomplishing these tasks. The joint Franco-German initiative on acceleration of European union and for a joint Community foreign and security policy in

April and December 1990 is a further encouraging sign of growing awareness of the problems ahead. If the historic opportunity
to strengthen the Europe of freedom and democracy is not to be
missed, then it is indeed time to set a course for a qualitatively-
new stage in Community policy.

In the opinion of an experienced American journalist, a
united Germany, with its federal, decentralised state system, is
particularly well prepared for the new requirements of a post-na-
tional Europe:

> Germany - the "belated nation", the political dwarf with a chronic
> identity crisis; it is Germany that is leading the trek to the future of
> Europe. Along this road, its own position could be normalised and at
> the same time a European unity emerge, as under Charlemagne, but
> now a decentralised, federative, post-national unity... In 1945 the Ger-
> mans lost their sovereignty and their national pride. They already have
> that painful loss behind them now the European Community is gaining
> in power and influence... Germany has at long last found its identity in
> Europe.[22]

The dynamics of German unification have caused the twelve
Community states to think seriously about the acceleration and
extension of European unification, so as to adjust the rates of both
processes to one another as far as possible. At the same time, as so
often in times of headlong change, a trend is emerging to regard
the nation as a sure value in the midst of unforeseen situations.
These divergent objectives make it possible to understand the
ambivalence of many responses to the affirmation by German
politicians that a "European Germany" is the real goal of unification
efforts.

In the sphere of financial and monetary policy, we already
have to deal with a "German Europe". The present European
Monetary System is so patterned that for stability it needs a
"leading currency". Weaker partners have - in part officially, in
part informally - tied their national currency to the D-mark and
more or less voluntarily take guidance from the will of the
German Bundesbank. From a French viewpoint, Alfred Grosser
opines in this connection that today the old joke from the 50's
that France wanted a German army that would at the same time

be smaller than the French one and bigger than the Russian one should be reworded as follows: "France would like a Germany economy weaker than the French one but much stronger than the Japanese one".[23]

André Fontaine, a convinced supporter of Jean Monnet's method of mutual linkage of national interests in a European framework, sees a return to this position as the sole possibility of averting a relapse into nation-state thinking: "The only policy still open to France if it is to prevent a German Europe is to support all those who - with the Chancellor and his friend Delors at their head - are pushing for a European Germany: a Germany whose sovereignty would be sufficiently restricted to make the risk that it might dominate the continent as small as possible".[24]

Of course, the desire to tie Germany down and keep checks on it has much to do with the project of European unification; but it was from the outset part of the nature of things, and was always part of the efforts at closer integration of Western Europe. Most Germans accept and support this connection between their unity and united Europe, but with an entirely positive aura. For them, Europe is a necessary alternative to the absolute dominance of the nation-state that they themselves carried **ad absurdum**. Today, however, the point is no longer fears at an eternal recurrence of past misconduct by Germany, nor even the irrational obsession with a "Fourth Reich". Instead, the point is much more the fact that a united Germany, because of its population size, economic potential and geographical position in the heart of the continent, unavoidably takes on a specific weight that is very difficult to balance out within the EC structures as presently available.

Which Europe is it to be?

The incorporation of the Federal Republic of Germany into the Western alliance system from the security viewpoint corresponded to a similar twofold objective; here too, the point was to tie down the heavyweight in the centre of the continent and at the same time remove the traditional German fear of encirclement. The post-war order that has been falling to pieces since 9 November 1989 was concerned not only to contain Soviet power but also to fence in the German question; and NATO membership for a united Germany continues this objective, though under changed conditions.

Before the USSR abandoned its resistance to the NATO solution in July 1990, Soviet diplomats and analysts had endeavoured to bring important arguments to bear against it. At a conference at the Woodrow Wilson Center in Washington in late April 1990, Viktor Shein, Director for Security Studies at the Moscow Institute for Europe, and author of several books on the Western alliance, presented his country's position at the time as follows:

> Nobody really wants to have in Europe a Germany that is unpredictable, nationalistic and - what is obviously implied - ambitious in a negative sense... In my view many of the speculations and anxieties concerning the future of united Germany are not totally valid. Is Germany going to cease to exist as a democratic country? Is membership in NATO the only way to keep it democratic?... A united Germany's participation in NATO could push events towards creating in Europe a superstructure with a possibility of including still other countries but with no place for the Soviet Union. This would amount to an exclusion of the Soviet Union from Europe.[25]

According to an opinion survey done in April 1990 in nine Soviet Republics, in spring 1990 60% of Soviet citizens were already positively disposed towards German unity, 24% rejected it, 16% had no opinion and only 11% regarded retention of Soviet troops in a united Germany as essential. These quite astonishing figures caused Andrey Kortunov of the US and Canada Institute of the Soviet Academy of Sciences to argue that German unification was all in all not a defeat for the foreign policy of Gorbachev and Shevardnadze, but an opportunity:

> But even if the Soviet role of superpower is coming to an end, Russia can become a full member of European politics, as it after all was for a full three centuries. Perhaps it will be easier for a smaller and therefore more homogeneous Russia to combine with Europe than for the huge Soviet Union. The new German opening eastwards gives Russia the

opportunity to participate in the creation of a comprehensive European Community. It would be imprudent to let that opportunity slip.[26]

This last argument addresses one of the major problems the West has to face in connection with German unification. The exclusion of parts of Eastern Europe and the Soviet Union from Western forms of economic and security co-operation, or their long-term incorporation into a network of international and supra-national mutual dependencies are, in a nutshell, the two strategies available to the West in order to cope with the changes in Germany and Eastern Europe. Union under a Western aegis is creating an entirely new situation, offering the Germans for the first time in their history the chance, as an integral part of the Western community of values, to be a bridge to the East too. The solution to the national question agreed with the four powers responsible for Germany as a whole also sweeps away the conflict of objectives between German unity and ties to the West that had weighed down Bonn's foreign policy in the period of dual statehood. The Danish security expert Ole Waever, author of a study on various concepts of Europe, felt in summer 1990 that the Germans had, in a headlong "overtaking manoeuvre on the Autobahn to German unity", left far behind them the French and the Russians with their competing plans for Europe, so that the point was now to harmonise the visions of the future of these two "losers of the post-war peace" with those of the Germans.[27]

The attempt to keep several balls simultaneously in the air and the impossibility of choosing, given the open national question, between the Atlantic, West European and Central European options, has now become reduced to the task of removing others' concern at the specific weight of a united Germany, and beyond that conveying to them the feeling and the certainty that the question of the shaping of the continent will continue to call for a joint response from Europeans.

References

1. Jean-Pierre Chevènement, speech at Institut des Hautes Etudes de Défense Nationale, 21 May 1990.

2. Only a few days after the fall of the Berlin Wall, General de Gaulle's long-time Prime Minister Michel Debré had sketched a vision of the future for Europe in which "Yalta" would be replaced by "Rapallo". See Michel Debré, "Quand Rapallo peut remplacer Yalta", **Le Monde**, 14 November 1989.

3. **The Economist**, 21 July 1990.

4. R. Gerald Livingston, "New Germany: Not Just a Bigger Federal Republic", **International Herald Tribune**, 16 July 1990.

5. Yevgeny Yevtushenko, "Das Gewicht eines Mauerstückchens", **Der Tagesspiegel**, 3 October 1990.

6. Francis Fukuyama, "The End of History", **The National Interest**, Summer 1989, pp. 3-19.

7. Pierre Hassner, "Response to Fukuyama", **The National Interest**, Summer 1989, p. 21.

8. Bernard-Henri Lévy, "Rückblick auf den Sozialismus. Mitteleuropäische Reisenotizen", **Kursbuch**, September 1990, p. 171.

9. Reprint of the minutes in **Independent on Sunday**, 15 July 1990.

10. **The Spectator**, 14 July 1990.

11. **The Economist**, 31 January 1990.

12. **Eurobarometer**, June 1990.

13. Václav Havel, speech at Prague Castle, 15 March 1990.

14. Henri Froment-Meurice, "Ein starkes Deutschland, den Nachbarn verpflichtet. Perspektiven einer europäischen Friedenordnung", **Frankfurter Allgemeine Zeitung**, 2/3 October 1990.

15. Kurt Georg Kiesinger, speech on the Day of German Unity, 17 June 1967.

16. Jean Hohwart (pseudonym), "Pour un autre regard sur les événements d'Allemagne", **Le Trimestre du Monde** 1, 1990, p. 74.

17. **Le Figaro**, 13 November 1989.

18. **Le Figaro**, 1 October 1990.

19. Adam Krzeminski, 'Was bleibt? Ein Deutschland, das keine Pranke zeigt, oder: Die Mauer ist noch immer da in Europa", **Frankfurter Rundschau**, 27 September 1990.

20. Jiri Dienstbier, speech at Harvard University, 16 May 1990.

21. **Ibid**.

22. Elizabeth Pond, "Aufbruch mit neuer Identität. Deutschland ist für das postnationale Europa gut vorbereitet", **Die Zeit,** 3 August 1990.

23. Alfred Grosser, "Es könnte doch viel schlimmer sein: Eine kritische Betrachtung aus Paris", in Ulrich Wickert (ed.), **Angst vor Deutschland** (Hamburg: Hoffmann & Campe, 1990), p.150.

24. André Fontaine, "Une Europe du possible", **Le Monde**, 6 July 1990.

25. Viktor S. Shein, "Implications of German unification for European security", in Samuel F. Wells Jr. (ed.), **The Helsinki Process and the Future of Europe** (Washington, D.C.: Wilson Center Press, 1990), pp. 95-97.

26. Andrey Kortunov, "Die Vereinigung Deutschlands: Niederlage Gorbatschows oder Sieg des neuen Denkens?" in Ulrich Wickert (ed.), **op. cit.**, p. 251.

27. Ole Waever, "Three competing Europes: German, French, Russian", **International Affairs** 66 (3), July 1990, p. 477.

Political and institutional implications for the European Community

Roger Morgan

1. Introduction

It is clear that the four-year period from 1989 to 1992 inclusive - in the EC's chronology, Jacques Delors' second term of office as President of the Commission - will go down in European history as a period of fundamental structural changes. The many changes now taking place, although they result from separate causes and proceed according to different dynamics, are inextricably linked with each other. The attempt to develop the European Community into a European Union, which was an objective of the Twelve long before the dramatic events of 1989-90, is naturally influenced by the simultaneous process of the unification of Germany - which is historically distinct in its origins and its dynamics. Further, both the Community and the German processes in turn interact with the broader and shared evolution of the military "Europes" of NATO and the Warsaw Pact into a new security system marked by greater elements of pan-European co-operation.[1]

This essay will attempt to analyse the political and institutional aspects of the interaction between, on the one hand, the European Community's further integration towards European Union, and on the other the process of the unification of the two German states. The concepts "political" and "institutional" are of course closely related: the future institutional structure of the Community (including the innovations which will result from the enlargement of its German member-state) will be shaped partly by processes of political bargaining within and between the member-states, and partly by whatever consensus may be reached as to the specific substantive policies, old and perhaps new, which these institutions are designed to "process" and to carry out.

The first thing to be noted, in relation to the interaction between the two processes of European integration and German unification, is that their respective timetables, which in 1989-90 looked for a time as if they might to some extent be synchronised, developed during 1990 according to sharply-contrasting dynamics. The process of the Community's further integration, despite the calls of some of its leaders for quick action, is inevitably a cumbersome and protracted one, involving twelve member states with a wide range of perspectives, as well as the various Community institutions, whose respective interests again are not identical. The two inter-governmental conferences scheduled for 1990-91 (one on Economic and Monetary Union, the other on institutional reform) have been preceded by a barrage of statements and counter-statements from the interested parties, and the task of reaching consensus is likely to prove a lengthy one. The results of this consensus will then have to be debated and ratified by the national parliaments of the Twelve before the reformed institutional structure can be put into place (at the precise moment, incidentally, when the internal market will in principle be completely liberalised, and when a new Commission takes office) in January 1993.

In contrast to this labyrinthine and stately procedure, it could be said that the tempo of the other process, that of German unification, accelerated, in the nine months between November 1989 and August 1990, from **allegro moderato** through **molto vivace** to **prestissimo**. When Chancellor Kohl issued his ten-point plan late in November, he proposed "confederative structures" linking the two German states, which would lead only after a long transition period to economic and political unification. In the event, the "economic, monetary and social union" of the two Germanies came into effect on 1 July, and political unification followed on 3 October, two months before the all-German parliamentary election (after much controversy concerning its date).

This acceleration of the German timetable has meant that

many of the various "scenarios" developed by the European Commission for the accommodation of the uniting Germany in the Community have been rendered not even obsolete, but still-born. The Strasbourg meeting of the European Council in December 1989 was able to consider three distinct options for the Community's relations with the GDR, all of them at that stage in principle open:

a) some form of Association Agreement with the GDR as a continuing separate state (despite the prospect that the existing inner-German trade arrangements would be subsumed in a vastly more comprehensive German economic and monetary union): the precise form of such an association could, as always in the EC, be flexibly defined, but the basic principle would clearly be that of the association of a non-member GDR with the Community;

b) the admission of the GDR as a thirteenth member-state, alongside the Federal Republic: this option, reflecting the view frequently expressed by President Delors that the GDR formed a special case among the formerly soi-disant "socialist" countries, was resisted by some member-states (especially the United Kingdom), but was perfectly thinkable;

c) the acceptance by the Community that Germany's unification would automatically bring the "new" territory of the enlarged German state into (Germany's) membership of the EC: a precedent for this was seen in the re-attachment of the Saarland to the Federal Republic in January 1957, which automatically brought the Saar territory within the (German) membership of the European Community as it existed at that time, namely the Coal and Steel Community.[2]

Much of this thinking was, however, rapidly overtaken by events, and the study produced by the Commission in April 1990, for the first of the two Dublin European Councils of the Irish Presidency,[3] already assumed that the third of these options was the one which would become reality.

By the time the second Dublin summit met in late June, only a few days before German economic, monetary and social union took effect on 1 July, it was clear that the political unification of Germany would follow within a few months, and in any case long before the institutional restructuring of the Community could be implemented or perhaps even formally debated. As the Belgian Socialist MEP Claude Desama expressed it in mid-July, the parallelism which had been expected between German unification and European integration, and which Mr Kohl had indeed promised, had become a parallelism "of variable geometry".[4]

This formula appears to have ironic undertones. The institutions of the united Germany are likely to have taken on their definitive shape long before the EC's intergovernmental conference on institutional reform, and its parliamentary sequels, produce their results. Even so, it is useful to consider some of the politico-institutional options which already figure in the Community-wide debate, since some elements of the developing European Union of the future, as they can already be discerned, will exercise an influence on the debate about Germany, however compressed its duration may be. Looking from the other side of the relationship of reciprocal influence - the more rapidly-moving process within Germany - it is also clear that developments at this level will exercise an influence on the EC debate.

2. What will "European Union" mean?

At this early stage of the current European debate, it is not possible to assess precisely what kind of "European Union" will develop during the 1990's - in other words, in what kind of European Community the citizens and the territory of the former GDR will find themselves. However, the probable general contours of the European Union are beginning to emerge, and some of them have a clear connection with the incorporation into this Union of the enlarged Germany.

As in earlier phases of the institutional debate which has characterised the European Community since its establishment - the most recent example being the debate on the European Parliament's Draft Treaty of European Union (1984), which led to the Single European Act (1986-87) - the central dialogue can be seen as one between the European institutions on the one hand (notably the Commission and the Parliament) and the governments of the member-states on the other. The former bodies, representing the European common interest of the present and its projection into the future, characteristically develop and present ambitious projects for the European institutions of the future; the national governments, composed of politicians concerned not to lose support in their national constituencies, tend on the whole to respond with reluctance to move too far from the existing status quo.

In the present case, as before, the European Parliament has put forward the most ambitious proposals. In its Martin Report (named after its rapporteur David Martin MEP, and adopted in July 1990), the Parliament called for a European Union whose four main features would be: firstly, the completion of Economic and Monetary Union; secondly, the extension of Community authority in policy areas related to the economic and monetary ones, where common action is needed to make EMU a success, such as employment and environmental policy; thirdly, the development of greater collective decision-making powers in the areas of foreign and international security policy (in other words proceeding effectively and actively with the review and intensification of the present European Political Co-operation system, which was promised in the Single European Act); and fourthly, the development of a common European citizenship to guarantee and protect the fundamental rights of all citizens of the future European Union.[5]

Although these demands are all expressed in terms of specific and concrete objectives, and avoid the grandiloquent phraseology of the Spinelli Draft Treaty which the Parliament adopted in 1984 (it has learned many lessons from that earlier experience), the Parliament's programme, as a whole, tends toward a "maximalist" project for the future. This far-reaching programme is most unlikely to be accepted **in toto** by the inter-governmental conferences of 1990-91. After the usual process of resistance on the part of some if not all of the member-states (who by definition have the last word in this conference between governments), what is likely to emerge is a diluted form of the proposals summarised above. The options chosen will probably include, concretely, some extension of the powers of the Parliament itself (an enlargement of the right of co-decision already available to it since the Single Act); perhaps a modest further development of the principle of majority-voting for certain decisions in the Council of Ministers (again, an extension of a principle already embodied in the Single Act); perhaps an up-grading of the role of the European Council, whose functions have been more latent than effective since it developed from the summits of the late 1960's and early 70's;[6] and perhaps a cautious extension of the procedures of political co-operation (EPC) towards a closer co-ordination of the foreign and security policies of the member-states.

This last point of possible development represents a long-standing problem among the Community's member-states: ever since the 1970's, when the EPC system was started, there has been permanent (and well-documented) disagreement between those who wished to see it develop into a military defence policy for Western Europe and those who - for a wide range of reasons - argued that the Community's member-states as a group should not take responsibility for this area of policy. Today, despite all the arguments put forward since the late 1980's for saying that they should now do so, and even despite the impetus given to these arguments by the Gulf crisis, there seem to be even more powerful reasons for expecting any advance toward West European security co-operation to be cautious in its approach and modest in its results.

There are in fact a number of powerful factors at work here, stemming from developments in the international situation as a whole, which are likely to tip the balance of the argument against any active promotion of a common Community-wide policy for military defence: differing points of view among the Twelve (of which their partially-divergent reactions to the Gulf crisis are only the latest example) suggest that the demarcation-line well established throughout the 1980's, whereby the EPC system limited itself to "the economic and political aspects of international security" (in other words, stopping well short of the military aspect) is almost certain to be maintained.

The existing reasons for this lack of any major change, it may be added, are likely to be reinforced by the new element under discussion here, namely the unification of Germany. Coming as it does in the context of - indeed as a result of - a massive East-West détente in Europe, the addition of the GDR's territory to the Federal Republic will be widely seen as reducing the need for military preparedness on the part of the former Eastern and Western alliance blocs in general; and the particular problems of adapting the former GDR territory to the Federal Republic's membership of NATO (a local membership without the presence of NATO troops) will certainly be a further inhibition against the addition of a military dimension to the Community.[7]

In the case of the other possible changes mentioned above - an increase in the powers of the European Parliament, an extension of majority-voting in the Council of Ministers, and an enhanced role for the European Council - the fact of German unification will again be present, though again its role will not be decisive. The main issue in relation to Germany and the European institutions is that of how far the enlarged Germany will be content to be represented, in Brussels and in Strasbourg, on the existing basis, which gave the "old" Federal Republic the same representation as France, Italy, and the United Kingdom. On the one hand, the fact of the GDR's incorporation into the Federal Republic under Article 23 of the latter's Basic Law obviates the need for any amendments to the Rome Treaty, and the Federal Government has made it clear that the "new" Germany will not ask for any institutional revision. On the other hand, the discrepancy in size between Germany and the other large member-states may create pressures for change.

The institutions where questions might arise are the Parliament, the Commission, the Council of Ministers and the Economic and Social Committee, all of which make provision for a degree of proportionality (sometimes very approximate), according to size, in their representation of the member-states. As far as the Parliament is concerned, this body itself, in the comprehensive resolution on German unification which it passed on 12 July, recommended that "the question of the representation in the European Parliament of the people of the present GDR should be resolved in the context of the revision of the relevant Treaty provisions due to take place before the next elections to the European Parliament in 1994 and such representation should be based on a balanced system in line with the structure of the Treaties".[8]

This prospective change in the representation of the voters of the member-states in the European Parliament may prove very difficult to put into practice, because of the questions it raises (what would happen, for instance, to the parliamentary representation of Luxembourg in a truly "balanced system"?). On the other hand, the way in which the 16 million people of the GDR are likely to be represented in the transitional period, by parliamentarians with observer status, can hardly be satisfactory in the long term. During 1990, indeed, the Parliament played an active part in considering the issues raised by German unification; and the Parliament itself, as Chancellor Kohl remarked during an informal meeting with MEPs, will look after its own interests as a representative assembly.

As regards the Commission, on the other hand, no increase in German representation is to be expected. The Bonn government has made it clear that it has no intention of asking for Germany's present allocation of two Commissioners to be increased, and this is absolutely understandable, not least in view of the argument which frequently recurs in the Community, that the number of Commissioners should in any case be reduced to one per member-state. (It will naturally be necessary, however, in future appointments to the staff of the Commission, to ensure that there are enough officials who can "represent" the former GDR area, or who understand its specific problems, but this question can be resolved separately).

At the level of the Council of Ministers, it could be argued that the enlarged German Republic has - as in the Parliament - a case for an increase in the weight to be given to its vote under the weighted system of the Community's treaties; but the circumstances of Germany's unification mean that, for the moment at least, Germany is not raising the issue. At the level of ministerial presence in the Council and related bodies, Bonn has been careful during the transitional stage to bring in GDR representatives at Community meetings (including the presence of East German Prime Minister de Maizière and Foreign Minister Meckel at the Dublin summit in June 1990) but such transitional arrangements obviously ceased with unity.

In the Economic and Social Committee, finally, it might be argued that the German allocation of seats should be increased, not only on the grounds that the present quota of 24 representatives cannot be expected to communicate with the greatly enlarged German territory and population, but also because of the particularly acute social and economic difficulties of the former GDR area.

3. The German *Länder* and subsidiarity

There is another issue of a political/ institutional nature where the interactions between events at the Community and the German levels may be of much greater significance, namely that of the growing role of the federal **Länder** of Germany (and, to a lesser extent, of regional authorities within other member-states) in the general development of the Community.

This question is important not only because of the essential role played in the practical implementation of EC policies by the "sub-national" units of government in member-states - most notably, of course, the Federal Republic - whose constitutions provide for them; it is also important because of the fundamental debate of principle now proceeding in the Community concerning the development of a "Europe of the regions", and of the allocation of political authority - according to the much-discussed principle of subsidiarity - at the different levels of government.[9]

Just as the principle of subsidiarity at the EC level means that the Community should only take over governmental functions when the function in question cannot be exercised effectively at the level of the member-states, so the same principle should mean that, in member-states which accept the principles of federalism, the individual provinces should only transfer upwards to the federal capital those functions which they themselves cannot effectively carry out. The principle of the priority of German **Länder** sovereignty is indeed suggested by Article 30 of the German Basic Law: "the exercise of governmental powers... shall be incumbent on the **Länder** in so far as this Basic Law does not otherwise prescribe or permit".[10]

In recent years, and especially since the entry into force of the Single Act in 1987, which was widely seen among the German **Land** governments as allowing the federal government to limit their due powers in the interest of achieving a unified German national position in EC affairs, there have been strong demands from the **Länder** for confirmation of their own right to a direct say in the formulation of Community policies.[11] These demands, pressed on the federal government from the level of the **Länder**, have been actively supported by the European Commission, which has a long tradition of fostering contacts - through its regional development policy and other means - with local and regional authorities within the member-states. The Commission President, Jacques Delors, in a working document which he presented for discussion at a conference of German **Land** Prime Ministers in Bonn in May 1988, personally called for a more active European role for the **Länder**. He said:

> I should like to mention to you the concrete areas in which the federal **Länder**, together with the Community, can actively support the process of European integration: culture, education and training, radio, televi-

sion, agricultural policy, health policy, environmental protection, food-stuffs law, transport policy, an active policy in support of small and medium-sized enterprises, an active policy for research.[12]

The **Länder** of the Federal Republic have in fact shown themselves more than willing to assert their right to a say in the development of EC policies in these and other areas. All of them have established liaison offices in Brussels for the purpose of obtaining early information about EC legislation, influencing it and benefiting from it. At the national level, the **Länder** have continued their campaign for more influence in relation to EC policies, which, as they quite rightly argue, increasingly touch on subjects where the German Basic Law clearly assigns responsibility to the **Länder** rather than the federal government.

On the level of the European Community institutions, the interest in establishing working relations with "sub-national" levels of political authority in the member-states, which has already been mentioned, is particularly strong on the part of the Parliament (one of whose current reform proposals is for a Consultative Committee of European Regional Authorities) and the Commission. The views of both bodies were summarised in a recent statement by Peter Schmidhuber, one of the two German Commissioners (the statement is of general application but has special interest when applied to Germany, not least because of Herr Schmidhuber's own firm base in the state politics of Bavaria):

> In a detailed Community charter for regionalisation the European Parliament is calling, among other things, for the regions to be given adequate powers to organise their own institutions and to promote and plan regional economic development... There is no reason why regional administrative traditions which have stood the test of time should be replaced in a politically-united Europe by the machinery of some distant and anonymous central body. By the same token, the regions must be left considerable room to manoeuvre when it comes to reducing local disadvantages or making the best possible use of local advantages.[13]

The territorial unification of Germany, and the re-establishment of the historic **Länder** in the area of the present GDR, are thus taking place at a time of substantial and growing co-operation between "Brussels" and the individual regional governments of the Community's member-states. This co-operation, while it is in principle taking place throughout the Community, takes on a particularly active form in the Federal Republic, for constitutional reasons; and it points in the direction of a particularly active role for the **Länder** of Germany in the future development of the Community.

There are several reasons why this matter will be of special interest and significance in the territory of the GDR. The newly-established or re-established **Länder** of this part of Germany will be finding their way into existence in conditions of particular difficulty and uncertainty: they will have lost the "national" institutions of the GDR and its official capital of East Berlin, and they will be component **Länder** of a very different kind of polity, namely a federal state whose government is in Bonn, even though its nominal capital is Berlin. Even if the current argument about the location of Germany's effective capital is resolved in favour of Berlin, the machinery of government will be essentially a continuation of what has been developed during the last forty years in Bonn: this will mean that the political and administrative élites of the "new" **Länder** (of Saxony, say, or of Mecklenburg-Vorpommern) will not have the same rapport with the federal ministries (or the same ease in performing their roles in the **Bundesrat**) as their counterparts in, say, Bavaria or Hamburg.[14]

The new **Land** governments and administrations of the former GDR area will thus be without any direct successor to the GDR to which they might relate, and without any of the "older" eleven **Bundesländer**'s automatic habits of co-operation with the **Bund** (fraught by elements of conflict though this co-operation has at times been). Mention of the eleven is a reminder that a partial exception to the previous statement should be made in respect of Berlin: it may be anticipated that the new **Land** to be assembled from West and East Berlin will be heavily influenced by the experience of the former, so that the considerable **acquis** of

Berlin's relationship with the institutions of the Federal Republic
can be exploited, whether the seat of the national government
stays in Bonn or moves to Berlin itself. However, the remaining
five states to be reconstituted on the former GDR's territory -
Mecklenburg-Vorpommern, Brandenburg, Saxony, Saxony-Anhalt, and Thuringia - will come into the world entirely without
any such useful heritage of close relations with the federal capital.

The relations of these **Länder** to their capital may indeed be
marked by mistrust, by a sense of deprivation, and by a burden
of demands on their part which "Bonn" (or "Berlin", as the case
may be) will not be able to satisfy. In particular their economic
expectations, reflecting the massive cost of renovating the exhausted economy of the former GDR, will be so great that disap-
pointment is almost inevitable (despite the very large budgetary
contributions which West German taxpayers are making and will
continue to make), and this will create a sense of distance for
years to come.

A second reason why the **Land** governments of the former
GDR area are likely to feel frustrated is that their counterparts in
the existing **Länder** of the Federal Republic appear to have dis-
criminated against them constitutionally, by limiting their weight
in national political decisions. It was reported late in August
1990 that the Federal Republic's **Bundesrat** had hurriedly voted
to change the weighting of the votes of the less populated **Länder**
in the chamber, principally in order, it appeared, to prevent the
five "new" states from exercising a blocking minority, and to
guarantee the five largest states (all of them in the old Federal
Republic) the option, by acting together, of vetoing any amendments to the Basic Law of which they might disapprove. If the
changes voted by the **Bundesrat** are put into practice, their two
main effects will be: firstly, that the five "ex-GDR" **Länder** (not
counting Berlin), which are together allocated 21 **Bundesrat** votes
out of the total of 79, will have no chance of acting as a blocking
minority on legislation (this would require 27 votes, so even the
21 plus the 5 votes of Berlin would be insufficient); and secondly,

that the four biggest states in West Germany (North Rhine-West-phalia, Bavaria, Baden-Württemberg, and Lower Saxony), now having 29 votes between them, will be able to block not only legislation but also amendments unwelcome (to themselves) to the Basic Law.[15]

Even though the leaders of the "new" **Länder** would certainly accept that their **Bundesrat** representation should be smaller than that of their big Western counterparts (the entire population of the GDR, at the time of unification, is approximately equal to that of the state of North Rhine-Westphalia), there is no doubt that they will resent the way in which the changes were so hastily adopted by the Western **Länder**, with the clear aim of preserving the existing power-relationships. It can be confidently predicted that this manoeuvre by the **Bundesrat** will add to the sense of alienation from Germany's national institutions on the part of the "new" **Länder**, and increase their propensity to look outside Germany to the European Community for support. This tendency will be strengthened by the action of the West German **Länder** in refusing, during the negotiation of the German-German State Treaty, to accept any financial commitments towards the former GDR area. The West German **Länder**, in other words, are asserting their interests with growing vigour, and the "new" **Länder** to the East will certainly do the same.

A third dimension in the ex-GDR's sense of distance from "Bonn" is related both to the area's economic deprivation and to its sense of political victimisation (both in such institutional matters as the one just mentioned, and in the general perception that during 1990 the GDR was being used for electoral purposes by the competing West German parties). One of the significant differences between the political culture of the former GDR and that of West Germany is the much more marked presence of the "social" dimension of the concept of "social market economy". The clear victory of the CDU over the SPD in the GDR's first free election on 18 March 1990 (repeated in **Land** elections on 14 October and in the all-German parliamentary election on 2 December) was due only in part to the promises of the CDU Chancellor

Kohl that unification would guarantee a better future for all: another important factor was that the CDU of the GDR heavily stressed the "social" dimension of Christian Democratic policies, in such vital matters as the security and conditions of employment, housing policy, and public-welfare provision of all kinds. Not at all surprisingly, in view of the previous experience and current insecurity of the former GDR's population, these issues are of great importance there, and play a large part in the CDU's popularity. As a well-informed observer of the GDR has put it: "If it is said that Helmut Kohl is the "political grandchild of Konrad Adenauer", then a personality like... Lothar de Maizière, who supports both a legal right to employment and to adequate housing, comes much closer to the socially-conscious traditions of Adenauer's greatest competitor, Jakob Kaiser".[16]

The strength of such a political approach (reminiscent of the early CDU's Ahlen Programme of 1947) will continue to set the political culture of the former GDR area apart from the prevailing West German consensus. In the CDU, it has been confirmed by the election of Professor Kurt Biedenkopf, a representative of the "left" of the CDU in the Federal Republic, as Prime Minister of Saxony.

It should again be emphasised that these aspirations, and others, on the part of the ex-GDR voters, will be expressed essentially at the level of their **Land** governments (the **Bundestag** they shared in electing in December 1990 will be much more remote from them), and that these governments will thus have a further incentive for turning to the European Community for both economic and "social" support. The Europe which is significant for the people of the former GDR is in part an economic and financial Europe, but it is above all the Europe of the Social Charter, which - in the thinking of Jacques Delors and its other promoters - derives from the same kind of Christian social doctrine as the programme of Lothar de Maizière's or Kurt Biedenkopf's CDU.

Even before the formal establishment of the "new" **Länder**, their unofficial representatives have been, quite understandably, preparing the way for their future relationships with the European Community. These emissaries have been visiting the Community's institutions in Brussels, and have been studying at first hand - in Munich, Stuttgart, and Hamburg - how the Western **Länder** manage their relations with the EC: the normal arrangement in Western **Land** governments, by which the same minister is responsible for European and for federal German affairs (in itself a significant combination of offices) is likely to be adopted in the East as well.

Meanwhile, it still remains to be seen how exactly the administrative staff of the "new" **Länder** will be recruited: as noted above, some of them will no doubt be found at a lower level of local government, the GDR's fifteen **Bezirk** administrations, and a few will no doubt be transferred from the defunct ministries of East Berlin, but certain key posts will have to be filled by experienced officials from the West German **Länder**. (Many of these, indeed, are already acting as advisors in the ex-GDR.) The need for this transfer of expertise from the West is clear when one considers the gaps in public administration which need to be filled: the GDR has not had, for instance, a ministry for environmental protection, and the expertise needed to manage value-added tax (hitherto unknown in the GDR) or the Common Agricultural Policy is totally lacking - not to mention any experience relevant to the running of the new **Land** banks which will have a central role in the financial system of the new Germany.

To handle all these areas of public policy and others - let us recall the list of **Land** government functions given in the statement by Jacques Delors, cited earlier - new political and administrative structures will emerge in the "new" **Länder**. They will naturally be heavily dependent on West German experience and support, but they will also - like the West German **Länder** themselves - have an increasingly important European dimension which will make the relationships between the EC institutions, the German national capital, and the **Länder** of Germany more intense, more complex, and more fruitful.

4. Conclusion

Among the political and institutional options which were presented in 1989 by the prospect of German unification, certain choices - for instance the association of the GDR with the EC, or its membership of the Community as a separate member state - have already been eliminated by the rapid march of events: the **Länder** of the GDR area will join the EC as component parts of the Federal Republic.

In certain policy-areas where choices are still open - for instance the form and degree of further integration of the Community, or its development into a Defence Community - we can observe that the factor of German unification plays a certain role: for instance, implying adjustments in the representation of Germany in some Community institutions, and probably acting, together with many other factors, to slow down any development of military co-operation between the Twelve.

In another connection, however - in the context of the campaign by West Germany's "old" **Länder** to gain greater control over policy-making - the creation of the five "new" **Länder** will give a powerful impetus to existing pressures for a more decentralised European Community. The attempt to construct a Europe of this kind, giving greater weight to the principles of regional responsibility and subsidiarity within member-states, as well as between them and the EC institutions, promises to be one of the most interesting and challenging developments of the 1990's. The process will have its dynamic centre in Germany, but its effects will be felt throughout the Community.

References

1. Some of these connections are explored in my article "Germany in Europe", **Washington Quarterly** 13 (4), Autumn 1990, pp. 147-57.

2. See Gerd Langguth, "Die Deutsche Frage und die Europäische Gemeinschaft", in **Aus Politik und Zeitgeschichte, Beilage zur Wochtenzeitung Das Parlament**, No. B 29/90, 13 July 1990.

3. Commission of the European Communities, "The Community and German unification" (Communication from the Commission), SEC (90) 751 final, Brussels, 20 April 1990.

4. Agence Europe, **Bulletin Quotidien** , No. 5296, 14 July, 1990.

5. Parlement Européen, Doc. A3-166/90, 11 July 1990.

6. See Juliet Lodge in Juliet Lodge (ed.), **The European Community and the Challenge of the Future** (London: Pinter, 1989), pp. 48-50.

7. The effects of unification on Germany's position in the WEU will also, of course, be complex, but here they can only be noted in passing.

8. European Parliament, Doc. A3-183/90/PART A, 9 July 1990 (para. 76).

9. See Caroline Bray and Roger Morgan, **The European Community and Central-Local Government Relations** (London: Economic and Social Research Council, 1985), for the background.

10. Quoted in Marc Wilke and Helen Wallace, **Subsidiarity: Approaches to Power-Sharing in the European Community** (London: Royal Institute of International Affairs, 1990).

11. See Wolfgang Renzch, "Deutsche Länder und Europäische Integration", in **Aus Politik und Zeitgeschichte**, Beilage zur Wochenzeitung **Das Parlament**, No. B 28/90, 6 July 1990, and further sources quoted there.

12. Text in **Europa-Archiv**, Bonn, Vol. 43, No. 12, (1988), pp. D340-343.

13. Peter M. Schmidhuber, "Regionalism and federalism in the Community's process of integration", in **Target 92**, Commission of the European Communities, July 1990, p. 1.

14. This will certainly be the case for the great majority of the officials of the "new **Länder**", even if, as seems likely, certain key posts in the early stages are in the hands of West German officials "on loan" to reinforce and guide the staffs recruited from the GDR's local administration, or - probably only to a small extent - from the disbanded ministries of East Berlin.

15. See **Der Spiegel**, 27 August 1990, pp. 28-29, and **Die Zeit**, 31 August 1990, p. 2.

16. A. James McAdams, "Towards a new Germany? Problems of unification" in **Government and Opposition** 25 (3), summer 1990, p. 315.

European security after German unification

Wolfgang Heisenberg

1. German unity in a process of security-policy change

The belief that the existing European security system has collapsed with the political changes in Eastern Europe, and that we ought now to set about creating a new one in line with political realities, belongs, like the metaphor of Europe's "security architecture", among the commonplaces of political rhetoric that call for clarification.

Firstly, there is no doubt that the institutions and strategies which have broadly determined European governments' security policies since the Second World War are in need of renewal. Not only the two military alliance systems in East and West, but also political and military thinking in their member states, was until the mid-1980's determined by the perception of an unbridgeable ideological and power-political conflict between East and West. The division both of Europe and of Germany appeared integral to that conflict of views. What, therefore, has changed?

The grave problems of the Soviet economy and the Soviet government's more liberal foreign policy under Mikhail Gorbachev's leadership, aimed at underpinning economic reforms, have led with amazing speed to the political collapse and break-up of the Soviet empire in Eastern Europe. The East European states have not exactly been transformed overnight into Western democracies with market-economies, yet practically all their governments have since embarked on the road towards liberalising their political systems, economic reforms and a loosening of their ties to the Soviet Union. Most are aiming at close economic and political relationships with the European Community. This has not yet fully eliminated the division of Europe, but it has certainly eliminated the dogma of that division's insuperability.

In the security sphere, these developments, along with a (till recently) very active Soviet disarmament policy, have contributed to the abolition of Western images of the Soviet foe. Though there has not yet been a drastic reduction in Soviet military potential, the Soviet Union is, rightly or wrongly, no longer perceived by broad sections of the Western public as a serious threat. This has removed one central element of the East-West conflict.

Changing threat-perceptions

The question of a military threat, therefore, on which all security analysis should be based, cannot be answered today for Western Europe as easily as before the mid-1980's. Nobody doubts that political revolutions such as those we are currently witnessing in the Soviet Union and large parts of Europe are always associated with security risks. The difference is that these risks are now much harder to specify in detail.

First, there is an obvious danger that the revival of ethnic conflicts in Central and Eastern Europe can develop security dimensions. These conflicts may be exacerbated by lack of economic development. The current instability of Yugoslavia provides an example of what might happen in Central and Eastern Europe, where the political revolution was triggered by the reform movement in the Soviet Union under Mikhail Gorbachev's leadership. This movement has, up to now, led to liberalisation in many areas of Soviet society, but also to considerable economic and political problems. Today, the disintegration of the country cannot be excluded. The dangers associated with such a development are, first and foremost, an internal Soviet problem. However, developments are conceivable which could also involve military risks for other countries in Europe. In this context, one could imagine a seizure of power in the Soviet Union by the military, and an attempt to draw attention away from internal political and economic problems by a re-establishment of the Soviet empire in Eastern Europe. Also, one could conceive of civil-war type situations, which could expand to the neighbouring European countries. Although at present only few Soviet experts regard such scenarios as realistic, they are realistic enough to be taken into account in any European threat analysis.

Second, as the Gulf crisis has reminded us, global economic interdependence may also imply threats to European security from other, less familiar regions of the world. Indeed, in the long run, military threats are likely primarily to emerge via Europe's relations with less-developed countries, particularly if these countries make an attempt to compensate for their economic weakness by the accumulation of military power and possession of weapons of mass destruction.

Third, the destruction of the environment through the actions of the industrialised world may involve security risks as well.

German reunification and European threat-perceptions

It is also true that in some European societies the reunification of Germany is still perceived as a dangerous event. There are arguments both for and against this reaction. The collapse of the GDR's political system was a predictable consequence of the political revolution in Europe. The wave of emigrants from the GDR, triggered by the dismantling of divisions in Europe, accelerated economic decline in East Germany and determined the speed of the German-German unification process. In East Germany, priority was given to democratic reforms rather than German unification, while the Federal Republic's government also assumed a slow rapprochement between the two parts of Germany.[1] German unity is, therefore, an inseparable part of the political revolution in Europe as a whole, i.e. an expression of a new growing-together of the two parts of Europe, and an indication that this process can no longer be reversed.

It cannot be denied, however, that German unity also has its own security implications. The restoration of German unity has reawakened fears in neighbouring countries that an over-strong Germany might fall back into old dreams of a great power and upset the delicate balance of the European post-war order. Therefore, many European politicians of a generation which grew up under the cloud of the Second World War see German unity itself as a security risk. Even those who regard these fears as unrealistic argue that, in conjunction with possible reactions within Germany, they could easily evolve into a self-fulfilling prophecy.

The agreement between the two German governments and the four victorious powers of the Second World War in Europe, on the final regulation of the German question,[2] concerns primarily the suspension of the rights and duties of those four powers, held since the time of the post-war occupation of Germany, as well as some other international aspects of German unification. It also, however, has security implications, since it attempts, by confirming the final German borders, German renunciation of weapons of mass destruction, the continuation in force of the Non-Proliferation treaty for all of Germany, and reductions in German military forces, to minimise the political risks which may be associated with German unity.

At the same time, the restoration of German unity has borne out the conviction of neighbouring countries that the possible dangers of German unity can best be removed by a deepening and broadening of the European integration process, while maintaining the existing transatlantic ties. The European Commission under Jaques Delors' leadership was the first to recognise this chance to accelerate the European unification process and therefore supported German reunification from the time when the decline of the GDR began to appear irreversible.

Of the two alliance systems, East and West, only NATO remains in existence. The Warsaw Pact has, with the collapse of the Soviet empire in Eastern Europe, lost most of its military functions and has been formally abandoned as a military alliance. It may nevertheless remain a political instrument, particularly in the area of arms-control. Meanwhile, there continue to be great differences between the economic systems in the former socialist countries and the western democracies of Europe. Even the Hungarian economy, which was already attracting attention some years ago with its introduction of market-oriented procedures, is at present still far removed from a market economy by Western standards. Most politicians in the EC therefore take the view, for economic reasons, that full membership of the European Community for the former socialist countries will not be possible in the near future, even if it is regarded as desirable for political reasons.

A glance at the literature in the field of international security, finally, shows the extent to which the thinking, particularly of experts, is still determined by the perceptions and thought-patterns of the East-West conflict. Even authors basically convinced of the need for a "rethink" frequently tend to base their assessments on concepts that betray their origin in the Cold War. Military planning is particularly largely determined by the East-West perspective, even if the concept of threat has since been replaced by that of risk.

The political revolutions of 1989, therefore, largely removed the ideological and power-political division of Europe and put the two German states on the road to reunification; but the political structures of the post-war period, of the Cold War, are still for the moment operative. They still overwhelmingly determine military planning and large areas of political practice. The new thing about the present political situation lies in the fact that their ultimate demise is in sight, and they are predominantly regarded only as a fall-back, as insurance in a period of transition to new structures.

Nevertheless, it is misleading to speak of a security architecture, still less a new security system, for Europe. Future security arrangements in Europe are not going to leap off the drawing-board, any more than the political changes in Eastern Europe were the outcome of rational planning. There are far too many competing models, with no consensus as to the selection procedure or the jury that is to make the selection.

Everything therefore points to the fact that Europe's future security structures will be far more complex and differentiated, and less ordered, than in the bipolar system that has obtained hitherto. The "old" security policy of the two military alliances will probably be increasingly overlaid by new "approaches", rather than replaced by them. Among these new approaches will presumably be limited co-operation between the alliances, particularly in the area of arms-control; a strengthening of the CSCE process and a detachment of the arms-control process from the existing alliance structure; a growing security-policy function for the European Community; and perhaps closer co-operation between, and a special security status for, some Central European states.

2. The future of NATO

In response to the extent and rate of political change in Europe, the conviction has spread among European political elites, even in some of the members of the Warsaw Pact, that NATO must for the moment be retained as a stabilising force in Europe. Consent to the Western alliance at present reaches far beyond the boundaries of specific political groupings.

Beyond that basic conviction, though, opinions diverge widely. Many conservatives tend to ascribe to the alliance a stabilising, peace-conserving function extending beyond the context of East-West conflict.[3] They therefore want to keep it alive as long as possible, irrespective of further political developments in Europe, and confine internal reforms to the necessary minimum.

By contrast, many left-wing and liberal groups see NATO as only a transitional solution, to be replaced as soon as possible by an all-European security system. NATO's stabilising function during the Cold War is not disputed; but these politicians hold that with the elimination of the conflict with the East, **both** alliances have largely lost their functions.

Alongside these positions there is a huge number of proposals for redesigning the Western alliance. Many of these go well beyond evolutionary "reform", in particular proposals to transform the alliance into a primarily political institution, or to give it an "all-European" character by incorporating into it the East European states or even the Soviet Union.

However, even those who continue to assess the security of Europe from the perspective of the East-West conflict and regard the Soviet Union as an "objective" military risk factor do not dispute the need for far-reaching reforms. They admit that the withdrawal of Soviet troops from Eastern Europe, the disintegration of the Warsaw Pact, and German reunification have clearly shifted the balance of power in Central Europe in favour of NATO. Even without taking account of Soviet intentions and of the political situation in Europe, some Western military experts accept as a fact that the Soviet offensive capacity has been significantly reduced and will fall further because of German reunification. A reduction in the size and combat-readiness of NATO forces is therefore regarded as possible even without arms-control. Additionally, in line with the CFE agreement, efforts are being made towards lighter armament with increased mobility.

Finally, the unification of the two German states is also compelling a rethinking of the composition of Western armed forces and defence strategies. Here there are at least four different overlapping themes.

Firstly, for both political and military reasons, the hitherto one-sided eastward orientation of Western forces should be abolished.

Secondly, the concentration of forces and defence installations close to the former inner-German border on the territory of the Federal Republic, in accordance with the principle of forward defence, has been rendered both politically and militarily obsolete by the unification of the two German states and the withdrawal of Soviet troops from Eastern Europe, and must therefore be eliminated.

Thirdly, the existing deployment of NATO forces in the Federal Republic is visibly derived from the period of Germany's military occupation after the war. Since reunification is intended also to bring the removal of all the Federal Republic's restrictions on sovereignty, the vestiges of the occupation period seen in the location of Western forces must also be removed.

Fourthly, the military drawbacks of the existing deployment of NATO troops - known in the jargon as the "layer-cake" (mainly problems of division of tasks and weapon standardisation) - should be reduced. But here the integration of NATO forces at lower levels too should be upheld. In this context, discussions are going on within NATO on increased deployment of multinational units and various concepts of in-depth defence.

In the area of defence strategy, at least the principles perceived by the East European countries as particularly threatening and aggressive should be changed. These include notably the concepts of hitting the Soviet air forces at their ground bases ("offensive counter-air") and attacking follow-up units of the Soviet army in Eastern Europe ("follow-on forces attack") as well as the directives on use of nuclear weapons, which allow "first use". The expected withdrawal of a large number of the American troops will in any case partly remove the basis underlying these concepts.

Even a few years ago, all these plans would have seemed Utopian. Today, they are more like the minimum of the changes that have become necessary. They are in any case still overwhelmingly determined by the perspective of the East-West confrontation. Any attempt to orient Western defence planning consistently towards risks **outside** the East-West relationship would require much more extensive changes. The planning of these changes would involve tasks of strategic restructuring and military planning in Europe on a scale comparable with those thrown up by the development of nuclear weapons in the late 1940's and the 1950's.[4]

NATO itself has announced that in future it will be increasingly concerned with political problems. US Secretary of State

Baker proposed in 1990 that the organisation should concentrate on co-ordinating the verification tasks arising in connection with European arms-control, and contribute to developing a common Western position on regional conflicts and arms proliferation in the Third World, thus helping to shape political and economic relations with the East. This proposal also met with a favourable response in Europe. NATO's London Declaration of July 1990 has testified to further progress in this direction and emphasised, in the first place, the dismantling of the now-obsolete East-West opposition and the reform of NATO strategy.

On the academic side, there are further proposals to abandon the integrated military part of the alliance entirely and return to the North Atlantic Pact of 1949,[5] or to transform the alliance into an all-European institution by taking in East European states.

Since NATO's defence tasks have lost significance with the decline of the traditional Soviet threat, the idea suggests itself that the alliance should bring its political functions more to the fore, especially since, after the Harmel decisions, these were always regarded as "equal-rated" parts of NATO's tasks. These political tasks have included, in the first place, arms-control. Other political tasks, while also considered, have never attained comparable importance. Since the substantive issues of military planning and of arms-control are very closely intermeshed, enhanced activity by NATO in the area of arms-control would be "technically right".

To date, however, arms-control has been regarded in the NATO countries as primarily a foreign-policy matter, internationally co-ordinated not exclusively in the NATO framework, but sometimes also bilaterally or even - in some cases - at West European level. There is therefore a danger that a stronger role for NATO in Western arms-control policy would be regarded among the public and by East European governments as a form of militarisation or - because of the still dominant role of the US in the Western alliance - as the Americanisation of arms-control, and for that reason rejected.

Despite the objective arguments in favour of NATO, the Western alliance will not find it easy even in this area to assert its interests against those of other "competing" institutions like the CSCE, the WEU or the European Community. There seems to be broad agreement that with the transition to phase two of the CFE negotiations, responsibilities will be transferred from the Alliances to the CSCE. In other non-military spheres, like those of economic and environmental policy, NATO's chances are even slighter.

The politicisation of NATO can, therefore, succeed at best if the Alliance manages to detach its work to a far greater extent than previously from the classical East-West perspective and from the overwhelming influence of the United States, and also make that visible externally. In this context, the London Declaration was a first step in the right direction. In particular, the admission of diplomatic representations from former Warsaw Pact countries to NATO, to which most of these countries have reacted very quickly, can contribute to the dismantling of mutual images of foes. Only once this process of "rethinking" is sufficiently far advanced should any enlargement of NATO to be thought of. Bringing in the Soviet Union or other East European states wou. of course be the most striking expression of a reform of the Western alliance, but it is not a suitable way of bringing about that reform.

A basic change in the function of the Western alliance would certainly not be impossible, but presumably requires more time than is at present available. But experience tends to suggest that big international organisations, particularly when they have long been successful, develop a considerable inertial force. While it is true that NATO was always more than just a defence alliance, common defence was unquestionably always in the foreground. This primary function has since taken firm root in NATO's organisation, its communication structures and, not least, in the minds of its personnel. Changes going beyond political declarations will therefore take time, and at present even their general direction cannot be reliably predicted.

NATO's capacity for obstinacy will therefore probably impose limits on the "politicisation" of the Western alliance, at least outside the sphere of arms-control. In this connection one must also ask whether further politicisation of NATO is actually necessary. Certainly, it looks at present as if NATO's former defence tasks will continue to lose significance. But this by no means eliminates the military tasks: even if the military defence of Europe is losing its present relative position, in many regions of the world military power will probably continue for some time to remain the "leading currency" of international politics. Recent developments in the Middle East confirm this, and even in Europe, at least the symbolic use of military power will continue to be significant.[6] In these circumstances, it will be neither possible nor desirable to make defence in Europe a primarily national task again.

Over and above this, the need for military analysis and planning has been sharply increased by the political changes in Europe. Although this has to do with tasks that should also be tackled at the national level and in the academic sphere, the Western alliance could in this process of policy-reorientation play an important co-ordinating role. Here, though, NATO ought to co-operate closely with East European states, including the Soviet Union, as in the area of arms-control.

3. Elements of common security in Europe

"Collective" security in Europe has been negotiated since the late 1960's in the framework of the CSCE, and all the indications are that the importance of this forum will continue to increase. The European conventional arms-control negotiations (CFE) are formally part of this process, although they have hitherto been taken over, to all intents and purposes, by the two alliances. This discrepancy reflects the academic dispute as to the possible contribution of arms-control to "collective" security in Europe. The new critics of arms-control assume that with the removal of the threat and the reduction of East-West conflict in Europe, the existing forms of arms-control have also become obsolete. For them, the ongoing negotiations serve primarily to maintain the old structures of confrontation and slow down the process of disarmament, which would go much faster unilaterally. Proponents of "traditional" arms-control, meanwhile, point to the contribution it can make to "collective" security in Europe.

It would exceed the bounds of the considerations being presented here to set out in detail the present state of negotiations and the effects on European security of the emerging CFE agreements. Positions on this have been adequately presented in the relevant literature. In connection with German reunification, however, some more general political questions are to the fore, as follows.

The end of the East-West confrontation is facing the European arms-control negotiations with heavy conceptual problems. Even now, it is clear that in some Warsaw Pact states (particularly Hungary and Poland), there is a preference for a security policy independent of the alliances. This would not only call into question the balance of military force in Europe as defined in the existing negotiations, but raise the more general question of whether the idea of a balance of forces between East and West constitutes a suitable basis for arms-control talks in Europe in future (for the planned second stage of the CFE talks), and if not, what criteria might replace it.

Additionally, the European arms-control negotiations have always, since the war, been bound up very closely with the German question. It is therefore to be expected that the restoration of German unity will decisively affect the course of negotiations and the interests of the participants. The old idea that military stability in Europe above all required some control over the military potential of the Federal Republic (and/or the Soviet Union) may reappear, applied to the whole of Germany, within some European governments. In the past, the governments of the FRG has always rejected such a "singularisation". In future, however, the very much more ambitious goal of guaranteeing a balanced relationship of forces between the major European "powers" (and to some extent between the superpowers operating from outside too) could grow in importance.

It certainly seems entirely reasonable in the short term to alleviate the historical fears of Germany's European neighbours, revived by unification of the two German states, through German arms restrictions, as agreed in the 'Two-Plus-Four" negotiations. This could even put the Bonn government in a position to employ savings on defence expenditure to offset the economic problems arising from the incorporation of the GDR.

On a longer view, however, difficult problems can arise for arms-control from restrictions on German military forces. If the CFE negotiations - in line with the actual threat-perceptions of some European governments - concentrate on such measures, there could be a dangerous upswing of nationalistic reactions domestically, leading to increasing fears outside Germany. Despite the very slight political importance of right-wing radicalism in the former Federal Republic, the danger persists that external discrimination against Germany could lead to nationalistic reactions in the country.[7] Such reactions could easily escalate into a process that would ultimately lead again to Germany's isolation and the political disintegration of Europe.

If, however, negotiations are oriented towards the general goal of defining a balance of forces between the major European "powers", this could enhance the tendencies already present towards the "renationalisation" of security policy in Europe. Moreover, it is a completely open question whether it is at all possible to define criteria for a multipolar balance of this nature that could gain consensus in Europe.

These dangers can only be completely avoided if we manage to create political conditions in Europe that let the question of relationships based on military power take second place. The opinion, at present very widespread in Europe, that military factors have largely lost their former significance may therefore for a while contribute to political stability. It will, however, prove lasting only if clear progress in the economic and political integration of the **whole** of Europe is achieved.

In that event, arms-control in Europe might be reduced to the task of formulating general guidelines for arms reduction (which would otherwise be unilateral) and the avoidance of crisis instability, as well as setting up joint monitoring and control institutions.[8] Until then, however, it is reasonable to keep to the idea of the (bipolar) balance of forces. Even after the combination of the CFE negotiations with the CSCE negotiations on security and confidence-building measures, it would be possible to continue the CFE negotiations as a working group with the existing range of participants, with the object of reducing remaining forces further and diminishing their offensive capacity. Here balance between the Central European partners in NATO on the one hand, and the Soviet troops in the western parts of the Soviet Union on the other, might serve as a basis.[9]

A first CFE agreement was signed in November 1990. It sets equal levels of battle tanks, armoured combat vehicles, artillery, combat aircraft and attack helicopters in Europe, slightly below the armaments level of the (hitherto) weaker side, NATO. At the time of writing, the agreement still has to be ratified, and on the way to ratification some difficulties have emerged.

By far the most serious controversy concerns the Soviet Union's shift of three motor rifle divisions to coastal defence units, and its claim that the 2000-3000 pieces of ground equipment involved are exempt from CFE limits. Although the treaty does not deal with naval units, the US and their allies argue that according to Article III of the CFE treaty, **all** tanks, armoured vehicles and the like within the area of application are subject to numerical limits. They fear that the Soviet interpretation creates a loophole which could be used by the Soviet military to undermine the political and military functions of the agreement.

Since the military value of the equipment in question is relatively insignificant compared to Soviet overall reductions, the allies' concerns are mainly based on political considerations. Many US observers, in particular, regard the Soviet interpretation as a sign of the growing influence of military and political hardliners on Soviet foreign policy. This has raised the question of whether the Soviet government - after Foreign Minister Shevardnadze's resignation - can still be regarded as trustworthy. According to US Secretary of State James Baker, the Soviet move "cuts to the heart... of [Moscow's] credibility and trust".

There are, however, indications that these difficulties can be resolved. In that event, the CFE talks will be continued (as (CFE-IA), with the object of reducing troop levels in Central Europe in accordance with the reductions in German forces agreed in the 'Two-Plus-Four" talks.

On a longer view (CFE-II) it is conceivable that arms-control can be used to cut forces in Central Europe further (to around 50% of present levels) and give them a more defensive structure. This could - along with a further refinement of "confidence-building measures" - help to reduce still further arms burdens and the fear of a surprise attack in Europe.

In any case, the latter danger is at present seen as very low even without arms-control. This is based on the (political) estimate that no Soviet government, in a period of far-reaching internal reforms, could harbour the intention to engage in military adventures in Europe. It is to be assumed that in future too, the influence of **political** changes in the Soviet Union and Eastern Europe on threat-perceptions in Europe will be stronger than that of possible arms-control agreements.

Whether arms-control can contribute to an awareness of "joint" responsibility for Europe's security remains to be seen. Experience with the arms-control negotiations of the 1970's showed that arms-control alone does not necessarily lead to the establishment of mutual trust and the setting-up of joint security structures. Admittedly, the climate for negotiations has radically improved since the INF agreement. But that alone is no guarantee of success in employing arms-control for the effective establishment of collective security structures in Europe. As an instrument for such **political** goals, arms-control remains largely untested.[10]

In today's conditions, it will depend above all on further political developments in Europe whether arms-control in this sense can be successful. There are a number of political requirements. Firstly, the further democratisation and economic development of the Soviet Union and its former allies in Central and Eastern Europe; secondly, further removal of the division of Europe that de facto persists; thirdly, a regulation of relationships with the Soviet Union, taking account of its historical ties to Europe while ruling out Soviet dominance on the continent; and finally, further progress in European unification, which must go hand-in-hand with an opening-up of the European Community to the East European states.

As a political means, then, arms-control can only be effective if tied into a comprehensive process of political integration in Europe. If one is to believe the numerous political declarations at present relating to the "renaissance of Europe", the enlargement of the European Community to the East of Europe or the "Common European House", then there is no lack of political will to all-European integration, though the way there is undoubtedly still very long.

If, however, it can be assumed that Europe is on that road, it may also be taken that agreed arms limitations and the setting-up of a joint control and monitoring system can act as the foundation stone for a system of "joint" security in Europe. It may well be that arms-control will tend more to slow down than speed up the process of reduction of armaments in Europe, and thus contribute to the maintenance of the existing security structures. But the incentive to unilateral arms reductions is so strong at present that this "braking function" is not likely to count for much. And the planned closer ties between the CFE negotiations and the CSCE will take into account the new political structures in Europe. The decisive point is that an effective arms-control system in Europe would give a solid foundation to the idea of "common" security, which is always at risk of petering out in political rhetoric.

This could also give further stimulus to the numerous recent proposals for giving more emphasis to the CSCE's security-policy function. Suggestions for equipping the CSCE with an institutional infrastructure; holding regular CSCE summit meetings or meetings of foreign and defence ministers; or giving the CSCE tasks of conflict prevention, dispute-settlement or verification, have met with very broad support in Eastern and Central Europe, the Federal Republic and other European states, and have partly been agreed by the "Charter of Paris for a New Europe" of November 1990.

The CSCE does indeed possess important prerequisites for playing a part in Europe's future security system: it covers both parts of Europe and the superpowers, that is, all the states on which a future "security system" in Europe will be based, and it has the reputation of already having made a useful contribution, in the sphere of security and confidence-building measures, towards overcoming the East-West confrontation and towards security in Europe.

There still are many voices warning against over-rating the idea of collective security,[11] and the assumptions about the nature of international relations underlying the idea are still quite widely regarded as unrealistic. Reference is made to the unsatisfactory security role of the League of Nations and the United Nations. Such arguments are, however, rather unconvincing: experience to date with **global** systems of collective security give no indication of the prospects for **regional** systems, from which greater coherence of security interests can be expected. Moreover, it is already becoming apparent that the reduction of the East-West opposition could considerably enhance the effectiveness of the UN security system. Finally, generalised statements about the nature of international relations have regularly proved wrong in specific cases.[12]

The greatest difficulties, in the specific case of Europe, surrounded the need to give the CSCE a formal treaty basis, if it is to be used for concrete military tasks, and the inevitable problems of reaching agreement in such a large negotiating body.

These difficulties do not yet, however, militate against an attempt to lend European security a collective component by revaluing the CSCE. Certainly, doubts as to its capacity for action in the event of crisis are basically justified, even if not every local conflict need lead to a crippling of the organisation. After the removal of the Soviet threat, moreover, security policy in Europe will increasingly rarely amount to decisions on military intervention or acute crisis management. Instead, longer-term political measures to settle or contain conflicts will acquire increasing importance. For these tasks, the CSCE is indeed a suitable framework.

If the CSCE is not regarded as a quick substitute for the existing alliance systems in Europe, but as a set of long-term objectives bound up closely with that of building a united Europe, then everything at present argues in favour of further extension of its security role.

4. Security through West European co-operation

In the shorter term, West European security co-operation probably offers better chances of coping with risks linked with the decay of the existing security system in Europe. Plans for this were developed after the war, chiefly in connection with the question of German rearmament. With the rapid intensification of East-West confrontation in the first post-war years and the outbreak of the Korean War in 1950, the view prevailed that effective Western defence in Europe could not be achieved without a German defence contribution. On that occasion, it was above all the great "Europeans" like Schuman, Monnet and Pleven, who called for the extension of Western European integration to the defence sphere (the Pleven Plan and proposals for the European Defence Community). These plans initially gave the French government the chance to avoid diplomatic isolation and postpone German rearmament indefinitely by linking it with West European integration.[13]

After the failure of the European Defence Community in the French National Assembly and the acceptance of the Federal Republic of Germany as a member of NATO, the idea of European co-operation on security policy retreated into the background. Only recently has the topic regained importance, in connection with the revival of West European integration efforts and American demands for a redistribution of Western defence burdens. Minor progress, like the setting-up of the Independent European Programme Group, the revival of the Western European Union, or first steps to military co-operation at a bilateral level, have aroused political expectations. Over and above that, the change in East-West relations and the revival of arms-control negotiations in Europe have created new incentives to closer co-ordination in European security policy. Altogether, too, the European feeling of dissatisfaction with the existing political dependency on the United States has tended to increase in recent years,[14] although the expected reduction of the US military presence in Europe has, at the same time, led to efforts to avoid severing transatlantic military relations completely.

The new interest in West European defence co-operation has, however, also revived old differences of opinion on the issue. This plurality of political opinions and objectives need not necessarily, however, as some observers seem to assume,[15] point to a stagnation of the integration process. All it does is to make clear that such co-operation is not an automatic consequence of European **economic** integration. Even if the present momentum in European unification is maintained, leading to new incentives to political co-operation in other spheres, co-operation in the security-policy area will remain a hard task.

Additionally, there are indications that some traditional reservations about European defence co-operation are losing weight.

Initially, the success of NATO probably constituted the most important cause of the lack of success of Western European defence co-operation. It limited Europeans' motivation for co-operation in the narrower European framework, particularly because any move in that direction was seen as potentially weakening NATO. Today, however, NATO has largely lost its primary function as a defensive alliance. It is in a process of far-reaching reform, the outcome of which is still uncertain. With the removal of the Soviet threat, the security interests of West Europeans are only in small part covered by NATO, and inside the Alliance the view has come to prevail that strengthening its European "pillar" will mean not a weakening but a strengthening.

The second reservation in decline is the view among proponents of European unification that the difficult integration process ought not to be burdened further by the special problems of military co-operation. It is becoming apparent today that even the limited objectives of the European internal market can probably not be achieved without clear progress in the direction of political union, which must include some collaboration in the field of international security. The question is no longer whether, but when, a start should be made on closer security co-operation.

Thirdly, fears that Western European defence co-operation might lead to a "militarisation" of the European Community have also abated. Under present political conditions in Europe, one cannot seriously expect any enhancement of the military activities of West European governments.

Approaches to West European co-operation in the security sphere have to date largely been confined to the political aspects of security. In the narrower military sphere and in that of arms-procurement, co-operation has so far scarcely got beyond general declarations. There has also been limited progress in the co-ordination of military activities in the Persian Gulf and in bilateral military co-operation. Yet it should be borne in mind here that the non-military areas of security in which Western European co-operation has already been developed have taken on considerably more weight with the changes in the East-West relationship. A stronger role for the EC in the formulation of the **political** goals of arms-control in Europe would in principle already be compatible with its present legal authority. Because of the relatively rapid progress of the CFE negotiations, military planning is now so closely bound up with arms-control that political objectives have gained considerable influence in the military area. Ever since the INF negotiations, in fact, military experts have been warning against the growing influence of "un-germane" political motives on the West's military planning. NATO's call for an "overall concept" was the attempt, only partially successful, to regain more effective military control over the arms-control process.

In view of the lasting change in threat-perceptions in West European societies, it can be expected that political considerations will in future gain increasing influence in the military area. Although the Gulf War temporarily strengthened European willingness to co-operate in the establishment of a joint European "Rapid Deployment Force" under WEU control - in close co-ordination with NATO - the future focus of European defence collaboration will probably lie in the political field.

While bilateral Franco-German military co-operation does have a political function in their direct partnership, it has also led to fears of a Franco-German special relationship that could perceptibly cramp the West European integration process. However, since the beginning of the reunification process the "Franco-German axis" no longer seems to have been functioning quite so smoothly as before. Certainly, both governments have managed to avoid the impression of any serious rift through their joint proposal to speed up the West European integration process. We should not, however, close our eyes to the fact that it has not so far been possible to restore the close process of mutual accord and trust that formed the core of Franco-German "friendship".

Finally, Franco-German co-operation in the military sphere has also shown how great the "technical" difficulties to be overcome in deploying multinational units still are. The most recent proposals by some pro-European politicians to set up multinational European forces will therefore not easily find adequate political support.

Better prospects for closer European co-operation are at present offered in the non-military areas of security policy, especially as many of these questions are so closely bound up with the development of the integrated European market that it is not possible to avoid them on the road to the common European market. This applies very generally to the sphere of European foreign relations, and here particularly to the European Community's relations with the US, the Soviet Union and its former allies. The question of whether intensification of West European co-operation in these areas should be brought about through a strengthening of European Political Co-operation or through an expansion of the European Community's foreign-policy powers, and an extension of the machinery set up to exercise those powers, cannot be discussed further here.[16] Strengthening the Community's foreign and security role would nevertheless be the most effective contribution to European security policy, at any rate until effective pan-European security structures have been successfully developed.

The issue of West European security co-operation is currently being debated in the framework of the Community's Intergovernmental Conferences. It is still too early to predict the concrete results of the conference on European Political Union, but recent meetings of the European foreign ministers in Luxembourg (March and April 1991) have shown a clear majority in support of a common European foreign and security policy. There now seems to be a real possibility of significant progress in this important field of European integration.

5. Conclusion

The factors of future European security mentioned here are in no way mutually exclusive; they are, on the contrary, complementary. Pan-European security structures can be effective only to the extent that the political integration of the whole of Europe is arrived at. The success of the European Community is, however, also the most important impetus towards a growing-together of the whole of Europe. It is therefore wrong to set up an opposition between advances in West European integration and the eastward opening of the European Community. Only if the Community is successful will it be possible to open it up towards the East. Strengthening its security role will thus in the longer term also further the development of pan-European security structures. Conversely, the development of the CSCE has shown that pan-European contacts can also be an incentive to enhanced West European co-operation.

For their part, the existing alliance systems must not be allowed to stand in the way of the building-up of West European and pan-European security structures. Even in the US and inside NATO, the conviction has now come to prevail that a strengthening of the European component in NATO will also help the Western alliance. The view that the security policy of the alliances and pan-European security structures are not contradictory but mutually complementary was already the basis for the Harmel decisions, but has not yet become widespread, because of a lack of adequate advances in arms-control. If it is finally possible to set in motion a process of political and economic integration for the whole of Europe, then it might in the longer term even be possible to give the elements of "joint" security in Europe the needed weight to confirm the idea underlying the Harmel resolutions.

References

1. Helmuth Kohl's "Zehn Punkte" plan did not lay down a time frame, but evidently assumed that the process would take at least several years.

2. **Vertrag über die abschließende Regelung in bezug auf Deutschland, Die Verhandlungen über die äußeren Aspekte der Herstellung der Deutschen Einheit,** Presse- und Informationsamt of the Federal Government, Bonn 1990.

3. Klaus-Dieter Schwarz, "Sicherheit durch Bündnissysteme" in Wolfgang Heisenberg and Dieter Lutz (eds.), **Sicherheitspolitik kontrovers,** Schriftenreihe der Bundeszentrale für politische Bildung, vol. 291/II, p. 279.

4. "It is the biggest military challenge at the time of the lowest military threat", Phillip A. Karber, cited in Michael R. Gordon, "New NATO Strategy Poses Major Test for Military Planners", **International Herald Tribune,** 9 July 1990.

5. Stanley Hoffmann, "From Old NATO to a New North Atlantic Security Structure", **International Herald Tribune**, 29 May 1990.

6. On this see Wolfgang Heisenberg, "Sicherheitspolitische Bedingungen und Handlungsmöglichkeiten im Zusammenhang mit der Vereinigung der beiden deutschen Staaten", Friedrich-Naumann-Stiftung 1990.

7. The usual reference in this context to the Treaty of Versailles goes too far in dramatising this danger. It would, however, be equally mistaken to interpret the reference to nationalist reactions in the Federal Republic as merely an attempt to improve the Republic's international negotiating position.

8. The idea already developed in the early 1980's of replacing traditional arms-control agreements aimed at setting quantitative or qualitative levels of armament by more general political or military rules of behaviour could gain importance in the new political conditions in Europe. See, for example, Christoph Bertram, "Arms control and technological change: elements of a new approach" in **The Future of Arms Control**, Part II, Adelphi Paper 146 (London: International Institute for Strategic Studies, 1978).

9. See Jonathan Dean, "The CFE negotiations, present and future", **Survival**, Vol. XXXII No. 4 (July/August 1990).

10. For a more detailed discussion, see Wolfgang Heisenberg, 'West European expectations from conventional arms control", in Keith Dunn and Stephen Flanagan (eds.), **NATO's Fifth Decade** (Washington: National Defense University Press, 1989).

11. A survey of the most popular arguments in the conservative critique of collective security can be found in Gerhard Wettig, "Zur Philosophie, Konzeption und Fragwürdigkeit eines Alternativmodells: Kollektive Sicherheit in und für Europa", in Heisenberg and Lutz (eds.), **op. cit.**, p. 315. This article was, however, still written in a Cold War perspective. Many of the questions addressed would have to be rediscussed today.

12. The "classical" theories of international relations, for instance, are still finding it hard to explain the relative success of European unification policy.

13. See Edward Fursdon, **The European Defence Community: A History** (London: Macmillan Press, 1980).

14. Stanley Hoffmann's description of European frustration in dealing with the superpowers is still apposite today: "The US and Western Europe: Wait and Worry", in **Foreign Affairs**, 63(3), autumn 1985. The relatively low-key European policy of President Bush and the fear by many European politicians of drastic reductions of the American presence in Europe have, however, taken the edge off the issue for the moment.

15. Peter Schmidt, **Europeanization of Defense: Prospects of Consensus?**, Rand Library Collection, 7 December 1984.

16. On this question see Henri Froment-Meurice and Peter Ludlow, "Towards a European foreign policy", in **Governing Europe,** CEPS 1989 Annual Conference Proceedings Vol. II, CEPS Paper 45, 1990.

Part III

Economic and Social Issues

Eastern Europe, Germany and the EC: a framework for analysing their economic integration

Giorgio Basevi

1. Introduction

In this paper I shall try to explore, with the help of simple models borrowed from international trade and growth theory, some of the effects that may derive, in the long run, from the integration of the economies of Eastern Europe within the existing fabric of the European Community (EC).[1]

On the one hand, attention will be focused on the integration of the two German economies and how it could affect the plan already under way to transform the EC into a full European Economic and Monetary Union (EEMU). The two sides of this plan - i.e. the economic and monetary sides - are represented, respectively, by the process leading to the integrated European internal market, to be enacted at the beginning of 1993, and by the design of European monetary unification (EMU), that gained momentum with the Delors Report (1989) and is currently the object of negotiations and debate.[2]

On the other hand, the focus will be on how the East European countries that are enacting market-oriented reforms of their economies may be integrated into world trade through association and eventually integration with the EC.

2. The static trade model

In this section I shall make use of the neo-classical trade model, first in its standard, Heckscher-Ohlin, version,[3] and then in its extension to economies of scale and differentiated products, which is mainly associated with the writings of Helpman and Krugman (1985). Let us consider a world made up of three countries, labelled FI (let us say an EC made up of France, Italy and other countries, except Germany); WG (let us say West Germany); and EG (let us say East Germany, and possibly East European candidates for EC association, which are likely to integrate more closely with Germany than with other EC countries).

2.1 East Germany as a closed economy

Let us assume, in the first step of the analysis, that EG is a closed economy, so that trade takes place only between FI and WG, which are the only other countries in the "world". The countries produce two homogeneous products, X and Y, with two factors, K and L, and linear homogeneous production functions, which are the same in all countries. X is assumed to be the labour-intensive product at all relevant factor prices. Consumers in the different countries have the same homogeneous utility functions. There are no distortions in any market, except those implicit in the closed-economy assumption about the EG economy.

Let us assume that the three countries are ranked as follows with regard to their endowments of capital and labour:

(1) $k_{WG} > k_{FI} > k_{EG}$

where $k = K/L$. Let us also assume that merging WG and EG in a unified G still leaves the new Germany a capital-abundant country relative to the rest of the EC, i.e.:

(2) $k_G = k_{WG} \dfrac{L_{WG}}{L_{WG} + L_{EG}} + k_{EG} \dfrac{L_{EG}}{L_{WG} + L_{EG}} > k_{FI}$

2.1.1 Incomplete specialisation

Let us assume, initially, that the partition of the "world" factor endowments between FI and WG reproduces, through trade, the same price equilibrium that would result in an integrated "world" made up of the two countries, i.e. that their factor-endowment point belongs to the factor/price equalisation (FPE) set as shown in Fig. 1.[4] Country FI exports X and imports Y from country WG. The vector of trade in factors incorporated in trade in products is E_1C_1, supported by the relative factor/price ratio corresponding to the angle ∞_1.

Figure 1

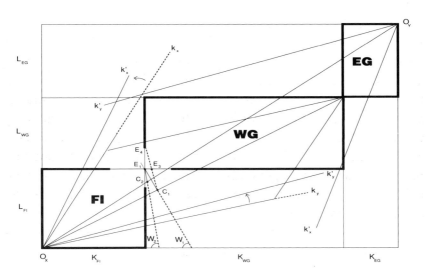

Now let us suppose that country EG merges with country WG, to become just one country, G. Consider first the new situation, but with the same prices as before German unification. Since the unification of the two Germanies is equivalent to an increase in factors in WG that is biased towards labour, we know (from the Rybsczynski theorem) that this implies that in G the production of X increases proportionally more than the production of Y. In FI the production of both sets of goods remains constant. Thus, with homothetic utility functions, prices cannot stay constant: the price of X must fall, and with it, the price of L must fall too. International trade between FI and G brings about a new factor/price ratio corresponding to the angle ∞_2 in Fig. 1. The FPE set gets larger and its sides rotate towards the L-axis: FI produces less of its export goods and more of its import goods. The factoral trade vector rotates and shrinks to E_1C_2: country FI exports less of its relatively-abundant factor L, but more of it per unit of imports of its relatively-scarce factor K. Thus the terms of trade and the welfare of country FI deteriorate, as shown by the movement of the consumption point from C_1 to C_2.

Because of the loss in real income that results from the unification of WG and EG, FI may be tempted to impose a tariff or some equivalent form of protection against G. This temptation is due both to (a) the deterioration of the terms of trade of FI relative to the unified G; and (b) the fact that the consequent loss of real income falls all on wage-earners in FI (according to the Stolper-Samuelson theorem), while owners of capital in FI actually see the real rental price of their factor rise. Insofar as in FI the lobby of workers is more organised that that of capital owners, protectionist pressures may be hard to resist. Moreover, because wage-earners in EG improve their lot relative to the previous situation - when they were working in a closed economy that was more labour-abundant than both FI and WG - they may oppose the threat of retaliation by G against FI that could, if credible, keep at bay the protectionist pressures in FI. On the other hand, capital-owners in what was the EG are as yet hardly identifiable and therefore unable to organise themselves as a lobby. All this makes it likely that protectionist pressures in FI will become effective following the unification of WG and EG.

Jumping from simple theory to complex reality, this analysis provides at least two initial hints. First, the improvement of the terms of trade that Germany must experience vis-à-vis its EC partners - if the empirical assumptions about this model are not too far from reality - will imply either an increase of prices in Germany relative to its partners, or a nominal appreciation of the DM, or both; in any case, a real appreciation of the DM. Considering the traditional anti-inflationary attitude of the German monetary authorities, the more likely development is a nominal appreciation of the DM. Thus the model suggests tensions and forces leading to one or more realignments in the EMS.[5] On the basis of this analysis, German unification does not bode well for the monetary side of EEMU, or at least for smooth progress without realignments into phase 2 of the Delors plan. Second, the forces pushing for protectionism may slow down the actual implementation of the integrated European internal market for goods and factors that is due to be completed by 1993.

However, the same theoretical analysis suggests a policy that may offset these protectionist forces, i.e. a transfer from G to FI such as would keep the distribution of real income between the two groups at point C_1 even with the new terms of trade. This may be brought about by transferring either a quantity of capital equal to E_1E_3 from G to FI, or a quantity of labour equal to E_1E_4 in the opposite direction. The second alternative means that the enrichment of Germany in terms of labour more than in terms of capital is partly shared with the old members of the EC. With another jump into reality, it would mean that some of the migration of labour from the East into Germany should be redirected towards the old partners of Germany in the EC. Clearly, any other combination of capital and labour migration that lies on the segment E_3E_4 is equivalent from this point of view.

2.1.2 Complete specialisation

Let us now suppose that the endowment point between FI and WG was initially lying outside the FPE set. In fact this might be interpreted as one reason for attempting to build the 1993 integrated market.

Now it may be that the unification of WG and EG, by shifting the FPE set in Fig. 1, could incorporate the allocation point of FI within the new FPE set. In this case, if the economic forces pushing for the integrated market were originating from non-equalisation of factor prices, they may be counteracted by German unification. Thus here again, as in section 2.1.1, although for different reasons, German unification may reduce the attractiveness of the 1993 programme for the old EC partners of Germany. The two factors - deterioration of FI's terms of trade and reduced differential in factor prices - work together, so that the threat to the internal market programme may be reinforced.

2.2 East Germany as an open economy

Let us now assume that, before the unification of WG and EG, some trade was already taking place between them; yet, for the sake of simplicity, let us also assume that no trade was taking place between FI and EG. Further, in order to model in the simplest way the fact that this trade was not part of the multilateral system of international payments, and that East European countries were somewhat isolated from world markets and market prices, let us assume that a given portion of the WG economy was exclusively dedicated to trade with EG. As a consequence, prices for this trade were different from prices in trade between WG and FI. To support this assumption, let us suppose that in WG factors of production were induced by taxes and/or subsidies to produce and trade at different prices when dealing with EG than when dealing with FI. Net receipts from such taxes and subsidies were redistributed in a non-discretionary way.

How much of the capital and labour endowment of the WG economy was dedicated to this sort of preferential trade with EG? Assuming that the purpose of the preferential treatment of WG vis-à-vis EG was to provide the latter with WG export products at prices lower than world market prices, we must partition WG into two parts (WG_1 and WG_2) and allocate WG_2 to this trade so that the sum of WG_2 and EG is more capital-abundant than the sum of FI and WG_1. Thus, with reference to Fig. 2, the partition of WG must identify an "endowment" point within WG - say point B - so that the diagonal joining O_X to B is steeper than the diagonal joining B to O_Y; in other words, B must lie north-west of the diagonal joining O_X to O_Y. However, we must also continue to assume that WG exports Y - the capital-intensive product - to FI. Thus B must also lie south-east of the ray originating from OX and passing through E. Hence West Germany must be allocated to the two parts of trade at a point such as B, lying in the shaded area of Fig. 2.

With the partition of WG at point B, factor prices were given by the angle ∞_1 as a consequence of trade between WG_1 and FI, and ∞_2 as a consequence of trade between WG_2 and EG: the

Figure 2

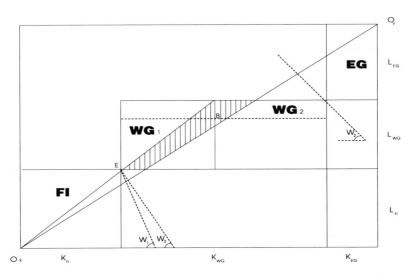

effective rental of capital and price of Y was relatively cheaper, while the wage of labour was relatively higher, in the portion of WG dedicated to trade with EG. As a consequence, this arrangement was leading, before German unification, to an excessive specialisation of East Germany in labour-intensive export goods.

Let us now suppose that WG and EG unify and trade with FI at a unique set of prices. Because the "world" made up of FI and WG was less capital-abundant than the new "world" made up of all three countries (now reduced to two, FI and G), the competitive world price of Y falls relative to what it was in trade between FI and WG, but rises relative to what it was in trade between WG and EG. The relative price of capital falls from that implicit in the angle ∞_1 to that implicit, for example, in the angle ∞_3, so that

(3) $\infty_2 < \infty_3 < \infty_1$.

Both X and Y become more K-intensive in FI and less K-intensive in EG (and in that portion of WG that was dedicated to trade with EG). The terms of trade of FI now improve. The FPE set of the whole integrated world rotates with its sides towards the K-axis. It could now happen that the endowment point E gets out of the FPE set as a consequence of unification between WG and EG. If this were to happen, the internal market programme for 1993 would become more attractive for FI, on two grounds: (a) the improvement in FI's terms of trade means that, for a given volume of trade, FI benefits more than before; hence it may now be more inclined to further develop its trade with G, by eliminating any residual obstacle to intra-EC trade (these obstacles, however, are not modelled here); (b) the possibility that E falls outside the new FPE set makes 1993 more attractive, if this programme, by extending trade to factors, in addition to goods, represents the means for bringing about FPE.

2.3 Inter-industry vs. intra-industry trade

Up to now I have considered homogeneous products, produced with constant returns to scale under perfect competition. With this assumption and within the framework of the Heckscher-Ohlin model, international trade is determined uniquely by relative factor endowments. The volume of trade is larger, the larger the difference in relative factor endowments. The relative size of countries does not affect the volume of trade.

If, following Helpman and Krugman (1985), we allow for differentiated products and economies of scale, the relative size of countries acts as an additional determinant of trade: the more equal the two countries in their size, the larger is the volume of intra-industry trade. More specifically, with reference to the two cases of sections 2.1 and 2.2, one should note that when EG was assumed not to have been trading with the other two countries before unification with WG (the case of section 2.1), the total world factor endowment was effectively enlarged by the inclusion of EG in the trading world. Assuming that FI was larger than WG, after German unification FI and G are less unequal in size, and, given our previous assumptions, less unequal also in relative factor endowments. Hence trade between FI and G tends to decrease in the form of traditional inter-industry trade and to increase in the form of the less traditional intra-industry trade, relative to the volume of trade previously observed between FI and WG.

On the other hand, in the case in which it was assumed that EG was already trading with WG (the case of section 2.2), FI and the new G, while still less unequal in size than before German unification, are now more unequal in relative factor endowments (in Fig. 2 the diagonal joining O_X with B is steeper than the diagonal joining O_X with O_Y). Hence, in this case, both intra-industry and inter-industry trade between FI and G will be larger than their previous level between FI and WG. If, with another, by now usual but still hazardous, jump into reality, we consider this as internal trade by WG before unification, then the analysis suggests that trade within the new EC will increase after German unification both in terms of intra- and inter-industry trade.

2.4 Non-traded goods

In the previous section reference to the 1993 European integrated market was made as if this could be interpreted, within the model, as the means to bring about factor/price equalisation through factor movements, when otherwise factor endowments would fall outside the FPE set.

An alternative way to interpret the 1993 plan is to consider it as a plan to reduce the number of non-tradable sectors within the EC. The elimination of all legal and institutional discrimination due to different national regulations, and the opening-up to foreign competition of traditionally protected sectors, such as some services and professions, make it unnecessary for factors to migrate in order to bring about their reward equalisation, as it effectively makes their products directly or indirectly tradable.

Under the traditional constant returns-to-scale assumption, the existence of non-traded products restricts the FPE set.[6] Again, if we assume that before German reunification EG was not open to foreign trade, then we have seen that merging the two Germanies into one country makes it more likely that the endowment point E could fall within the FPE set, and therefore reduces the attractiveness of 1993 for FI. However, the widely-different legal provisions of the East European countries, and more specifically of East Germany, could be interpreted to enlarge, at least for some time, the number of non-tradable goods in the newly-integrated Europe, and thus reduce the size of the FPE set. This, while making it more worthwhile to redesign and push forward the integration of the European market beyond 1993, will probably, in the meantime, induce more migration of the factors that could legally resettle themselves in the various countries of Europe. A similar reasoning applies to the case where EG was already trading with WG before unification.

2.5 Association/integration of new countries with the EC

Let us now consider a different problem from those examined above with the example of German unification. Let us assume that there is a set of countries waiting to be associated and eventually integrated into the EC. These countries, in reality, may be the EFTA countries, or the countries of Eastern Europe that are moving towards a new economic order based on markets and international trade. An assumption I shall make is, however, more appropriate to the East European countries: I shall assume that, before considering association or integration with the EC, none of the candidate countries was trading with the Community or with the other candidates. Clearly this assumption is extremely far from reality; yet, because I want to reason on the dramatic changes in institutions, policies and economic structures that are being experienced by Eastern Europe, and because certainly those countries were less oriented towards the market and world trade than the EFTA countries, the assumption is at least less far from reality for them than for the EFTA countries.

Two questions may now be asked: (i) is there a preferable sequence for these countries' association with the EC? and (ii) is there a preferable sequence for their integration with the EC?

In order to give meaning to these questions, the concepts of association and integration must first be defined, and it must be explained why there has to be a sequence, rather than a joint movement, towards association or integration on the part of all candidate countries. A criterion must also be selected for ranking alternative sequences as preferable. It is assumed that the countries newly appearing on the stage become associated with the EC when they enter into free trade with it. They become integrated with the Community when factors too, and not just products, are allowed to move freely between the previous EC members and those countries. Thus, through integration, these countries become full members of the integrated market that should result from the 1993 programme.[7]

The assumption that there has to be a sequence is exogenous to the model of this paper, i.e. it is based on considerations that fall outside the realm of its analysis. Such considerations could refer to bureaucratic or political opposition to an enlargement that, if it were to take place all at once, may endanger the present equilibrium in the political and constitutional structure of the EC. Reference to this or other elements of a political nature justify the assumption that the enlargement of the EC to include a series of new candidates cannot be considered a one-step process. Political considerations are particularly relevant for the accession of East European countries, but also some EFTA countries, as reference is made, in the former case, to their degree of progress towards democracy or, in the latter, to their status of political neutrality.

Finally, as to the criterion for ranking alternative sequences, this will be based on the economic gains to be reaped from trade and integration, and on the transitional costs that are involved in reallocating productive resources, both internally (within the existing EC and the new applicants) and internationally. Such costs are particularly important when the factor to be relocated is labour.

One should note that, given these definitions and assumptions, association does not require integration if the candidate for association to the EC has a K/L ratio such that the FPE set of the new "world", inclusive of the applicant country, contains the point that separates the endowments of the EC and of that country. If it does not contain it, then association would not equalise factor prices between the applicant and the EC, so that there will be pressures for factor migration and, eventually, integration.

2.5.1 Sequence of association

Let us assume that the applicants are all more labour-abundant (relative to capital) than the EC, and rank them in order of decreasing labour abundance. Both the EC and each applicant stand to gain from opening up trade between themselves, and the gain is larger, the larger the difference in pre-trade prices. On the basis of the Heckscher-Ohlin model, we can therefore say that, with reference to the order of gains from trade, the sequence of countries to be associated should be determined by the difference in relative factor endowments between each applicant and the EC. First should come the most labour-rich countries relative to the EC, and the order should follow that of increasing K/L ratios. Moreover, for a given difference in K/L ratio, the gains for the EC are reduced the smaller the size of the new applicant, as this will reduce the improvement of the terms of trade for the EC. Thus, from the point of view of the EC and of the gains from trade based on comparative advantage, the countries to be associated first should be the larger ones and/or those with the most divergent K/L ratios relative to the EC.

However, an additional element in the assumed criterion for determining the sequence of associations is based on the costs of reallocating productive resources. This would suggest that the sequence of countries to be associated with the EC should follow a rank opposite to the previous one, with respect to the K/L ratios of the applicants, so as to minimise the transitional costs of redirecting factors of production towards the export sectors. Moreover, in order to avoid tensions in the factor markets that may give rise to migration of factors (particularly labour), countries must keep wide of the complete specialisation point; thus they should select the sequence so as to keep the point that divides the total "world" endowment between the EC and each new applicant within the FPE set or as close to it as possible.

Considering the costs of adjustment, the sequence of countries should therefore present an order opposite to the one that would follow from consideration of the gains from trade: first associate the countries that are less different in terms of K/L ratios, and/or smaller in size, relative to the EC.

One should note that the comparative-advantage element in the selection criterion tends to develop first the largest opportunities for inter-industry trade between the EC and the new applicants, because the volume of inter-industry trade is the larger the greater is the divergence between factor endowments. Moreover, selection of the largest countries as first candidates on the basis of the same element also tends to develop more significantly the volume of intra-industry trade between the EC and the new applicants, because the volume of this type of trade is larger the more similar in size are the partners in trade: presumably the candidates are smaller than the EC, so that they are closer to the EC size the larger is their size.

Following the second element in the criterion - i.e. the one based on reducing the costs of factor-reallocation and the pressure on their migration - has the opposite effect on trade to the first: it tends to slow down the development of both intra- and inter-industry trade between the EC and the sequence of applicants for association.

2.5.2 Sequence of integration

While, in reality, political reasons may be the main determinant, the need for integration with the EC arises, in this model, uniquely from the fact that international trade between the EC and the newly-associated countries is not sufficient to equalise factor prices internationally. Integration is therefore meant to avoid distortions, by allowing factor movements within the integrated EC.

On this basis, the countries to be integrated first should be those that are more likely to locate outside the FPE set the point that separates their factor endowment from that of the EC. Thus the larger and/or the more different countries in terms of K/L ratios relative to the EC should be integrated first. This would give a ranking of countries for integration that is the same only with respect to the first of the two elements suggested for the criterion of association. Unless we were to assume that an associated country, before becoming integrated with the EC, has to wait for the country that preceded it in the queue of association to be integrated first, the sequence of integration would not be the same as the sequence of association. This leaves us in a theoretically-ambiguous situation.

In order to be more specific on the sequence of integration, we could assume that integration is considered the only viable choice when association is insufficient to equalise factor prices. In other words, if association (i.e. free trade of products) were to generate a trade equilibrium with a FPE set not containing the endowment point, the only choice is assumed to be immediate integration instead of association. Let us also assume that the costs associated with the movement of labour are larger than those associated with the movements of capital.[8] The preferred way to bring the endowment point within the FPE set will then be through movements of capital from the EC (the capital-abundant "country") to the candidate-countries, rather than of labour in the opposite direction. It follows again that the sequence of integration will be determined by the size of the candidate country and its K/L ratio. However, it is now possible to be more specific.

For a given equal K/L ratio of the two candidates, when a larger country is a candidate for integration with the EC (e.g. when the north-east origin shifts to O_{Y2} in Fig. 3), the endowment point E would be more horizontally distant (K is measured horizontally) from the FPE set than when a smaller country is the candidate (e.g. when the north-east origin shifts only to O_{Y1}), if factor prices were the same in the two alternative situations, so that the sides of the FPE parallelogram would keep the same slope. However, factor prices cannot be the same in the two alternative situations: the larger country also makes the "world" more labour-abundant than a "world" made up of the EC and the smaller country. Thus, with a larger candidate-country, the relative price of labour will fall further and the FPE set will rotate its sides towards the L-axis. This tends to reduce the horizontal distance of the E point from the FPE set, if the candidate-countries are smaller in size than the EC.

Figure 3

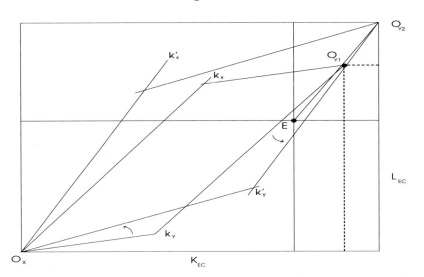

Thus, contrary to intuition (which is based only on the effect at given factor prices), the net effect of size is to make smaller the movement of capital implied by integration, the larger the candidate to be integrated with the EC, provided it remains smaller than the EC and in any case more labour-abundant. If we add the consideration of different K/L ratios, it simply follows, for two candidate-countries of similar size (defined by the length of the diagonal of their factor endowment rectangle), that the more labour-abundant the candidate country, the larger the required movement of capital implied by integration.

On the whole, therefore, the sequence of candidates for integration should follow, from the point of view of the EC, the decreasing order of their size and/or K/L ratios: first the larger countries and/or the ones that are more capital-abundant.

3. A dynamic trade model

In section 2 it has been possible, on the basis of admittedly simple and heroic assumptions, to reach conclusions that are suggestive of some implications of German unification for the European Economic and Monetary Union, and of the order in which East European or EFTA countries could be associated or integrated into the EC, with minimal problems for the latter. Such conclusions were in any case founded on the exogenous assumption that neither association nor integration could be applied at once to the whole set of candidate countries, but that these should follow an individual sequence.

I want to explore, in this section, whether there are theoretical economic (besides political) reasons to suggest that a sequential process is preferable to a simultaneous enlargement of the EC to all candidate countries. In order to do so, the model must be made dynamic; as this increases its complexity, the analysis will make use of a one-product model. The question that is approached with this model is also relevant to the current debate on whether the movement towards monetary unification in Europe should proceed at one speed for all participating countries, or whether a "two-speed approach" should be followed.[9]

Dellas and De Vries (1990) distinguish two strands of thought in previous economic literature on this field, and propose a third one. The first two rely on "second best" arguments for a gradual movement towards integration, whereas the third relies on "first best" arguments. Second best arguments identify in market frictions or market failures the basis for moving toward integration in a gradual way; thus, where no frictions or failures exist, a gradual approach to integration would seem unjustified.

According to the first strand of literature, these frictions are due to costs of adjustment or of delay, so that countries may want to move faster or slower, depending on their particular cost functions. Similarly, according to the second strand, frictions could be different for different markets, with some markets finding their equilibrium faster than others, thus requiring countries to integrate first the markets that adjust less rapidly towards equilibrium (such as the product and labour markets), and only later integrate the fast-adjusting markets.

One should note that this second strand of literature relates different speeds of integration not to different countries but to different markets. However, insofar as different markets may find their equilibrium more or less efficiently in different countries, this argument may also suggest internationally-differing speeds of integration. Thus labour markets may be more or less regulated in different countries, and their variables (wages and salaries, or employment) be more or less sensitive to market disequilibria. Countries with more efficient labour markets could presumably integrate at lower costs than countries with less efficient ones.

One should also note that, according to this line of thought, it seems difficult to understand why labour markets in the EC have been integrated less or later than product markets: insofar as they are less efficient than product markets they should have been integrated first. Also, if they are less efficient, trade theory cannot be invoked to argue that it is enough to integrate product markets, in order to reach the same equilibrium that would result from integrating factor markets. Hence, as I have already mentioned above, the very rationale of the 1993 internal market is that it has not been enough to allow free trade of products throughout the EC: unless other factor markets - both capital and labour - are also fully integrated, and unless non-tradable sectors are opened to indirect competition from other member countries through freedom of establishment, full economic integration of the EC will not be achieved.

However, it is necessary here to disentangle positive from normative analysis. On the positive side, it could be argued that more efficient markets are easier to integrate, at least economically: thus capital markets should come first, product markets second, and labour markets last. On the normative side, because of the costs of adjustment, it could be argued that countries should first integrate slow-adjusting markets, in order to avoid a backlash from efficient markets on less efficient ones, with the overshooting effect so familiar from the exchange-rate literature.

In any case, the relationship between the cost of integration and its speed must be clearly specified: in the end the analysis should involve both the sequence of costs and benefits, and the social versus the political rates for discounting that sequence. Thus the discounted value of social and political objective functions could provide a normative evaluation of the results.

Broadly speaking, the process of integration already followed or still planned in the EC appears to be a compromise between positive and normative points of view, insofar as tradable product markets have been integrated first, general labour markets second, money and financial markets third, and nontradables or other artificially-protected markets last. A question that arises with respect to the new challenges from Eastern Europe - in particular with the migration of labour from those countries - is whether the same sequence will also be adopted with respect to the eastward enlargement of the EC.

The third strand of analysis is cast in terms of a growth-theoretic model, with two periods overlapping generations.[10] Originally the model was used in terms of positive theory (identifying the sustainable sequences in the integrating process), but the analysis can hardly avoid normative implications (identifying the optimal sequence). Dellas and De Vries focused their attention on the difference between an international liberalisation of factor markets that immediately leads to an integrated endowment of factors (one-stroke or "precipitous" integration), and a liberalisation that must be preceded or accompanied by steps aimed at making sustainable the eventual merging of the factor endowments (gradual or "piecemeal" integration).

As already mentioned, this analysis does not rely on market frictions or failures, but on the possible existence of multiple equilibria, in order to justify a gradual movement towards international economic integration. Thus the approach, although grounded on theoretical characteristics that may be difficult to test, has the advantage of being a "first best" argument for gradualism; as such it is complementary to, rather than a replacement for, "second best" arguments for gradualism, like those discussed by Willms (1990) on the basis of the theory of "optimum currency areas".

3.1 Integration between two countries

The gist of the argument is captured by Fig. 4, where the function g is the capital-accumulation function that, on the basis of the production capacity and saving behaviour of a country, relates current to previous period capital/labour ratios. Even with a well-behaved neoclassical production function there could exist more than one equilibrium point.

In fact, let us assume that

(4) $y = f(k)$

with $k = K/L$ and a function such that $f(0) = 0, f' > 0, f'' < 0$. Then

(5) $r = f'(k)$

and

(6) $w = f(k) - kf'(k)$

determine the real rental of K and the real wage of L. If we assume that the younger generation saves all its income, for completely consuming it when old, then we obtain

(7) $k_{t+1} = S_t = W_t = f(k_t) - k_t f'(k_t) = g(k_t)$

An example of this function g is represented in Fig. 4, where - since the conditions on f do not give a definite sign to g'' - it has been assumed that there exist three positively valued equilibria, with the low and the high K/L ones being stable and the intermediate one unstable, as can be checked by projecting successive K/L ratios through the diagonal: if a country's K/L ratio happens to be to the left of point B, it will progressively step down to point A; if it is to the right of B, it will progressively step up to C.

Figure 4

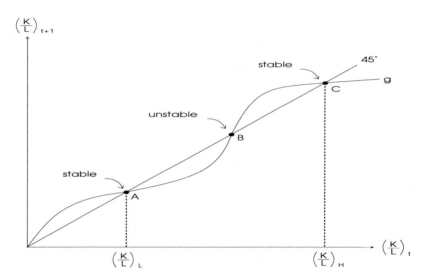

A worrying possibility is that two countries that find themselves in equilibria separated by an unstable one (as at points A and C in Fig. 4), may - by deciding to integrate their capital and/or labour makets, i.e. to merge their separate K/L ratios into a common weighted one - end up in one stroke to the left of the unstable equilibrium point B, and thus converge together at A, the lowest of the two stable equilibrium points.   In this case the low capital/labour ratio country (i.e. the one with the $(K/L)_L$ ratio) attracts the high one (i.e. the one with the $(K/L)_H$ ratio) into its low original position, as if it were a "black hole".   This position is considered less efficient than the one with the high capital/labour ratio, insofar as, with given labour endowments in the two countries or given equal rates of their growth, it corresponds to smaller production possibility sets.

In this case it can be shown that, while a precipitous (i.e. one-stroke) integration of the two countries' capital and labour makets may lead to the low equilibrium point, there may also exist a preliminary transfer of capital from the high to the low K/L ratio country (or a contrary transfer of labour from the low to the high K/L country), followed by an integration of their factor markets, so that the two merged countries would land to the right of the unstable equilibrium point, and jointly converge from there to the highest K/L equilibrium point.

One should note an interesting implication of this case: all other things being equal, precipitous factor-market integration is more likely to be efficient the larger is the capital-abundant country relative to the labour-abundant country - where size is measured by the ratio of a country's labour force to the total of the two countries' labour forces. This suggests that countries of similar size should be more careful in integrating their factor markets in a precipitous way, whereas countries of smaller size could, with higher probability of success, proceed to one-stroke integration of their factor markets with larger countries. With the usual hazardous application to the real case of new candidates for integration with the EC, the suggestion is that, if there has to be a sequence in considering the application of countries, the first ones to be admitted should be the smaller ones.

Although obtained from a simple theoretical model - where clearly many empirical economic and political elements are missing - such a result is suggestive of why smaller countries clustered around a larger one - such as the Benelux countries and Denmark, not to speak of East Germany - have already found it easier than larger countries to integrate their economies with that of the largest country (e.g. West Germany). This result is in line, although for different theoretical reasons, with an element of the theory of optimum currency areas, i.e. the one based on the degree of trade openness of a country vis-à-vis its prospective main partner.

According to this model, it could be against the interests of a large country (e.g. Germany) to integrate with countries of not much smaller size (such as France and Italy), since these could be large enough to attract the large country into their "black hole". The large country may instead be indifferent, and thus possibly willing, to integrate with much smaller countries (such as, again, the Benelux and other small countries neighbouring Germany). On their side, the smaller countries would be indifferent to the choice between precipitous and gradual integration - indeed between integrating or not with the large country - if integration were to attract the larger country into the smaller country's "black hole"; they would be interested only if integration, gradual or otherwise, were leading them to the higher position of equilibrium. Thus the large country would be attracted by integration only if it could eventually obtain from its partners a compensation for bringing them up to its higher level.

These results fit only part of the actual experience of the EC. In fact relatively large members, such as France and Italy, until recently objected to fast integration of their capital markets with that of WG, while smaller ones were more inclined to proceed quickly. More in line with the analysis' results is the higher willingness of WG to integrate closely with smaller than with equal-sized countries.

Even though political elements were clearly dominant, the model could also be stretched to explain the desire by EG to proceed to fast integration with WG, as well as some initial attempts by the latter to slow down that process. In fact the German case seems to fit the "transfer cum integration" approach: it is likely that, in the long run, the larger country (WG) will be "compensated" for the transfers that it has to grant initially to EG in order to implement a successful integration.

Clearly, other elements must be introduced into the model in order to capture the complexities of the German case. A possibility is to consider that German unification, by making the capital stock of EG suddenly obsolete, and thus to be partly scrapped, would land the country to the left of a lower and unstable equilibrium, whence it would move to an even lower one (see the movement from point $(K/L)_M$ to point $(K/L)_L$ in Fig. 5), possibly attracting down to that "black hole" also WG (initially located at $(K/L)_H$), unless the latter were to assist it with transfers high enough to take the joint K/L ratio to the right of the unstable point D.

Figure 5

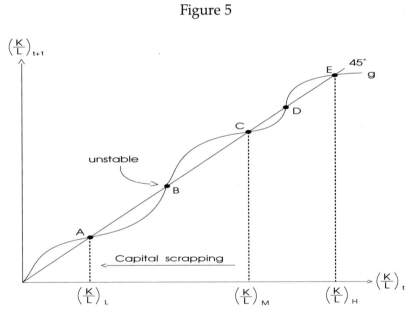

3.2 Integration of different countries with a third

As already pointed out with respect to "second best" arguments for gradualism in economic integration, it is not easy to distinguish between gradualism relating to different markets or different countries. This can instead easily be done within the "first best" model just discussed, since in its simpler formulation there is just one homogeneous product and the two factor markets (labour and capital) play a symmetrical role in the process of integration. Indeed, this model provides a simple but elegant theoretical basis for arguing in favour of the so-called "two-speed approach" to European economic integration. This approach - particularly discussed in relation to integrating capital markets in the European

Monetary System (EMS) countries and to moving ahead towards narrower bands for exchange-rate fluctuations - is now, as already recalled above, again in the foreground of debate concerning the fate of the Delors plan.

In order to meaningfully analyse the "two-speed approach" we need to consider in our model at least three countries and three stable equilibrium points. An example is shown in Fig. 6, where, of four stable equilibrium points, three correspond to the K/L ratios of three different countries before integration of their factor markets.

Apparently, with three countries, there are five possibilities: (i) precipitous integration of all three countries, (ii) gradual integration between all three countries, (iii) precipitous integration between countries 1 and 2, followed by their gradual integration with country 3, (iv) precipitous integration between countries 1 and 3, followed by country 2, and (v) precipitous integration between countries 2 and 3, followed by country 1. Clearly, for the "two-speed approach", only possibilities (iii)-(v) are of interest. Upon closer consideration, however, a larger set of possibilities can be identified. The two countries to be selected for merging their factor markets before integration with the third country may themselves move to such a merger with or without a preliminary transfer (i.e. by piecemeal or by precipitous integration), and then successively integrate in a precipitous or piecemeal way with the third country. Conceptually, therefore, each of the three pairings of countries gives rise to four possibilities. Thus there are in total twelve possibilities in which a "two-stage" (rather than "two-speed") approach could be applied to a community composed of three groups of countries.[11] In any case, whether the two-speed approach should encompass, with three countries, either three or twelve different possibilities, I shall only consider, in the following, the three different pairings of countries, without further specifying whether between them (and subsequently with the remaining country) integration is one-stroke or gradual.

It is also clear, from the enumeration of all possible cases, that their number grows rapidly with the number of countries involved. This, in addition to casting doubt on the usefulness of such theoretical analysis, should induce us to be cautious before jumping to conclusions about what seems to be, even on purely economic grounds, the best or most likely reaggregation of countries within the existing or a larger EC, for the process of gradual and differential movement towards European Economic and Monetary Union.

Figure 6

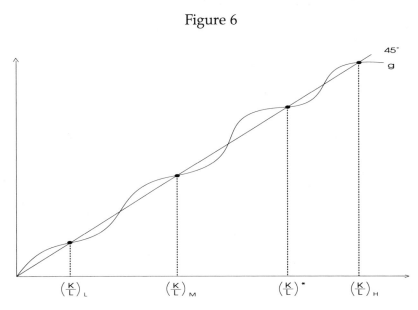

In any case, returning to the three countries example, which of these cases is preferable, i.e. which of the three countries (groups of countries) should integrate first, depends upon (a) the shape of capital-accumulation, function g, in particular the distance between the stable equilibrium points from which the countries start considering integration, and (b) the countries' relative economic size. However, the choice cannot be based only on such positive elements: in the dynamic setting of the model, the choice must also involve the present value of their social welfare or policy-objective functions, and weigh them appropriately.

Some interesting questions arise in this context, two of them strictly interconnected. A first is whether two countries with capital/labour ratios at opposite extremes (ratios $(K/L)_H$ and $(K/L)_L$ in Fig. 6) may find it advantageous to integrate their economies at a stable equilibrium point **lower** than the one from which the highly-placed country starts, in order to be able to integrate, subsequently and gradually, with a third country that was placed at an intermediate ratio (ratio $(K/L)_M$ in Fig. 6). This might be possible, if there are more than three stable equilibrium points and if the mid-country starting point is below the one to which the two fast-integrating countries decide to step (e.g., point $(K/L)^*$ in Fig. 6). This point, although lower than the starting one for the highest-placed country, would be more efficient for the three countries as a whole, if the highest-placed equilibrium could not be reached by any combination of one-stroke and gradual integration of the three countries' factor markets.

A second question is whether a country may efficiently proceed to **gradual** integration with the other two, only if these are allowed to move to their integration first and in one stroke. If it were so, the two-speed approach would also be in the interest of the country left behind waiting for its turn.

The analysis of these two questions could again be applied to the German unification process. It may be generally advantageous for WG (possibly the highest K/L country in the EC) to integrate its economy first and/or faster with EG (possibly the lowest K/L country, as compared with the rest of the EC), in order to make it subsequently viable for the united Germany to integrate with the rest of the EC. The WG "sacrifice" would be necessary in order to make it possible for the rest of the EC to integrate with the united Germany.

Perhaps more suggestive with reference to the other prospective members of the EC - such as Czechoslovakia, Hungary and Poland - is to apply the analysis and argue that stricter integration of their markets with only some of the present members of the EC is a prerequisite to making it subsequently possible also for the other present members to integrate with them.

A third question is whether, out of the multiple pairings of countries (or groups of them, when they are more than three) to be candidates for faster integration, more than one pairing leads to the same stable equilibrium. If so, the choice between alternative country pairings should, as mentioned above, be based on the higher present value of the sequence of steps leading to the steady state. In other words, and again applying the analysis to German unification, it could be that both a precipitous integration of EG and WG, and their alternative integration at the same pace as with the rest of the EC, would have eventually landed all EC countries in the same steady-state position. However, the paths leading to that position would have been different under the two alternatives: presumably the present value of the integration path that has led to German integration first is (at least when discounted at the German political discount rate) higher than the present value of the alternative path.

The arguments developed in this section on the basis of a dynamic trade model[12] emphasise structural (rather than economic policy) differences between countries as the basis for proceeding towards integration gradually and at different speeds for different countries. The model is clearly abstract, and empirical research is in order before accepting it as a relevant additional framework for explaining the difficulties currently experienced in the movement towards European Economic and Monetary Union and the problems that may arise in enlarging the EC to new entrants. However, before rejecting it as just theoretical or simply artificial, we may want to consider how relevant it could be in order to explain historical experience, such as that of the North and the South of Italy, where some economic historians have argued that their precipitous integration in the nineteenth century - accompanied by an immediate monetary unification - did not so much contribute to lifting the South up to Central European standards of development, as to pulling the North down to a level lower than the one it could have reached with a different choice of partners for political integration, or with a transitory monetary arrangement short of full monetary union with the South.

3.3 Different saving functions

In the model of section 3.1, countries had the same production and saving functions, and they only differed in their K/L ratios. In reality, countries also differ in their saving propensities -as often discussed with reference to Japan or Italy, as opposed to the US. In the German case it is likely that, leaving aside a temporary adjustment of a long-repressed propensity to spend, the saving ratio will be higher in East than in West Germany or the other EC partners, at least for a number of years during the necessary catching-up period. A higher saving rate, other things being equal, makes for a higher g function, and thus a higher steady-state K/L equilibrium for a united Germany than for its EC partners. The merging of the two Germanies may therefore lead to a joint steady-state situation above the one that could have been reached by West Germany alone. While beneficial to Germany, this could have opposite effects on the inducement to complete EC integration. On the one hand, it should enable Germany's partners in the EC to reach in due time a higher steady state, by successfully merging with the new Germany. On the other hand, the larger distance that would separate the united Germany's steady state from its partners' could give rise to points of unstable equilibrium that would, in the absence of transfers, make it no longer viable for the new Germany to integrate with the other EC partners.

In other words, here we may find a theoretical argument in support of the fear that German unification may water down German interest in moving further towards European integration.

4. Summary and conclusions

This paper has attempted to analyse some aspects of German unification by emphasising that their significance goes beyond the internal problems of German political economy, as it extends to the whole process of European unification. In fact, in some respects German unification has triggered a movement towards the enlargement and restructuring of the whole European Community, particularly with regard to East European countries.

The latter countries are already - or will soon be - knocking on the door of the EC, to become associate or even full members. The experience of German unification, though unique, contains lessons and suggestions as to how these new candidatures may strain, or reinforce, the movement already under way towards full European Economic and Monetary Union.

The approach of this paper is theoretical, so that it leaves out many elements, particularly those of a political nature. Even so, if these reservations are borne in mind, its results may raise some issues of which further empirical analysis and judgment is necessary. One initial conclusion of interest deriving from a static and non-monetary analysis is that German unification should contribute to a real appreciation of the mark, and possibly to increasing obstacles on the way to the full integration of the European internal market.

The analysis also deals with the issue of how the traditional partners in the EC will alter their trade with the unified Germany. It appears that intra-industry trade - i.e. trade in similar products that are differentiated by quality and produced under economies of scale - could develop more than inter-industry trade - i.e. trade in widely-differing products, where specialisation depends on countries' factor endowments rather than economies of scale.

Moving on to the issue of the relative ease with which Germany is becoming economically unified, the paper examines, by analogy, how the EC could meet the challenge of associating, and possibly fully integrating, new countries within its economic fabric. The paper tries to find indications for determining the optimal sequence of such associations. The analysis is based first on a static model for identifying the costs and benefits that derive from this process, and the characteristics that candidate countries should have, in terms of their factor endowments and economic size, in order to minimise the costs and maximise the benefits.

A dynamic model is then used to show how, in a framework

of growth, simultaneous integration between a set of countries may not be advisable, as it would lead all of them to a lower position in terms of capital per head. A better approach is to associate first those countries that are sufficiently different in size and/or differently endowed in terms of their capital/labour ratios. A suggestion that results from this analysis is that, while the two Germanies may have been a good example of countries that by integrating will improve their long-term position, the same may not occur with the association of other pairs of countries or the enlargement of the EC to take in all would-be members. The analysis also provides a new theoretical basis for the so-called "two-speed" approach to economic and monetary unification - an approach that is often coming to the surface in the debate on how fast and between which countries it is advisable to move towards European Economic and Monetary Union.

The growth model and its application to the analysis of this paper are clearly in need of further refinement. In particular, consideration of different saving propensities seems in order, both for theoretical reasons and because the new applicants to join the EC are indeed likely to contribute to it a higher propensity to save and a different demographic pattern - as is the case with East vis-à-vis West Germany.

References

1. I am grateful to Casper de Vries for the discussions we had on the implications of his work for the problems analysed in this paper. Vincenzo Denicolò has also provided useful comments.

2. In another paper (Basevi, 1990) I concentrated on the short- to medium-run implications for the evolution of the European Monetary System of German unification and the possible enlargement of the EC to include EFTA and East European countries.

3. Use of the Heckscher-Ohlin theoretical framework to analyse some of the aspects of German unification can also be found in Fitoussi and Phelps (1990) and Siebert (1990).

4. On the construction of the FPE set, see Dixit and Norman (1980), ch. 4; for its extensive use, see Helpman and Krugman (1985).

5. This possibility has been suggested by many authors, but often on the basis of different models. Gros and Steinherr (1990) argue for a possible appreciation of the DM on the basis of the disequilibrium created in the goods market by the need to expand demand in the East and contract it in the West, in a tradeables-non tradeables context. In my paper mentioned above (Basevi, 1990) I do the same, but with reference to the transfer theory model in an exportables and importables context. Begg et al. (1990) provide a more detailed analysis of the dynamic consequences of German unification for the exchange rate of the DM; see also Melitz (1991).

6. See Helpman and Krugman (1985), ch. 1.

7. The analysis does not consider the rest of the world or the existence of tariffs. Thus the choice is between trading or not trading goods and/or factors. As a consequence, the analysis does not refer to the theory of customs unions, which is the traditional basis for discussing problems of real integration between countries. On the other hand, because of the focus on factor and product market integration, the analysis comes closer to the theory of optimum currency areas, which is the traditional starting-point for discussing problems of monetary integration between countries.

8. Again, the model does not incorporate an economic analysis of these costs: they may be considered social utility costs, and considered from the point of view of the EC social utility function.

9. This approach has recently been advocated by the Bundesbank, and opposed particularly by the Bank of Italy, with reference to who should proceed and when to the second phase in the Delors plan for European monetary unification.

10. The model used here is borrowed from Dellas and De Vries (1990), and is a simple version of the Diamond (1965) model, presented also in Blanchard and Fischer (1989), ch. 3.

11. The first stage is when a pair of countries (or of groups of countries) integrates first (whether precipitously or gradually); the second stage is when that pair of countries, having completed integration of its factor markets, decides to integrate (in a precipitous or piecemeal fashion) with the third one.

12. One should note that, in this one-product dynamic model, international trade in products (and international movements of factors, if necessary) is only a temporary phenomenon, since it takes place only until the steady state is reached.

Bibliography

G. Basevi (1990), "Some implications of the developments in Eastern Europe for European Economic and Monetary Union", paper presented at the International Symposium on "A quest for a more stable world economic system", Osaka, October 22-25.

D. Begg et al., **Monitoring European Integration: the Impact of Eastern Europe**, CEPR Annual Report (London: CEPR, 1990).

O.J. Blanchard and S. Fischer, **Lectures on Macroeconomics** (Cambridge, Mass.: MIT Press, 1989).

H. Dellas and C.G. De Vries, "Piecemeal versus precipitous factor market integration", mimeo, May 1990.

(Delors Report) (1989), Committee for the Study of Economic and Monetary Union, **Report on Economic and Monetary Union in the European Community**.

P.A. Diamond, "National debt in a neoclassical growth model", **American Economic Review**, 15 (5), December 1965, pp. 1126-1150.

A. K. Dixit and V. Norman, **Theory of International Trade** (Cambridge: Cambridge University Press, 1980).

J.P. Fitoussi and E. Phelps, "Global effects of Eastern European rebuilding and the adequacy of western saving: an issue for the 1990's", paper presented at the 2nd Villa Mondragone Conference, mimeo, July 1990.

D. Gros and A. Steinherr, "Macroeconomic management in the new Germany: its implications for the EMS and EMU", mimeo (Brussels: CEPS, September 1990).

E. Helpman and P.R. Krugman, **Market Structure and Foreign Trade** (Brighton: Harvester Press, 1985).

J. Melitz, "German reunification and exchange-rate policy", mimeo.

H. Siebert, "The economic integration of Germany", **Kiel Discussion Paper** No. 160, 1990.

M. Willms, "German monetary unification and European Monetary Union: theoretical issues and strategic policy problems", paper presented at the Conference on "European monetary integration: from German dominance to an EC central bank?", American Institute for Contemporary German Studies, The Johns Hopkins University, Washington, D.C., mimeo, July 1990.

Macroeconomic management in the new Germany: implications for the EMS and EMU

Daniel Gros and Alfred Steinherr

Introduction

The broad goals of macroeconomic management in the "new" Germany are no different from those of the "old" Federal Republic: price stability and sound growth. However, the conditions under which these goals will be pursued are quite different. On the monetary side there is uncertainty about the behaviour of the financial sector in the new eastern part of the country, and on the fiscal side there is even more uncertainty since it is impossible to estimate the likely cost of reunification at present. In this paper we concentrate on the monetary side because in this area there is a clear potential for repercussions at the European level.

Federal German economic policy in general now has an additional and overriding goal: to equalise living conditions in the two parts of the country. However, it should be obvious that this goal cannot be reached with the tools of **macro**economic policy, i.e. monetary and fiscal policy. It requires a mixture of income transfers, investment subsidies, public infrastructure investment programmes, wage restraint and social legislation. We do not deal with these more **micro**economic policies except one, which we consider of primary importance, namely the issue of privatisation.

1. The benefits of monetary unification

Monetary union has already been effected, but it is still useful to emphasise its benefits because this shows that the decision to introduce the Deutschmark in the former GDR can be defended on economic grounds, even if the main motive was political. We recently argued that monetary union would have two main advantages: i) it would create overnight an efficient capital market that would facilitate international trade and domestic investment, and ii) it would replace the need for a comprehensive price reform.[1] This is indeed what has happened.

Currency union creates an instantaneous capital market

The importance of an international currency for the East German economy can be illustrated by considering the growth rate in foreign trade required for the territory to become as integrated into world markets as the "old" FRG was (let us say within a decade or so). This can be estimated crudely by comparing exports per capita. West German per capita exports to (and imports from) the OECD area were about 28 times higher than those of the GDR.[2] In order to come close to the level of West Germany, the exports (and imports, both with the rest of the world) of East Germany would have to grow for the next 10 years by over 40% in real terms each year. This would be much higher than the growth rates achieved by West Germany in the 1950's (whose real exports then grew by "only" about 15% annually), but with the help of totally free access to the markets of the EC it would be much easier.

The importance of an efficient capital market for investment can also be illustrated by looking at the investment rate which the East German economy would need in order to catch up with the West within a decade. This can be estimated by starting from the generally-accepted observation that the GDP per capita of East Germany is about one half of that of the West. To catch up in ten years, growth rates in the East would have to be about 7% above those for the West. Growth in the West has averaged about 2 to 3% recently; if this is extrapolated and if one allows for a 10% income-differential between the eastern and western **Länder** by the year 2000, the "required" rate of growth of GDP per capita in the East would be about 9%.[3] Using a capital output ratio of two and a depreciation rate of 12% (as in West

Germany),[4] this implies that the ratio of investment to GDP in the East should be about 30%[5] for the next ten years.

The very high growth rates of trade and investment necessary for East Germany to catch up with the West can only be achieved if the former's domestic capital market is well-enough developed to provide financing to existing and new firms and if the financing of exports and imports is not hampered by controls. Foreign financing of investments will be particularly sensitive to a stable monetary framework. The introduction of the DM in East Germany has been sufficient to fulfil both of these conditions. On the external side, all capital controls are gone and the financing of trade is no longer a problem. Without the DM as the basis of the banking system, the new **Länder** would not only have had to cope with a system of capital controls, but would also have had to learn how to operate in international financial markets, which would certainly have slowed down the process of trade integration.

On the internal side, firms in the East, many of which are new and small, now have access to the Federal banking system. Introducing the DM was thus equivalent to immediately creating an efficient capital market, which would otherwise have taken some time to develop. The West German banking system that "conquered" the territory of the GDR is already now providing the bulk of financing for new firms. In addition, with the DM as the common currency the large current account deficits which East Germany will have to run become invisible (like those of, say, Bavaria in the West) and can be financed by private capital without any difficulty. With two currencies the current account deficits would have been highly visible, and probably always a cause for concern for policy-makers and therefore a source of expectation of exchange-rate changes.

The only alternative that would have allowed the new **Länder** authorities to abolish capital controls immediately was flexible exchange rates. This solution would have had the advantage that the real exchange rate would have been established in the market and could therefore have reacted to shocks even if nominal wages were rigid. But given the great uncertainty surrounding the success of the transition to a market economy and eventual monetary unification, this rate might have fluctuated greatly and overshot in the transition. Moreover, under flexible exchange rates the monetary policy of the former GDR's **Staatsbank** would have been the only anchor for prices and inflationary expectations in the East. Given that it would have taken some time to build up a banking system and establish procedures of monetary control, monetary policy would have been highly uncertain, and over- and under-shooting of the exchange rate would probably have been the result. Even in the absence of political considerations, therefore, flexible exchange rates would not have been a viable alternative to the adoption of the DM as a common currency for a reunited Germany.

Currency union makes price reform superfluous

Introducing the DM in the new **Länder** had the additional advantage of being equivalent to a comprehensive price reform. Prices needed to be freed anyway, but without the price system of the West German **Länder** prices might have taken longer to find their equilibrium level. Moreover, the reforms that have the most immediate effects are the freeing of the price system and **Gewerbefreiheit**, i.e. the freedom to create new firms. What is happening now confirms what experience suggested anyway, namely that it takes time to privatise. The existing state-owned factories will therefore account for the bulk of industrial output for some time to come. Since these firms are in most cases local monopolists they might have used their power when setting new prices. With the DM as the common currency and open borders that is impossible.

As predicted, not all prices went immediately to the West German level. Even after the introduction of the DM the prices for non-tradables, i.e. personal services and real estate, continue to be lower in the East. There is apparently also some overcharging in rural areas, but these transitional problems are minor compared to the massive distortions that existed previously.

Before July 1990 it was often argued that the elimination of subsidies would raise price levels, according to some estimates by as much as 30%, and that this would imply a cut in real wages. However, this prediction was never appealing from a theoretical point of view since the savings from the elimination of subsidies can be used to lower taxes and increase direct income-transfers. Price reform and the elimination of subsidies should therefore lead to a redistribution of income, but should have little effect on the average level of real incomes. Events so far have shown that on the contrary, price levels in the former GDR have fallen if one compares June 1990 to December 1990.[6]

A fixed exchange rate between two separate currencies would have had a similar effect of equalising prices. But the link would not have been as strong, since the exchange rate might be changed over time and this would allow inflationary pressures to develop in the East, especially since at the outset a tight monetary policy would have been difficult to implement.

The main economic argument against the introduction of the DM in the former GDR was and is that it would make it difficult to change the real exchange rate if it was too high, because wages cannot be reduced in nominal terms.[7] However, the danger of an overvaluation would not have been avoided even in the absence of monetary union since the newly-reformed trade unions would probably have "seen through" the effects of a devaluation of the Mark and adjusted their wage demands accordingly.

2. Currency union and the choice of conversion rate

In order to implement currency union it is necessary to specify the rates at which current payments and stocks of financial assets are to be converted. We do not discuss the former, i.e. the conversion rate for wages. Many have argued that this was politically imposed and represents an overvaluation. However, we recently argued that converting wages at much less than 1:1 would mainly have led to inflation without solving the competitiveness problem of the old GDR.[8] Subsequent events have borne out the view that the conversion rate for current payments would anyway hold only for "a logical second". The substantial wage increases that have already taken place in the former GDR show that the conversion of wages at less than 1:1 would have anyway been "corrected" immediately. The conversion rate for wages was therefore irrelevant as an issue.

One of the most contentious aspects of the introduction of the DM in the territory of the former GDR was the rate at which financial assets, especially the savings deposits of East German citizens, were to be converted from Mark (east) into D-mark (west).[9] The **Bundesbank** proposed converting financial assets at 2:1 while providing all East German citizens with a lump sum called **Kopfgeld**.[10] The balance sheet of the consolidated credit system of the GDR before reunification provides a convenient background for a discussion of the economic impact of the choice of conversion rate for financial assets and liabilities.

Consolidated balance sheet of the GDR credit system
(31.12.1989, in billion DDR-mark)

Assets			Liabilities		
Credit to the domestic sector		418	Deposits		260
of which	households	23	Of which	households	176
	firms	260		firms	60
Claims on external sector		45	Foreign liabilities		162
Other Assets		4	Cash in circulation		17
			Capital and reserves		28
Total		467			467

It is apparent that the balance sheet total is much larger than one would expect from the figure of about 176 billion in savings deposits that had been known for some time. Firms also held deposits of 60 billion. However, the large "foreign" assets and liabilities are mainly the result of complicated internal accounting conventions which have little to do with the $18 billion net foreign debt of the GDR.

Public attention focused for a time on the most important item on the asset side, i.e. "credit to firms" of 260 billion. We argue, however, that this was not warranted since in the GDR there were only two sectors, households and the government. The latter comprised firms (all government-owned) and the "external" sector (through the government monopoly on foreign trade). The distribution of assets between the state, firms and the external sector was therefore irrelevant and arbitrary under the old system.

The fact that the government controlled all firms (and still controls many through the **Treuhand**) implies that from an economic point of view it is irrelevant how much firms owe to banks and at what rate this debt is to be converted. If debts had been converted at 1:1 many firms would not have been able to repay them and the government would have had to pay up. If firms had been able to service their debt, their privatisation value would have diminished by a corresponding amount and the government would have lost in sales revenues what it received indirectly through the banks in the form of debt-service payments. The rate at which the debt of firms was converted therefore had few economic implications. It determined only what one part of the government sector had to pay the other. Converting the debt of firms at 2:1 or lower did, however, have advantages from an accounting point of view: fewer banks and firms became technically bankrupt.

In this situation the main economic impact of the choice of the rate for currency conversion came from the net creditor position of households (vis-à-vis the government sector). This "exposure" of households was equal to 176 billion GDR-marks in savings deposits,[11] not the 46 billion of credit to the state that appear on the asset side of the balance sheet. Conversion at 2:1 instead of 1:1 did therefore reduce the implicit transfers from the

Bundesbank (through so-called compensatory items) by about 88 billion DM (not taking into account the **Kopfgeld**). The **Bundesbank**'s proposal nevertheless aroused a storm of protests in the old GDR. It was justified on the grounds that a conversion of the 176 billion mark in deposits at 1:1 (into DM) would lead to a massive "monetary overhang", whereby the increase in the DM money supply would exceed the increase in money demand coming from the old GDR's economy.

The increase in the money supply can be mechanically calculated from the existing stock; however, the additional demand for money is very difficult to estimate. Most of the difficulties came from the fact that it was and still is not clear what kind of "money" is represented by the savings deposits,[12] i.e. whether or not they can be considered equivalent to "sight" deposits (M1 in technical terms) because they can be cashed without notice. If they were to be viewed as such, the additional demand for DM would be only about 40 billion and conversion at 4:1 would have been appropriate. If they were to be considered "true" savings deposits (M3 in technical terms), the additional demand for DM would then be about 80 billion and conversion at 2:1 would have been appropriate. Finally, if they were to be considered as representing the sum of all financial assets (because no other savings instruments were available in the old GDR), households might use them partly to buy other financial assets and even at a conversion rate of 1:1 there would not have been a monetary overhang.

A concern that was frequently raised until recently was that a favourable conversion rate would generate inflationary demand pressures. We did not share this concern, which with hindsight appears unfounded. The reason for not expecting important inflationary demand pressures from this source was that the larger deposits were accumulated to top up the extremely meagre pensions most East Germans have been able to expect. Even if pensions are somewhat increased by the new Federal government, many pensioners will need the interest income from their savings for some time. Moreover, savers in the new **Länder** will for the first time have access to a range of alternative real and financial investments and might also wish to insure themselves against unemployment. All this increases their propensity to save, making it highly unlikely that East German citizens will plunder their savings to go on a spending spree.

Events so far do not indicate that there is any monetary overhang. Interest rates have risen, rather than going down as one would expect from a monetary policy that was temporarily too loose. There is no sign, either, of demand pressures in West Germany originating in the eastern part of the country. German unification therefore appears not to be leading to uncontrollable inflationary pressures.

3. German unification and European exchange rates

It is widely expected that German unification will lead to a large reduction in the current account surplus of Germany[13] because of the huge investment needs in the eastern part of the country.[14] The crucial question for the European Monetary System is whether this requires a real appreciation of the DM. If it does, a realignment would be desirable to forestall the tensions that would otherwise arise inside the EMS.[15] Given the unprecedented nature of the event it is dangerous to hazard any predictions, but it is still useful to apply some simple basic tenets of economics to see whether German unification is likely to produce tensions in the EMS. In doing so it will be convenient to distinguish between the demand effects that arise in the short run and the supply effects from factor movements that might take longer to occur. Finally, this section will also speculate about the effects of German unification on the leadership position of the **Bundesbank** in the EMS.

The short to medium run: demand effects

The crucial point to be kept in mind in the ensuing analysis is that at given West German wages, the exchange rate of the DM - against, for example, the French franc - determines the price of

West German relative to other European goods. It is therefore essential to distinguish between the effects which German unification will have on the demand for goods produced, respectively, in East and West Germany, because their relative prices may change through changes in wages in East Germany, which, at least for the coming few years, will be negotiated independently from wages in the West.

The widespread hypothesis that German unification requires a real appreciation of the DM is usually based on the conventional "tradables versus non-tradables" framework. In this an increase in overall demand goes partly towards tradables, thus reducing the external surplus, but also partly towards non-tradables, whose supply is not infinitely elastic (or at least much less elastic than that of tradables), thus requiring an increase in the relative price of non-tradables. At given nominal wages such an increase requires an appreciation of the nominal exchange rate.

If this standard model is applied to the problem at hand, however, it does not lead to the conclusion that a real appreciation of the DM is required. It would be required only if the demand for West German non-tradables were to go up, which can happen only if West Germans spend more. However, this is not a necessary consequence of German unification since West Germans lend or transfer large accounts of purchasing power to East Germans. There is therefore no reason why the relative price of, say, French and German non-tradables should change.

On the contrary, one could even argue that, despite the denials of the Bonn government, citizens in the western part of Germany expect to pay higher taxes to cover the interest on the approximately 100 billion DM fund that is supposed to cover the cost of reunification. This might lead to a reduction in demand in the West, part of which would fall on non-tradables, requiring a real depreciation of the DM. This might explain why the DM is currently weak inside the EMS.[16] If this hypothesis is true, keeping the nominal exchange rate of the DM unchanged would mean that inflation must fall in Germany, rather than increase as is often argued.[17] This argument does not mean that in the case of Germany "full Ricardian equivalence" applies and that therefore all future taxes are immediately taken into account by consumers. All it implies is that in the present special circumstances the German public is very well aware of the burden on the public finances that will come in the next few years. This public awareness, coupled with higher interest rates, should dampen expenditure in West Germany, thus reducing the need for a realignment.

The relative price of East German non-tradables (goods that cannot be traded between, say, Germany and France can presumably be considered also as non-tradables between East and West Germany) may of course have to change. And it can change easily because a large jump has already occurred through conversion at 1:1 for wages, and further adjustments can take place through wage increases in East Germany.

Another framework often used to argue that German unification requires a real appreciation of the DM is one in which there are nationally-differentiated tradable goods. In this framework there would also be a need for a real appreciation of the DM only if East Germans (as the ones receiving the additional purchasing power) have a higher propensity to acquire West German tradables than those produced by other members of the EC. The extent to which East Germans do in fact prefer West German goods is impossible to determine a priori. Casual observation suggests that, with the possible exception of West German investment goods, most of the spending seems to go towards goods supplied by other members of the EC and the newly-industrialised countries of East Asia.

The only way to make actual data bear on this question is to use the experience of other European economies of a size comparable to that of the former GDR, such as the Netherlands and Belgium. These countries take no more than a quarter of all their imports from the Federal Republic. Applying the same percentage to East Germany implies that even if the latter runs a current account deficit with the West of 80 billion DM per annum (i.e. about 30% of its own GDP) the additional demand for West German exportables would be only about 20 billion DM (and the reduction in the German current account surplus would be 60 billion DM).[18] This represents only about 3% of overall West German exports in 1989, i.e. prior to unification, a total of 600 billion DM, which is not likely to require a large price change.

The long run: factor movements

A different way to look at the implications of German unification for the EMS is to take into account not only its effects on demand, but also factor endowments and movements using the standard Heckscher-Ohlin framework.[19] The crucial point in this framework is that East Germany starts out with a much lower capital-labour ratio. This should lead to capital flows into East Germany.[20] However, given that the German capital market is open to the rest of the world, most of the capital will come from the rest of the world (hence the lower external surpluses). Movements of goods and factors can equalise prices and consequently there will again be no need for a change in the relative price of (West) German exports relative to imports.[21]

Implications for the EMS

It has been argued so far that German unification might not really imply a need for a large exchange-rate adjustment, basically because it represents above all an inter-regional shock inside Germany itself. However, it might still have considerable implications for the European Monetary System if it were to affect the leadership position of the **Bundesbank** within the System.

German unification brings with it the possibility of a large financial shock, because it implies a considerable increase in uncertainty about the demand for DM balances. It can be argued that this reduces the usefulness of the anchor function of the DM and makes a more symmetrical EMS desirable. However, this uncertainty should not persist too long, since the West German banking network is already implanted in the East. After an initial adjustment period during which the East German public learns to adapt to this network, its demand should become as predictable as that of the West German public before unification.

A more serious reason why the leadership of the **Bundes-bank** might become less strong, however, is that, at least in the eyes of some, its anti-inflationary credibility has been reduced. The Bonn government's offer, early in 1990, to introduce the DM in the GDR already showed clearly the limits of the **Bundes-bank**'s independence. Moreover, it is widely perceived that if the shock treatment administered to East Germany's economy leads to politically-unacceptable unemployment there, the **Bundesbank** might not be in a position to resist the pressure for a softer policy stance, in the form of lower interest rates and/or debt-relief for firms in East Germany.

However, these are also factors that might actually strengthen the position of the **Bundesbank**. If the process of integrating the East German economy proceeds smoothly, the relative economic weight of Germany and therefore that of the **Bundesbank** should increase. Moreover, it may be expected that some of the Eastern European countries (Czechoslovakia, Hungary, and perhaps Poland) will adopt the DM extensively in their foreign trade, a large share of which will be with Germany. This should also increase the special position of the DM in the European system. But these factors are likely to become important only after an initial adjustment period of several years, when the current EMS has been superseded by stage II of the Delors plan incorporating a European monetary institution that will take over the leadership role currently exercised by the **Bundesbank**.

German unification as a regional issue

German unification will lead to large shifts of demand and also to large factor movements within one small area that constitutes an economic and monetary union. This will require large shifts of relative prices **within** Germany. But these are possible (in one direction at least) since due to the exceptional circumstances, wages can move independently in the two regions bound together by the German EMU. The purpose of this section has been to argue that the need for a change in the price of goods produced in one part of Germany (the western part) relative to the rest of Europe will be minor (if not necessarily zero). If the arguments used to justify the need for a realignment of the DM today were correct, it would follow that once economic and monetary union has been achieved within the European Community, any large increase in regional aid to finance large public investments in Southern Europe should lead to a stronger Ecu. Few would accept this corollary.[22]

4. Privatisation and growth perspectives

Reunification implies a thorough institutional reform in the old GDR, with a realignment of property rights to conform with those existing in the old FRG. Whilst there may be no issue of principle, there certainly is the issue of the modalities for carrying out the institutional change. Privatisation needs to be seen in terms of both efficiency and its distributional effects. Distribution is particularly important in order to ease the hardship of transition and give East Germans a sense of fair treatment. Acceptance of the wealth distribution at the start of a market-based system is all the more important as labour incomes will remain well below those in West Germany during the transition period and uncertainty about job requirements and availability will be quite high.

One important political goal of rapid integration has been to reduce the flow of **übersiddler** (migrants from East to West Germany). Since the time when subsidies for accommodating such migrants were phased out (i.e. when this category was eliminated), the flow has fallen drastically. Nevertheless, it may be feared that with real income differentials at the present level of about one to two and the prospect of increasing unemployment, there is still a risk of renewed emigration from the East.

Of course, emigration is costly and depends not simply on an individual's or a family's current income, but rather on per-manent income. Therefore, it becomes important to achieve a credible growth programme for the East which will bring permanent income closer to West German levels. However, given the economic and psychological costs of migration, incomes do not need to be perfectly equalised. As argued earlier, credibility was achieved through currency union and this is a major factor.

The prospects for permanent income (the present value of future earnings) depend on two main factors: growth in East Germany and its distribution. We now consider both in turn.

The effect of growth

It was argued in Section 1 that it is entirely feasible to bring per capita income in the former GDR up to the level of West Germany. This would require growth rates of about 7% above those of West Germany. A one-percentage point of growth represents an increase of per capita permanent income of about 10%. This is roughly equivalent to a transfer from West to East Germany of 30 billion DM. As long as an average growth rate of 10% remains a credible target for the next ten years, permanent income would double and should provide enough incentive for East Germans to stay at home.

What this argument neglects, however, is how the growth in income is to be distributed. It implicitly assumes a neutral di. tribution. Whether this assumption is warranted or not depends, of course, not only on labour income but also on the initial distribution of wealth.

Privatisation

Historic examples of ownership structure can be usefully grouped into four stylised classes: a "colonial" regime where assets are predominantly owned by foreigners; state or "social" ownership, as was the case in the old GDR; direct ownership by national citizens, as has been the case in West Germany; or indirect ownership through unit trusts to whom investment choices and managerial control are entrusted.

What is going to happen in East Germany? The ownership of 8,000 major firms and **Kombinate** has been transferred to **Treuhand**, whose task it is to privatise these firms or groups after an evaluation of their future viability and "market" value. An effort has been made by **Treuhand** to establish contacts with firms in West Germany and other countries with the aim of arranging shareholding, joint ventures or takeovers. As there is very little scope for sell-outs to East German residents, there is a danger of getting close to a "colonial" system of ownership which would be deeply resented.

A further issue which has not been tackled is raised by the implicit social contract of the old GDR. Presumably social ownership of the means of production meant that the state managed productive assets but that these belonged to the people. Even if one rejects this concept, it may not be wise to dismiss the substance of such a social contract completely. **Treuhand** will, of course, hand over its net receipts to the Bonn government, which in turn will provide financial transfers to German citizens in the East. But the latter will not hold extensive ownership of the territory's productive assets.

On the operational side, **Treuhand** also faces serious difficulties in proceeding rapidly with privatisation. It is a Herculean task to evaluate 8,000 firms in an environment characterised by profound structural change. Either the job will be done somewhat superficially or it will take a very long time. Neither option appears attractive. We therefore strongly believe that an alternative solution should be given serious consideration. This consists of distributing ownership of the capital stock (state-owned houses and productive assets) to citizens along the following lines.

Firstly, the ownership of housing would be transferred to present occupants. Rents would continue to be paid for, say, 10 years and they would be considered as instalments towards the acquisition price. They could be indexed to average wage rates and therefore rise only in line with purchasing power. Houses could be bought and sold but ownership rights would be lost in the event of emigration.

Secondly, the same system would be applied to the agricultural sector, with co-operatives (**Genossenschaften**) free to split up or stay together.

Thirdly, individual and small firms would be turned over to their present managers and workers, who would continue to pay taxes and rents to acquire the buildings.

Fourthly, most of the **Kombinate**, or holding companies, now in the **Treuhand** portfolio would be turned into joint-stock companies. Some would be sold to foreigners when technological modernisation, economies of scale or the acquisition of marketing and management skills could not be achieved in any other way. For the remainder, each **Kombinat** would issue a number of shares equal to the number of citizens with voting rights. Each citizen would receive one share in each **Kombinat** and thus a highly-diversified portfolio of the economy of the former GDR. The value of these shares could and need not be known a priori: they would be distributed freely. Thus at the end of the socialist experience, at least, collective ownership would have acquired a concrete sense. Such shares would be tradable. Their current book value might not amount to much, but after currency union the present value of future earnings could be a multiple for at least some of them. Therefore there is an incentive for holding on to them.

The **Kombinate** would own, say, 50% of the **Volkseigener Betrieb** (VEB), or individual holdings, comprising the **Kombinat**. The remainder would be given to the workers in the VEB. These shares would not be tradable for, say, two years and would be lost in the event of emigration, in order to provide incentives to stay in the GDR. Workers would thereby also be encouraged to take a greater interest in the performance and management of their firm. **Kombinate** would be closer to a holding company, as they already are to a large measure today. VEBs are legally independent entities, frequently with an independent finance plan. **Kombinate** could provide management or financial expertise or sell their shares to a Western firm. VEBs would also be free to opt out of a **Kombinat**, which would then be reduced to the role of major shareholder. One implication of this proposal is that government employees would receive shares in the **Kombinate** but not in VEBs. Therefore they would receive fewer shares than workers or members of co-operatives. This differentiation can be seen as a premium for the job security they enjoy.

With such widespread share-ownership, all citizens of the former GDR would overnight become "capitalists", an objective actively pursued in West Germany - without, however, complete success. The creation of a stock market would be greatly stimulated and long-term gains would probably be important judging by the experience of the old FRG. Few people invested in stocks in the late 1940's but those who did have never regretted it, nor would they have regretted staying where they were.

What are the pros and cons of this proposal? First of all, it would put capitalism on a broad basis and create a starting point for tradable productive assets. As privatisation progressed, each citizen would hold an increasingly-diversified portfolio. Obviously, not all citizens would be interested in holding all the shares they received and an informal market would therefore arise. This would provide the basis for an over-the-counter market and eventually for an organised stock exchange. Any investor wishing to obtain control over a company would then have to acquire shares at market rates or with a takeover proposal. Whether the investor was a resident or non-resident would then be a question of secondary importance. Citizens, as shareholders, would decide and cash in now rather than later, as in a referendum, about each sale to foreigners, with the clear advantage that each citizen would have the same endowment of "voting" rights (one). A possible sell-out to foreigners could not be critised because it would not be a political decision in any centralised sense.

Second, such a privatisation programme would be flexible enough to accommodate worker participation if so desired. Instead of union power in versions of the West German **Mitbestimmung** (worker-participation), workers could be allocated part of the shares of their firm, as outlined above, and thereby exercise their votes and benefit from the firm's profits. Of course, they should not be in any way constrained from disposing of such shares for reasons of better risk-diversification or otherwise. One implication of such a differentiated scheme would be that all workers in privatised firms would get their allocation of shares in all privatised firms plus a special allocation of shares of the firm in which they worked. Employees of the public sector would not get that second allocation. Economically one could consider the firm-specific allocations as a risk premium, because the risks of bankruptcy or job reductions are higher in the private sector. Moreover, as the public sector in East Germany has been greatly overstaffed, some incentives to leave would be appropriate.

Third, it would be consistent with social justice. In fact, for the first time the terminology of social ownership of the means of production would be given a real, as opposed to rhetorical, meaning. In such systems it would certainly be impossible to compute the social contributions of each individual and make share allocations accordingly. How would one compare the marginal social productivity of a civil servant with that of a coal miner? Similarly, young people would inherit the goods as well as the problems of older generations. Therefore there should not be any discrimination and everybody should obtain one share.

This proposal has the additional attractiveness of making a **tabula rasa**. The new starting point would be one where social capital is distributed according to the principle of equal starting conditions. Capitalism would then also be perceived as a system with a potential not only for greater dynamism but even for greater social justice. This is a notion well accepted in West Germany, where privatisation is often aimed at spreading share-ownership as widely as possible. One could argue that citizens endowed with a portfolio of shares in national industry definitely become convinced capitalists and recognise capitalism's "human face". In a document on reforms needed in the USSR, Professor Stanislav Shatalin expressed this point very aptly: "A person who has his own home and his own plot of land... a person who owns shares and other financial instruments, is objectively interested in the stability of society, and in social and national harmony."

Fourth, control over companies would obviously not be exerted by the whole population. In this respect the problem is no different from that of large Western companies with hundreds of thousands of shareholders. There are several options for the practical setting-up of share ownership. The choice depends on whether one favours direct or institutional ownership. If shares are held directly, a system of proxy-voting exercised by banks and unit trusts could fulfil this function on a permanent basis. This option has the advantage of contributing to the active development of the stock market, but the possible disadvantage of insufficient incentives for effective managerial control. Alternatively, **Treuhand** could remain the owner of the shares and itself be transformed into a joint-stock company whose shares were distributed as outlined above. One disadvantage would be excessive concentration of control by **Treuhand**. If this were a serious matter of concern, **Treuhand** could be split into several units competing with each other. Such a splitting-up would in any case make sense as it does not seem possible for one institution to control several thousand companies effectively.

Finally, for privatisation purposes no assessment of the value of the firm would be necessary. This job would be taken over at a subsequent stage by the stock exchange. Nor would a decision at a stroke be required. Companies could be privatised one by one.

5. Conclusion

In this paper we have investigated several issues on which opinions and interpretations have not yet settled down to a widely-accepted view. We argue that the sequence of integrating the GDR's and the FRG's economies, starting with a currency union, was the best economic choice. It made reforms easier and quicker than under any alternative.

The concerns about the risks of monetary destabilisation and dramatic exchange-rate repercussions, requiring a substantial appreciation of the DM, were in our view misplaced and unsupported by economic analysis. The evolution of inflation and of the exchange rate since currency union became effective fully supports our view.

Many commentators considered conversion at 1:1 to be excessively harsh and now point to rising unemployment and the financial difficulties of firms in the old GDR as consequences of the chosen conversion rate. We strongly reject this view. Given the inefficiencies of the GDR's economy and the need for drastic restriction, the only choice concerned the timing. Rather than delaying necessary structural changes it always seems better to reform right away. Financial difficulties, the closures of some firms and a transitory rise in unemployment were unavoidable under any circumstances. What conversion at 1:1 could, however, avoid was massive social conflict and a wage-price spiral whose dynamic instability was to be feared.

Even if the present situation in the old GDR is difficult (and who could argue that this would have been avoidable?) the prospects for rapid improvement are excellent. A dramatic increase in permanent income has occurred and currency union provides the necessary stability for projecting a future growth path. Reaching West German levels of income within 10 years is an altogether feasible and reasonable prospect. The sharp drop in emigration to West Germany suggests that citizens in the East subscribe to this view.

Less reassuring is the process of privatising real assets in the East. Here we have two concerns. First, the task of privatising 8,000 companies one by one cannot be carried out quickly and in an economically rational way by any bureaucracy, let alone the **Treuhand**, which has to rely on a large number of old **Kader**. We fear that the process will be too slow or that economic rationality will suffer. Second, 100% private ownership per se is neither economically efficient nor socially desirable.

We argue that the previous social contract of the GDR should be respected, which implies that ownership should be transferred freely to the former GDR's citizens. The current operations of the **Treuhand** suggest that privatisation may result in a sell-out to non-GDR residents, leading to serious reactions motivated by the feeling of having been carpetbagged. We therefore elaborate a practical proposal to avoid such repercussions and give the residents of the former GDR a place in the new system.

References

1. See Gros and Steinherr (1990a).

2. This figure is a result of the extreme CMEA orientation of the former GDR's economy. It can be assumed that this market will disappear with the generalised move to trade based on world prices and convertible currencies.

3. For comparison: West Germany achieved 8.8% overall GDP growth and about 7% on a per capita basis in the 1950's. Foreign investment and Marshall Aid combined, however, represented only a fraction of the potential investment flows from West Germany to the GDR.

4. This does not account for the fact that most of the existing capital stock in the former GDR is obsolete.

5. For comparison: FRG in 1960 about 24 and in 1988 about 20%.

6. Hans-Werner Sinn, "Macroeconomic aspects of German unification", NBER Working Paper No. 3596, January 1991.

7. This effect is also considered the main potential cost of European monetary union.

8. **German Unification in European Perspective**, CEPS Working Document No. 49, March 1990.

9. This section is based on Gros and Steinherr (1990b).

10. The amount finally agreed varied between 2 and 6000 Mark depending on age classes.

11. The exact exposure of households is 176 billion plus 17 cash minus 23 billion of real-estate credit.

12. For more details on the following calculations see Gros (1990) which uses data from the FRG in the 1960's.

13. In 1990, before unification, the FRG had a large surplus and the GDR a small deficit. After reunification the former GDR region had a large deficit so that all of Germany had a much lower surplus.

14. This section is based on Gros and Steinherr (1990c). For a different view see Wyplosz (1990).

15. A real appreciation of the DM could also be achieved without a realignment if inflation in Germany were to increase considerably. It is assumed that the Bundesbank will not let this happen.

16. The entire group of EMS currencies is strong vis-à-vis the rest of the world because of the current boom in Europe as a whole.

17. That is, the West German Consumer Price Index should increase less. However, the weighted average of the East and West German index can be expected to show a higher inflation rate, since wages in East Germany are likely to increase at a faster rate than in the West.

18. These crude calculations do not take into account the import content of West German exports into the former GDR, estimated to be as high as 40%, implying that each DM of exports from West to East Germany reduces the current account surplus by 0.4 DM. However, preliminary calculations suggest that this effect is more or less offset by the fact that exports from the rest of the Community (and EFTA) contain imports from West Germany.

19. The demand-side story takes place implicitly at given factor endowments.

20. Perfect, i.e. instantaneous, mobility of both factors would, of course, lead to instant equalisation of the capital-labour ratio. However, since movement of both factors involve adjustment costs the ratio will not be equaliseu immediately.

21. This is true as long as the East German economy is in the factor-price equalisation region.

22. In a similar vein: who would expect the US dollar to strengthen if the US absorbed Mexico?

Bibliography

Paul De Grauwe (1990), "Currency union between East and West Germany: what should be the conversion rate?", in **German Unification in European Perspective**, Centre for European Policy Studies Working Document No. 49, March 1990.

Wolfgang Gebauer (1990), "German monetary union: on implicit theories and European consequences", **Geld und Währung** Working Paper No. 15.

Daniel Gros (1990), "The DM for the GDR: why and how", mimeo, Brussels, February 1990.

Daniel Gros and Alfred Steinherr (1990a), "Currency union and economic reform in the GDR: a comprehensive one-step approach" in **German Unification in European Perspective**, Centre for European Policy Studies Working Document No. 49, March 1990.

Daniel Gros and Alfred Steinherr (1990b), "A German compromise that makes economic sense", **Financial Times**, 21 May 1990.

Daniel Gros and Alfred Steinherr (1990c), "Relax, GEMU Poses no Problems for EMU", **The Wall Street Journal**, 23 July 1990.

Horst Siebert (1990), "The economic integration of Germany", Kiel Institute of World Economics Working Document No. 160, May.

Charles Wyplosz (1990), "A note on the real exchange-rate effect of German unification", mimeo, **INSEAD**, August 1990.

The economic integration of Germany: two tales based on trade theory

Paul De Grauwe

The monetary union between East and West Germany launched on 1 July 1990 was opposed by a majority of economists. They argued that monetary union should come as the last step in a long process of economic unification. The gradualist approach towards monetary unification has also been the cornerstone of the Delors Report.

Germany decided otherwise, and turned this gradualist approach upside down. Whether the right decision was made will be difficult to determine, and is likely to remain a subject of academic debate. The question analysed in this paper concerns the prospects for the economic integration process in Germany.

Our forecasts of the future development of countries or regions that integrate with each other depend very much on the theoretical model at the back of our minds. We have basically two models of the effects of the integration process. One is the traditional trade model based on comparative advantage; the other can be called the "increasing returns" model that has received more attention recently. These two models lead to drastically-different predictions of how the integration process will take place.

The comparative advantage model

This theory postulates that with free trade, regions will specialise in the activities in which they have a comparative advantage. Most poor regions have an abundance of cheap labour. Therefore free trade and economic integration will lead them to specialise in relatively labour-intensive production. This in turn will put upward pressure on wage levels in these poor regions. The opposite occurs in rich regions, which are usually endowed with a large capital stock. These regions will specialise in capital-intensive activities which tend to depress the level of wages. This phenomenon leads to a narrowing of the income gap between rich and poor regions.

Similar forces are at work tending to equalise the return on capital in different regions. In rich regions, capital is abundant so that its return tends to be low. In poor regions, capital is scarce so that its return is high. The process of market integration will therefore lead to outward investment from rich regions towards poor ones. This will lead to a dynamic tending to equalise rates of return.

This view of the regional effects of economic integration has a long tradition in economics. It is based on the Heckscher-Ohlin trade model.[1] It also leads to the conclusion that economic integration contains a dynamic tending to reduce regional income inequalities.

The increasing returns model

There are, however, other forces which work in the opposite direction, and which may lead to greater regional inequalities following a process of market integration. These phenomena have to do with economies of scale, both static and dynamic, and with externalities. Let us concentrate on the static economies of scale first.

The enlargement of markets makes it possible for firms to exploit economies of scale, close inefficient plants and concentrate their activities in fewer and larger plants. It is clear that this process must lead to divergent regional effects. Some regions (or sub-regions), where activities are concentrated, will gain, others may lose. The phenomenon of economies of scale leads to "agglomeration effects" in some places. The reverse of that coin is depopulation in others.

Dynamic economies of scale lead to similar agglomeration effects. Large-scale production leads to the accumulation of experience and technological know-how. Over time, this allows for productivity gains, which in turn increase competitiveness and stimulate more production. Economic growth becomes a cumulative process in a world where dynamic economies of scale are important.

This process of cumulative growth and concentration of production is reinforced by external effects. First, producers in the same region profit from the existence of a pool of specialised labour and specialised suppliers. This makes it possible to respond flexibly to changing market circumstances, and to quickly exploit new profit opportunities. In the absence of such a pool of resources firms have to raise their prices in order to attract them from elsewhere.[2] Second, producers in the same place benefit from the technological and scientific performance of other producers. Workers trained in one firm will, when moving to others, bring their technical expertise with them. These externalities have the effect of creating economies of scale for the industry as a whole. They are therefore called "economies of scale external to firms".

Thus, once a region is able to attract a significant amount of productive activities, it may find itself on a cumulative growth path, while regions unable to attract or to engender these activities will experience difficulties in taking off. These phenomena of increasing returns and externalities lead to the conclusion that market integration may result in increasing divergences in regional income levels.[3]

One important feature of these "increasing returns" models is that the prediction of where exactly these economic activities will be concentrated is difficult if not impossible to make. Much depends on historical accidents. A region may obtain a small initial advantage based on some unique historical event, and start a process of cumulative growth. This process will also lead to a regional concentration of economic activity.

When we compare the comparative advantage effect and the increasing returns effect, we must conclude that the process of economic integration does not have clear-cut results for regional development. The former effect leads to a convergence of regional incomes, the latter to a divergence. Which of the two effects will prevail is difficult to predict a priori.

Some empirical evidence of the integration process in Europe can be useful here. If we look at sufficiently large regions, e.g. the Iberian peninsula versus northern Germany and the Low Countries, the equalising effects of economic integration will tend to dominate, because these regions are large enough to be able to attract "increasing returns" industries. Comparative advantage becomes the more important integrating force. As a result, the Iberian peninsula is catching up on the northern part of Europe. In much the same way Italy as a whole has been catching up on the northern part of Europe since the early 1960's.

Evidence of this catching-up is presented in table 1. During the last thirty years Italy and Spain have experienced a higher growth rate of real GDP than West Germany, which has allowed them to narrow the income gap with the latter country. Thus, if we combine regional effects, say, for the north of Europe versus the south, there seems to be evidence of a convergence of real incomes over long periods of time.

Table 1: **GDP per capita in southern Europe**
(expressed as % of West German GDP per capita)

Year	Italy	Spain	Greece	Portugal
1960	66	28	33	23
1970	71	36	37	24
1987	73	39	24	19

Source : European Commission, **European Economy**, July 1987, table 7.

However, if we analyse the regional effects themselves, the economies of scale and the cumulative growth effects may become more important, leading to increasing income gaps. This may have been the phenomenon underlying the divergence in economic growth between the north and the south of Italy in the postwar period. It may also explain the fact that in southern Europe, two small countries, Portugal and Greece, have experienced increasing income gaps with the north, as is also made clear in table 1.[4]

The comparative advantage model and German unification

Comparative advantage effects depend mainly on future developments in wages and productivity in East Germany. At the start of monetary union on 1 July, labour was considerably cheaper in the eastern part of Germany than in the western part. It has been estimated that East German wage levels were only about 40% of West German ones.[5] At the same time average productivity in East German industry was estimated to be also about 30 to 40% of the West German level. This led some observers to believe that unit labour costs in East Germany were at a comparable level to those in West Germany, so that East German industry could be said to be broadly competitive at the start of monetary union.

Subsequent events have destroyed this optimistic view. The large-scale collapse of East German industry during 1990 suggests that the productivity statistics given vastly overstated the true productivity of the East German worker. This probably derives from the fact that productivity measures were based on physical productivity, and not on the market value of output per worker. To give an example, if the East German worker produced, on average, one Trabant per unit of time, and his West German counterpart two Volkswagen Golfs during the same time, one could conclude that the East German worker's productivity was half the West German one. The market value of a Trabant compared to a VW Golf, however, is much lower. As a result, the (value) productivity of the East German worker was substantially lower than the (physical) productivity measures led us to believe.

A first conclusion emerges. At the start of German monetary union, labour (in efficiency units) was expensive in East Germany compared to West Germany. Thus, the dynamics of comparative advantage effects, predicting that low-wage regions attract labour-intensive activities, and that these regions' real incomes can catch up quickly with others', did not apply to East Germany. The opposite was more likely to be true.

The question of whether the comparative advantage effects will lead to a catching-up process in East Germany, of course, depends on the future evolution of wages and productivity. As far as the latter is concerned, there are certainly major untapped sources of improvement in East Germany. The introduction of market discipline will increase the organisational efficiency of the East German economy. It will also improve motivation and incentives to work. Finally, it will lead to the introduction of new technologies. All this should lead to dramatic increases in productivity in East German industry.

At the same time, however, the unification process is likely to lead to significant increases in nominal wages. In fact, this is already happening. Nominal wage increases of 20 to 40% since the start of the monetary union have not been uncommon. This wage push has several causes. First, the use of the same currency in a region which is now a full part of Germany leads to demonstration effects. East German workers will not easily accept lower wages "for the same job." Second, the introduction of a relatively favourable social security system in East Germany raises the "reservation wage" of East German workers.

The upshot of all this is that while productivity improvements are going to be substantial, so are nominal wage increases, and it is difficult to foresee whether productivity growth is likely to outstrip wage increases. My prediction, however, is that this will not happen easily, so that the East German economy is likely to remain one with relatively expensive labour. Thus the incentive to do business in the East is unlikely to be based on the existence of cheap labour. In this sense the integration process of East Germany will be different from that of southern Europe, where the abundance of cheap labour has been a major driving force in increasing the growth rates of southern European countries and helping them to catch up with the north of Europe.

Paradoxically, it is much more likely that the catching-up properties of the comparative advantage model will apply to other East European countries that have switched to market economies. Productivity increases are likely to be pronounced there (as they are in East Germany). However, the wage push now visible in East Germany will probably be much less import-ant in other East European countries, since there are few demon-stration effects on wage formation nor are there wage-push effects induced by a favourable social security system. As a re-sult, their labour costs are likely to be much lower. This will attract the kind of labour-intensive industries that lead to the convergence of real income levels predicted by the comparative advantage model.

The increasing returns model and German unification

From the preceding section it follows that most of the integration effects between the East and the West of Germany will come from the increasing returns dynamics described earlier. The question which then arises is whether concentration effects will occur and, if so, what form they will take. Is it likely that a "core-periphery" relationship between the West and the East will be the outcome?

At this moment most manufactured goods consumed in East Germany can be produced and shipped from the West. What, therefore, are the incentives for West German firms to move to the East? The theory tells us that in increasing-returns industries, these incentives will depend on the existence of a pool of spe-cialised labour, on the existence of a network of firms able to supply intermediate goods, on technological know-how and on such collective amenities as infrastructure and communications.

It is clear today that the West is far better endowed with all these than the East, so that the incentives for firms to move East and to create little cores of economic activities which can then spread around them is small. In addition, and more important, new emerging Eastern firms may face the same incentives. The incentive for many of them may be to set up shop in the West to profit from the externalities provided by the "core".

A possible outcome of the integration process between the West and the East, therefore, provided that market forces are left to play freely, is a core-periphery arrangement as a permanent feature of intra-German relations, in which West Germany continues to attract resources from the East, in particular labour.

The question which now arises is whether policies can change this outcome. There is no doubt that the German authorities today are fully committed to preventing any core-periphery relationship from developing in Germany. This they will do by massively subsidising the construction of infrastructure and communications and by providing financial advantages to firms locating in the East. Such advantages will be necessary to compensate for the great disadvantages inherent in such relocation. The issue therefore boils down to the question of whether these flows of subsidies will be sufficient to overcome the handicaps of a periphery. Here the experience of other countries with such regional policies is not very favourable. In Italy, for example, many years of such subsidies have failed to eliminate the core-periphery relationship between the north and the south.

There is a good chance, however, that Germany's experience will be different. For one thing, it appears that the German authorities are committed to outspending the Italian authorities by a wide margin. In addition, the historical tradition of industrialisation in East Germany is quite different from that of the **Mezzogiorno**. Third, the geography of Germany is very different from that of Italy. Large parts of East Germany are physically close to West Germany (including West Berlin), making it possible for firms starting their operations in East Germany to profit from the externalities produced by the proximity of the West.

More particularly, it is quite unlikely that East Germany as a whole will develop as a peripheral region to West Germany. It is much more likely that some regions within East Germany will be able to develop and to be absorbed into the economic network of the West German economy. By the same token, however, one has to take into account the possibility that other regions will experience protracted problems in catching up with the rest of the German economy. This will to lead to continuing substantial migration. It will also induce the German authorities to transfer substantial resources to the lagging regions for many years to come.

References

1. For a presentation, see e.g. Balassa (1961), Ethier (1988) and Caves and Jones (1986).

2. This externality is a "pecuniary" one, i.e. it can be priced in a market. In perfect competition models these pecuniary externalities do not really matter. Things are different in models of imperfect competition. See P. Krugman (1990), p.4.

3. This view of the unequal regional effects of economic integration has been elaborated by Myrdal (1957). See also N. Kaldor (1966). In the French economic literature, this view has found an expression in François Perroux's "pôle de croissance" (1957). These ideas have been very influential in devising regional policies in southern Europe,and were recently formalised by Paul Krugman (1990). The "new" growth theory has also incorporated some of these ideas (see Romer 1986).

4. There are alternative explanations, however, for these two countries. Both have until recently heavily protected their domestic markets. The increasing income gaps may be the result of these inward-looking strategies, which have left their domestic producers very uncompetitive. Another explanation is that these two countries have followed very volatile macroeconomic policies, which may have led to an environment not very conducive to growth and investment.

5. See **Sachverständigenrat** (1990).

Bibliography

B. Balassa, **The Theory of Economic Integration** (New York: Irwin, 1961).

R. Caves and R. Jones, **World Trade and Payments** (Boston: Little, Brown, 1986).

W. Ethier, **Modern International Economics** (New York: Norton, 1988).

N. Kaldor, **The Causes of the Slow Rate of Growth of the United Kingdom** (Cambridge: Cambridge University Press, 1966).

P. Krugman, "Increasing returns and economic geography", NBER Discussion Paper, No. 3275, March 1990.

J. Myrdal, **Economic Theory and Underdeveloped Regions** (London: Duckworth, 1957).

F. Perroux, "Les formes de concurrence dans le Marché Commun", **Revue d'Economie Politique** 1, 1959.

P. Romer, "Increasing returns and long-run growth", **Journal of Political Economy** 94, October 1986.

Sachverständigenrat zur Begutachtung der Gesamtwirtschaftlichen Entwicklung, Sondergutachten vom 20. Januar 1990, mimeo.

Horst Siebert, "The economic integration of Germany", **Kieler Diskussionsbeiträge** 160, May 1990.

Adaptation problems in the former GDR: an economic analysis

Jürgen Kröger

1. Introduction[1]

In the past various models have been developed to describe the transformation of a capitalist into a centrally-planned economy, but no such model exists for the reverse process. Consequently economic theorists and politicians have had difficulty in keeping up with the rapid development towards a market economy in Eastern Europe. Here, internal German development is playing a rather special role. A German monetary union was concluded between the Federal Republic and the GDR on condition that the framework was created for a market-orientated economy in the latter. The fundamental political aim was that the promotion of economic prosperity in the East, rather than administrative measures by the Federal Republic of Germany, would put an end to the tide of migrants which followed the opening of the inner-German border. German economic, monetary and social union was seen as a promise that differences in living standards would be reduced in the foreseeable future, with the awakening of positive expectations for the economy of the former GDR.

The late government of the GDR accepted the Federal German offer of monetary union on certain conditions, and economic, monetary and social union came into force on 1 July 1990. The conditions related to the basic foundations for a market economy, the prime requirements being freedom of contract between economic actors; deregulation of controlled prices; autonomy of employers and employees with regard to wage rates (independent trade unions and employers' associations); reform of the law of private ownership; and the introduction of a tax and social-security system on the West German pattern.

The offer also included ancillary measures to cushion the transition period. These consist primarily of financial aid to the state budget (German Unity Fund) and to the newly-created social-security system, mainly unemployment insurance and pensions (initial funding). Financial help was also promised for the improvement of the East German infrastructure, together with financial and technological backing for measures to reduce its severe environmental pollution, in the interest of both sides.

The most diverse opinions are to be heard concerning the likely effects of German economic, monetary and social union. They range from optimistic predictions that the Eastern economy will quickly catch up to warnings that the West German economy might be destabilised, chiefly as a result of the massive transfers of resources needed to support the East. Financial markets, for their part, reacted sceptically, and this was reflected in a distinct rise in interest rates, particularly for the Deutschmark. Questions regarding the effects of the union on the Eastern economy and the means by which an economic catching-up process could be initiated were largely ignored.

2. Analogies for an economic catching-up process

The "economic miracle" of the FRG
At first glance it seems as though the development of the former GDR's economy could follow a course similar to that taken by the Federal Republic of Germany at the end of the war. Here too, a currency reform marked the transition from a planned economy to a fully market-orientated system. Wartime production had led to the capital stock being misdirected and in part destroyed. The economic starting conditions prevailing in 1945 are comparable to the present situation in the new German **Länder**, where the capital stock is economically obsolete. However, the present position in these **Länder** may be much more serious, and the financial backing provided by the Federal Republic of Germany to help the East catch up greatly outstrips the financial support provided to West

Germany's post-war economy by the Marshall Plan, generally seen as having applied the initial spark for West Germany's economic "miracle".

The dynamic of the West German takeoff stemmed basically from a number of factors. The influx of workers from the former German areas in the East, combined with a high performance potential, created a fertile environment for investment. What is more, the Federal economy had the benefit of strongly-expanding demand, not least because of an undervalued currency. Important domestic sectors were protected from the competition of the world market, not least because of the relatively modest integration of the commodity (especially financial) markets. In the course of the 1950's and early 60's the efficiency of the West German economy was also favoured by a relatively modern capital stock compared to that of other countries.

Although a similar course of events would be desirable for the former GDR, the differences between the starting conditions of the new German **Länder** and those of post-war West Germany are obvious. Essentially there are three basic considerations arguing against a repetition of the economic miracle. In the first place, unification means that the East's economy has been immediately exposed to world competition. Because of greater market integration and an overvalued currency - measured in terms of East German productivity - the effects of this will be far more serious. Secondly, important preconditions for an expected high yield on capital do not exist: wage-levels measured against labour productivity seem too high, and there are considerable industrial-location problems due to the inadequate infrastructure. It is therefore likely that government incentives will be required to produce an autonomous investment boom. In the third place - and this is perhaps the most crucial difference - economic actors (entrepreneurs, employees and consumers) in the former GDR are now able to choose between an economically-developed area - the Federal Republic of Germany - and their own, which is faced with a time-consuming catching-up process. In the 1950' and 60's this choice did not exist in the Federal Republic of

Germany. It can be expected to trigger major socio-economic transformations, which will be reinforced by German cultural links. All in all it must therefore be assumed that an independent economic catching-up process will not take place within the area of the former GDR.

A German Mezzogiorno?

A lack of investment in the new German **Länder** carries with it the danger that the territory could, like the **Mezzogiorno** of southern Italy, become an economically-backward region, supplied by producers from the West or by other European countries without any need to set up major new production units. Highly-trained and adaptable workers would migrate to the economically more prosperous West, while less adaptable workers and the older population would stay at home. The region would become heavily dependent on government transfers without itself being able to make any substantial contribution to prosperity.

Against this, there are weighty considerations which argue against the new German **Länder** falling into a state of permanent underdevelopment. Firstly, there is the fact that Eastern Germany was an important German and European hub of industry before the war. Just as other East European countries are now improving their economic situations, so this part of Germany will probably be able to pick up the threads of this tradition. Secondly, the opening-up of Eastern Europe is likely to quickly eliminate the peripheral status which the former GDR occupied. The area could now work itself into a central position on the European stage. Thirdly, it may also be assumed that centres like Berlin or the south of the new **Länder** will be able to develop their own economic pull. The general economic trend towards the service sector may be of distinct benefit here. Indeed, a more than proportional share taken by Eastern Germany in service and leisure activities falls into line with the future structural requirements of German economic development as a whole. In the fourth place, the area has a reservoir of qualitatively well-trained labour, which, if fully mobilised, could prove as economically successful as the labour force of the Federal Republic of Germany has been.

Thus, while the danger of the former GDR becoming a **Mezzogiorno** cannot be entirely dismissed, this outcome can be avoided by suitable policy measures.

West Berlin

In some ways, the present state of the new German **Länder** is comparable with West Berlin in the 1950's. Because of its marginal position, West Berlin had no attraction for manufacturers. The market could be supplied from West Germany, and the labour force was increasingly migrating to more prosperous areas. Extensive, long-term financial aid was needed to reverse this trend. It follows from this that the former GDR needs a massive regional development programme offering a wide range of short-term attractions, especially investment incentives, to persuade people not to emigrate. The incentive scheme for zonal border areas provides a further example for a programme of this kind. Unlike the former situation of West Berlin, however, in the medium term the East Germans can overcome their peripheral status, both in regional terms and with regard to the technical and organisational facets of economic life. This means that assistance should be on a massive scale in the short term but be planned to run down thereafter, as prosperity ensues.

3. The macroeconomic view

Effects of German monetary union

The present economy of the new German **Länder** has been deeply affected by a policy which, mainly because of a permanent shortage of hard currency, was aimed at minimising dependence on Western countries. It is therefore not highly specialised. Autarky resulted in a number of notably misguided developments. Firms were encouraged not merely to produce the capital goods they required; large concerns were even forced to carry out their own repairs and to produce a certain proportion of consumer goods apart from their main production lines. This gave very large firms themselves an autarkic character. There was no competition; there was even a marked diminution in cross-industry integration by way of primary and intermediate products. Recent decades have seen little change in the sectoral composition of the former GDR's economy compared with Western industrialised countries. At the time of German monetary union the sectoral structure of GDR industry greatly resembled that of the Federal Republic of Germany at the end of the 1960's.

It is generally accepted that labour productivity in the new German **Länder** amounted to approximately 40% of that in other parts of Germany, although there are admittedly wide sectoral disparities and large differences no doubt occur between individual enterprises. This productivity-differential is ascribed to three main factors: the organisational shortcomings of central planning, the lack of motivation as an incentive to performance and a technologically-obsolete capital stock. The seriousness of the last-mentioned problem grew markedly in the 1980's. The net investment rate dropped and this contributed to a further deterioration in the value of plant. In addition, the strong links binding the former GDR's economy to the state-run CMEA economies, combined with its marginal trade with Western industrialised countries, aggravated the acknowledged inefficiency of its economy. The need for that economy now to adapt is plain to see. The output structures and the product range may very well meet the demands of the early 1960's, but are hopelessly out of date for the markets of the 1990's.

The possibilities of adaptation flow from the conditions brought about by monetary union and the creation of the framework for a market economy. Monetary union signifies giving immediate mobility to the factors of production and setting aside the exchange-rate tool. The mobility of capital and a uniform currency imply that the real interest level on financial assets and the yield on capital will even out over the whole currency area, the former with immediate effect and the latter at least in the long term. In view of the relatively high mobility of labour as a factor of production, it is also likely that wage-levels in the new **Länder** will quite quickly come into line with those of West Germany. In the short and medium term there is even liable to be a further increase in mobility on the East's labour market, thanks to improved transport facilities and better training opportunities.

Rapid wage-alignment will have a critical impact on the adaptation process of the former GDR's economy, and therefore deserves closer consideration. Various mechanisms favouring such a development are conceivable: price reform, together with the introduction of a system of taxing consumption, leads to a rise in price-levels - a rise which may provoke an exaggerated subjective response. This is already giving rise to wage claims which are in fact incompatible with the productivity level. An aggravating factor is that the prices for East Germany's products will probably have to be substantially lowered in order for them to be sold at all. The periods for which the new wage agreements are to run are extremely short, and the wage rises have mainly been agreed in terms of basic rates. Adaptation of wage structures will be necessary to step up motivation and hence the performance of labour. This will probably lead to a further rise in average wage-levels. To the extent that employees in areas close to the border can also find a job in other parts of the Federal Republic, there will be repercussions in the new **Länder**. The Berlin labour market will probably be very seriously affected. In the civil service, large pay differences cannot really be accounted for by differences in productivity. New investments in the former GDR will create high-productivity jobs and demand well-trained labour. It is likely that wage-levels for such jobs will approximate to those of West Germany. Furthermore, it is probable that in many areas the middle management will come from the former parts of the West. If the salaries of corresponding employees in the new **Länder** remain well below the level of such staff, this could lead to a pay pyramid exhibiting an unacceptable degree of distortion. In other words, the model of a "colonisation" of the former GDR is hardly plausible. It must be assumed that the trade unions in both economic areas, though motivated by different aims, will press for rapid wage-alignment.

The cost-alignment of the most important factors of production - except for the special case of land - would mean alignment of the market capital/labour ratio throughout the currency area. Essentially this could take place in two different ways: either by the increased offer of labour by former GDR workers in the West or by investment in the new German **Länder**.

If movements of labour generated no social costs, it would largely be a matter of indifference which of the two strategies was adopted. In practice, however, things are liable to be different. Any massive East-West migration would encounter lively resistance in West Germany, as it would aggravate housing problems, jeopardise entrenched positions on the labour market and impose an additional load on the social fabric. In the former GDR a large-scale emigration of labour would aggravate the regional problem. The least mobile and efficient workers and the older population would stay at home. Here again social tensions could not be ruled out - though the reasons would be different. It follows that it is in the public interest that capital flows be directed towards the former GDR in order that any one-way movements of labour be offset. In the short term, however, the difficulty arises that movements of labour can take place more quickly than the transfer of physical capital. Consequently the alignment of wages between the two regions as the result of private decisions, that is to say, job-seeking in West Germany, could happen more rapidly than is in the overall public interest.

In view of these factors it is unlikely that a West German economic miracle will be repeated in the new parts of Germany. The geographical proximity of a prosperous economic area and the possibility of participating in its prosperity, the immediate and complete convertibility of the currency (which measured against the productivity level of the former GDR seems overvalued) and a real wage-level which, set alongside the production potential, does not ensure the high return on capital regarded as essential, add up to fundamentally different starting conditions. It therefore seems indispensable that the nominal signal given by the introduction of the Deutschmark should be accompanied by macroeconomic measures of a practical character.

Economic union and the catching-up process

The improvement of the former GDR as a productive environment will be critical to the economic catching-up process. Because of the probably rapid integration of labour markets it is unlikely that East Germany will remain a low-wage area. Therefore investment will presumably not be directed at labour-intensive industry.

The first necessity is to eradicate the problems which currently beset the industrial sites of the former GDR and, wherever possible, create advantages which attract investment. In the short term the aim must be to eliminate the most obvious deficiencies affecting living conditions. The introduction of the Deutschmark is likely to go a long way towards overcoming shortages in supply. The modernisation of housing will probably get under way quickly thanks to the availability of high-quality materials. The rapid introduction of owner-occupation would reinforce self-motivation and provide an incentive to stay put.

As regards the protection of the environment, the marginal returns on investment should be high, even if the standard of the West German economy can be attained only in the medium term. The same applies to the waste-disposal sector. Traffic is likely to generate increasing difficulties. It is to be expected that the level of car-ownership in the East will increase rapidly, and growing integration into the West German economy and the expected tourism will impose considerable additional burdens on the road-transport infrastructure. Although a solution can only be achieved in the medium term, the relevant planning and investment should be set in train at the earliest possible moment. The possibility of mobilising private resources should be examined, but this should not be allowed to disadvantage the new **Länder** as a productive environment. This would occur if, for instance, charges for road usage were levied solely within the area of the former GDR. The miserable state of its communications system demands a large-scale replacement of the entire infrastructure. However, this also offers the opportunity of establishing a very modern system which could assume the character of a model beyond the boundaries of the former GDR. But in the short term it will be necessary to find transitional solutions to improve communications between business centres.

The announcement of extensive measures aimed at improving the infrastructure in the new German **Länder** will no doubt produce a positive response. At the same time it must also be borne in mind that the absorption capacity of the area's economy is still very limited. This means that a major infrastructure programme will be practicable only if suitable building capacity is shifted from West Germany. Additional resources could also be made available by the increased use of public tendering on a European level, as envisaged in the internal market programme.

Nevertheless, the transitional phase for the former GDR's enterprises is liable to bring greater risks than in other EC countries. This is truer of industrial undertakings and investment in production plants than in the service area (trading firms, hotels and catering). An investigation should therefore be carried out to determine what further investment incentives are needed to trigger the catching-up process. As noted earlier, these incentives should be large in the short term, but not open-ended. If there is a failure to generate expectations of high returns together with a prospect of improved economic conditions for the people of the former GDR, there is the danger of another build-up of East-West migration.

There seems therefore to be a need for a comprehensive regional support programme for the new German **Länder**. Similarly-orientated examples could be the promotional schemes for zonal border areas and Berlin. The programme could comprise the following elements: **a)** generous short-term investment incentives in the former GDR, the impact of which could be reinforced by lowering investment incentives in the West; **b)** incentives for establishing new firms, which could be backed up by income-support for new, small-scale entrepreneurs during the start-up phase; c) greater flexibility with regard to the regulations governing working hours in the former GDR in order, for example, to allow individual employees to work longer hours and firms to introduce multi-shift operations; d) substantial public investment in infrastructure, particularly in the communications system. In view of the limited absorption capacity of the Eastern economy, this would probably mean that such investment in the West would have to be postponed; and e) rapid adaptation of production structures, notably the speedy scrapping of non-viable structures and the overhaul of enterprises capable of survival.

The overall conclusion is that there is a need for a general review of Germany's regional policy. The substantial financial resources made available in the past for the economic survival of West Berlin can serve as a pointer to the magnitude of the funds in question. Against this, there is the long-term prospect of the former GDR economy's overcoming its present peripheral position and becoming a dynamic region within Europe.

4. Adaptation problems in particular sectors

The individual sectors of the economy in the new German **Länder** are undergoing a major structural adaptation process, following their exposure to the full force of world market competition. It is now clear that considerable portions of the capital stock have become obsolete. Decisions regarding the scrapping or resuscitation of production plants must therefore be taken very quickly to ensure that the fresh start is not impeded by prolonged and ultimately fruitless attempts to support unviable structures, and that the considerable financial risks being envisaged do not lead to a trade-off between subsidisation and the promotion of new investment or investment in infrastructure. A brief sector-by-sector review of the specific economic problems of the new **Länder** and the consequences of their integration into the European and world markets can indicate where their comparative

Table 1
Modernising the economy of the former GDR: analysis of selected sectors

Sector	Situation in 1990	Requirements and prospects
Energy	2/3 based on brown coal (heavily-polluting). All nuclear power stations declared unsafe by EC standards and due for closure; GDR has high per capita energy-consumption	Increased imports of primary energy will be needed to replace obsolete and environmentally-hazardous technology
Steel	No pre-war capacity owing to transport problems and lack of raw materials. Post-war capacity obsolete, producing low-quality steel	Large-scale scrapping inevitable
Chemicals	Based on pre-war coal-tar chemistry. Plastics expanding but far behind Western standards	Modernisation raises severe environmental problems. New investment rather than privatisation seems desirable
Machinery, vehicles	Large workforce (1m). Machine-tool industry the most competitive (30% of all CMEA exports to West) but hampered by CoCom prohibitions especially in electronic control systems. Vehicle industry insignificant and low-quality	Some jobs in vehicle industry (components manufacture and assembly) might be saved, but doubtful owing to low quality
Micro-electronics	Heavy investment was made to build up monopoly position for GDR in Eastern bloc; but sector remains obsolescent by Western standards	Joint ventures with Western firms could help to save markets in East. Software-production the most promising because of available high-quality programmers
Opticals, precision engineering		Prospects good for international competitiveness
Construction	Orientated towards large prefabricated living units	Construction of new individual homes and groups of home will require larger workforce and medium-sized firms; selective help to such firms is desirable
Textiles	Mainly devoted to standard, mass-produced articles competing on world market with Third-World countries	Successful restructuring of FRG's textile industry, towards high-quality articles, should be imitated
Agro-food	Large-scale production, labour-intensive and inefficient in use of land	Rapid economic catching-up should be possible given smaller farms and workforce, product-diversification and better market-orientation towards the individual consumer

advantages might lie in a world economy based on the division of labour (see Table 1.)

The development of the service sector will also be critical to the reform of the former GDR's economy. The pruning-off of service activities such as repairs which are not company-specific would be a first step towards the increased transparency of company structures. The setting-up of new small and medium-sized firms in business, building and trade must be promoted by the creation of a suitable environment (regulations governing property and competition). However, as there is also a substantial need for an autonomous effort to catch up in this area, it may be assumed that an efficient service sector will come into being without major problems and can help to cushion the negative effects of structural changes in the primary sector of the economy.

The restructuring of the existing service sector is likely to be comparatively simple thanks to its relatively low capital intensity. Furthermore, no great need for "overhaul" exists, as the primary issue is to build up a new and effective sector. With the introduction of the two-tier banking system, efficient banking services will presumably be on offer quite quickly, especially as West German banks are present in the East, though there is admittedly a need for a fundamental improvement in the training of the former GDR staff.

The region's foreign trade will undergo obligatory adaptation similar to that experienced by the internal supply structures. For a region of its size, it is only weakly linked to the world trading system. About two thirds of the GDR's trade was conducted with CMEA countries and therefore did not have to contend with the conditions of market economics. The introduction of the Deutschmark has led to marked adaptations in foreign trade. It is open to question whether the former GDR's economy will continue to demand the goods - with the possible exception of energy products - which are on offer from CMEA countries. Internal consumer demand will refashion itself to Western standards, and investment will probably be undertaken primarily with Western know-how.

As far as exports to CMEA countries are concerned - mainly machinery and equipment - these must now be paid for by the latter in convertible currency. They are therefore in direct competition with Western goods, which are better in quality and can presumably also be offered more cheaply owing to the low productivity in the new German **Länder**. It follows that without massive subsidies, the latter's foreign trade is likely to decline sharply in the near term.

The creation of new trading relationships should be left to market mechanisms, and existing distribution channels should, wherever possible, be left untouched. As the former socialist European countries become integrated into the world economy, the former GDR could assume a key role thanks to its experience and geographical proximity. Trade policy measures could facilitate the process of reform in Central and Eastern Europe, whereas clinging to present trade structures, such as guaranteed purchases of specific quantities of goods and supply-commitments for exports, would only bring an unjustified need for subsidies.

5. The need for short-term action and the prospects for success

The need for the adaptation of the former GDR's economy is enormous, as in all the centrally-planned economies, but it has already been greatly increased by German monetary union. Although the negative consequences of adaptation will be alleviated for a large proportion of the population by massive transfers from West Germany, a marked decline in production, high unemployment and financial imbalances between various sectors in the former GDR are nonetheless highly likely. In order to avoid a destabilisation of society and the economy, it is important that this process - in line with Schumpeter's thinking - be moulded into a "creative destruction" process.

The Trusteeship Agency, or **Treuhand**, as a public legal body, is responsible for the whole range of privatisation and reorganisation of what were hitherto public assets. This responsibility will be crucial. The dismantling and privatisation of existing enterprises must proceed quickly. An effective market stance is possible only if competition operates and private entrepreneurship with the necessary risk capital provides for the effective allocation of resources. There is therefore a danger that the Trusteeship Agency, in attempting to reorganise wide areas of the enterprise sector by itself, will be unable to cope. The relatively high credit-granting and guarantee facilities which already exist bring with them the danger that necessary structural adaptation will be postponed. In the final analysis, this means a wasting of capital and therefore of productive jobs. So long as truly private risk capital is not involved, the danger persists that the "joint irresponsibility" of the economic actors which has greatly contributed to structural distortions will continue.

The rapid privatisation and dismantling of state monopolies and the establishment of new enterprises are also preconditions for effective competition. In the short term there is a need to strengthen competition in trade. This is difficult, as even the retail trade is made up of monopolies, and the number of retail businesses is limited. This means that consumers often have no possibility of withholding their custom and retail businesses behave like small regional monopolies. There is also the danger that co-operation agreements between Western trading companies and former GDR firms will lead to the supply being unilaterally directed towards Western goods. Deficiencies in the former GDR's distribution system reinforce this tendency. The market access of its suppliers must therefore be improved. On the part of the suppliers this means rethinking in the direction of better marketing; at the level of economic policy, statutory regulations on competition must safeguard access to the market. Use of the pricing instrument should be managed flexibly on behalf of former suppliers.

In the medium term, an effective market economy demands a large measure of primary and intermediate-product exchange across industry. This requires, firstly, a high degree of specialisation in companies' product ranges and, secondly, effective competition. These demands can only be satisfied by a broad industrial spectrum at intermediate level. A structure of this kind is probably not easy to build, nor does it come into being of its own accord, as there are heavy capital requirements even at this level. The privatisation and dismantling of the state combines does, however, make it possible to establish the foundations for a broad stratum of medium-sized firms. The combines should therefore be examined to determine which of their parts or specialised production facilities could rationally be brought together to form such firms. The danger of creating "bequeathed" market structures by the sale of entire industrial sectors should not be underestimated.

A delay in privatising the existing industrial potential could, in the medium term, lead to undesirable effects on the European market from the standpoint of competition policy. If the Trusteeship Agency should fail in the thorough reorganisation of certain sectors, and if the scrapping of unviable concerns were to be blocked, subsequent privatisation would become more difficult, and conceivably could then only take place on the strength of additional inducements to companies. This in turn might lead to distortion of competition on the European market, if the effect were to unilaterally confer favours on companies in West Germany; these would be simultaneously improving their position on the internal European market and receiving additional output subsidies. The wholesale adoption of West German labour law even during the transition phase, during which the only option open to firms for improving their productivity is the more efficient use of labour, will prove to be a further obstacle in the path of companies adapting themselves to competitive conditions. The notices of redundancy written into some current wage agreements intensify this problem. All in all, the reduced flexibility at company level resulting from the adoption of the labour law provisions will render the change to market-orientated behaviour more difficult. This reduces the prospects for existing firms of being able to move quickly out of loss. The need for subsidisation is increased, and the assessment of whether, after reasonable adaptation, an undertaking is basically profitable becomes more difficult.

A similar complex of problems arises from the treatment of company debts. Although the 2:1 conversion resulted in an at least nominal reduction of company indebtedness, the servicing of the residual company debt at market rates will impose a heavier burden on the profit-and-loss account than before the currency conversion. As the allocation of debts in the past had only very little to do with the real economic efficiency of the enterprise in question, the problem of a distortion of the starting conditions arises anew. There is no doubt that individual verifications and assessments are beyond the capacity of the Trusteeship Agency.

All in all, a contradiction is discernible between the introduction of the Deutschmark, the resulting pressure on companies to adapt and the still-narrow room for manoeuvre available to them. Instead of trying to reorganise enterprises from the top down, what is needed is a rapid increase in the self-reliance of company management, an improvement in the starting conditions of enterprises at a stroke, so as to facilitate speedy privatisation, and the closure of unviable concerns in order to husband resources for new investments. Any delay in rapid adaptation is fraught with dangers which could lead to permanent subsidisation.

The action guidelines for the Trusteeship Agency should therefore run as follows: **a)** privatisation of portions of state combines as quickly as possible; **b)** rapid, systematic and realistic analysis of the prospects for particular enterprises or areas of their activity; **c)** development of adaptation strategies by Western consultancy firms; **d)** rapid closure of unviable concerns to husband resources for new investment; and **e)** encouragement of new investment in areas where the risks involved in taking over existing facilities are too great. The general principles to be applied to structural policy are the speedy initiation of measures aimed at the infrastructure to herald an improved economic environment, and the drafting of a regional development programme covering the whole former GDR area.

6. Conclusion

Compared to other former socialist countries, the former GDR is in a position to carry through its adaptation process without a drastic reduction in real purchasing power. This does not mean, however, that painful structural changes can be avoided. In particular, the pressure in the short term to increase labour productivity and improve product quality will be distinctly greater than in other countries of Central and Eastern Europe. This may lead to very high unemployment in the short term. A rapid transformation of the economy also demands greater flexibility in restructuring. The prospects for success will depend not least on how the various economic actors use the opportunities presented by German monetary union. Will the primary outcome be an intensified drive to make demands or will a spirit of initiative gain the upper hand - a spirit which in practical terms might need, or have needed, an initial spark to accompany monetary union?

In the long term there is the possibility of creating in Central Europe a region of economic prosperity which advances the division of labour in Europe as a whole to the advantage of every country. The territory of the former GDR can perform more than its due share in this process, acting as a bridgehead between the countries of the European Communities, as they have existed hitherto, and the reforming countries of Eastern and Central Europe, always provided that the governing parameters are consistently geared to market-economic structures and use is made of the possibilities offered by the market economy.

1. This essay is written in a personal capacity and does not necessarily conform to the views of the Commission of the European Communities.

Environment policy for the former GDR

Ernst Ulrich von Weizsäcker and Helmut Schreiber

The political changes in 1989-90 in Eastern Europe have affected no other country in the region so lastingly as the former GDR; unlike the other socialist countries, where the continued existence of the state is guaranteed, the GDR as such no longer exists. In the environmental sphere, the unification of the Federal Republic of Germany and the GDR presents considerable opportunities, but problems too.

Over the last twenty years the former GDR has developed into one of the biggest environmental polluters in Europe. Its air and water pollution reached peak levels, and crossed borders into other countries. During this time, governments in the GDR declared their environmental data more "secret and confidential" than in any other socialist country.

Through the unification of the two German states, the Federal Republic of Germany is taking on the enormous task of directing and at least partly funding environmental rehabilitation in the new German **Länder**. This essay will first take a brief look at the most important environmental problems in these parts of Germany, then present possible rehabilitation strategies, and finally go into prospects for environmental development there.

1. Environmental problems in the new *Länder*

1.1 First environmental sector: clean air

Concerns about air pollution are concentrated overwhelmingly on processes in the energy sector and in heavy industry. Here sulphur dioxide emissions are the most environmentally-burdensome proportion of emissions to the air. Out of 5,209 kt total emissions in 1988, 5,031 kt were accounted for by the energy sector. The districts with the highest SO_2 emissions are Borna, Görlitz, Cottbus, Weisswasser, Bitterfeld, Merseburg, Spremberg, Hohenmölsen and Calau. Together in 1988 they emitted 53% of total emissions in the former GDR.

The greatest difficulty in reducing SO_2 emissions has proved to be rigid adherence to an energy economy based exclusively on indigenous brown coal, without simultaneous modernisation of power stations or consideration of ecological requirements in building new ones. It has not yet been possible to achieve the voluntary reduction of SO_2 emissions by 30% in accordance with the protocol to the Convention on wide-ranging border-crossing air pollution, since the necessary financial resources are lacking. Meeting this obligation in the new German länder has been calculated at 14,400 million DM.

Clean-air measures are essentially confined to dust-retention installations. But the actual requirement for such installations was only 30% met. Smoke de-sulphuration installations and nitrogen oxide removal equipment were not covered by the GDR's economic plans. Only for smoke de-sulphuration installations were investments begun, in 1986, but success has been minimal since effective installations are not yet, or not sufficiently, available.

One important problem that cannot at present be calculated is the pollution caused by private and commercial vehicle transport. The recent clear-out of used-car markets in the Federal Republic, moreover, suggests that used vehicles, with an outdated technical level, in the new parts of Germany will add still more to the existing problems of air pollution.

With German unification, however, a structural decline in the rate of emissions can be expected in the near future. Furthermore, the Bonn government has drawn up a list of measures to guarantee more environmentally-tolerable energy supplies in the new German **Länder** in the long term. It provides for the furthest possible replacement of lignite by lower-emission fuels (gas, oil); increased use of "environmentally-friendly" energy-production plants (nuclear energy, renewable energy sources); intensified application of rational energy-use and more effective employment of all energy sources, using high prices and tariffs; the reconstruction and modernisation of major power stations, combined with higher energy-conversion efficiencies, and retro-fitting with denoxing, smoke de-sulphuration and dust-filter equipment; and increased recourse to alternative energy sources at selected sites.[1]

1.2 Second environmental sector: clean water

The natural potential water supply in the new German **Länder** amounts in hydrologically average years to 17,700 million m^3, and in a year of drought to 8,900 million m^3. This corresponds to water consumption per head of some 1085 m^3 per inhabitant per year. This area, therefore, with its relatively sparse water supply, has had the tightest water budget in Europe. A direct consequence of this necessarily-intensive water utilisation is that surface water is exposed to extreme burdens. Serious problems have arisen in providing drinking water in adequate quality and quantity. The classified surface waters break down as follows: only 20% of bodies of water are usable for procuring drinking water using normal purification technologies; 35% are purifiable with complicated, economically very costly technologies; and 45% are no longer usable for procuring drinking water.

In many cases the water is not even usable for industrial processes without major, costly purification processes, and does not meet the quality requirements for service water and irrigation water. The classification is in detail as follows:

Quality class 1 (suitable for all uses): only 1% of surface waters meets this quality standard.

Quality class 2 (suitable for drinking water and service water uses after simple treatment): 14%.

Quality class 3 (suitable for drinking water and service water uses after complicated treatment): 38%.

Quality class 4 (unusable for drinking water or for watering vegetables, only partly usable as service water): 47%.

The black spots for water pollution are the lower courses of the Black Elster, the Mulde, the Saale with the Unstrut and the White Elster.

The pollutant load on ground water has also dramatically increased. In particular the nitrate burden has increased to such an extent that in some places tapping of ground water for drinking-water supplies has had to be stopped. It is to be expected in the future, given leaching rates and the accumulation of pollutants underground, that a number of pollutants will be having negative effects on drinking-water supplies in the next few years.

1.3 Third environmental sector: soil protection

One factor considerably influencing water pollution is the unecological use of land. Although the Constitution of the former GDR and legal provisions based on it placed areas usable for agriculture and forestry under protection to guarantee the ecological balance at high, stable yields and ensure human recreational needs, it was not possible to put these legal provisions into practice.

The area withdrawn annually in the last few years covers 16,000-20,000 hectares of usable agricultural land and some 3000 hectares of land usable for forestry.[2] Some 10% of the area lost have gone to the sector of mining and energy (lignite extraction), and 4% each to the areas of housing construction and agriculture.[3] To work against this phenomenon, a few ground-water regulation measures, mainly in northern and central regions of the former GDR, were carried out. But the methods used caused too great a fall in the ground-water table.

Additionally, the careless application of fertilisers in agriculture has caused acute dangers to ground and surface waters. A number of measures will be required to protect the soil and in the broader sense agricultural land, such as avoiding affecting the soil/water budget by subsoil compaction as a result of use of heavy agricultural machinery; the reduction of nitrogen and phosphorus wash-out from fertilisers and pesticides; pushing back soil erosion in northern and central districts; and reducing animal stocks in over-large stabling complexes, to gain better control over dung removal.

2. Environmental strategies for the new *Länder*

Environmental policy strategies must be developed against a background of the manifest errors that led to the present situation. In our view, four interrelated problem areas can be identified:

1. The concentration of economic and structural policy on energy-intensive and raw-material-intensive heavy industry; the high use of lignite; high energy-consumption; and outdated production processes.

2. The neglect of the environment and the absence of administrative and legal environmental protection.

3. The neglect of environmental technology.

4. The disintegration of economic and environmental policy; wrong economic policy signals; and the subsidisation of wastefulness.

The concentration of economic and structural policy on energy-intensive and raw-material intensive heavy industry is a typical characteristic of Stalinist economic systems. The high use of lignite, by contrast, is specific to the former GDR, since lignite was the only indigenous energy source available in adequate quantities. Energy-consumption per inhabitant in 1988 was 7.7 TCE,[4] while in the Federal Republic it was 6.3 TCE.[5] Outdated factories are again a characteristic of Stalinist economic systems.

In our view the problems listed above will gradually be solved "by themselves". The mere need of a unified Germany to compete on the world market will initiate great structural change (with considerable social costs) in the new German **Länder** that will do away with outdated production structures in the foreseeable future. The concentration on lignite, based primarily on autarkic considerations, is likewise obsolete after unification. Energy wastage will be brought down to the level of other parts of Germany by adapting industry to the world market and through the considerably increased energy prices to be expected in the foreseeable future.

The neglect of the environment and the absence of administrative and legal environment protection is likewise a problem which will be resolved automatically through German reunification. The furthest possible adoption of the Federal German legal system will give the new states binding provisions for dealing with the environment. The main obstacle to their adoption might be the simultaneous take-over of the existing bureaucratic apparatus. Since the state of the environment is so catastrophic in the new German **Länder**, valuable human resources must in no way be allowed to be lost here.

The same applies to environmental technology. Setting a price on the environment will trigger a massive avalanche in the new German **Länder**. Many firms, because of technically long-outdated plants, will no longer be able to stay in business without massive investment in new technologies. As seen above,[6] the old regime had great difficulties in developing new technologies; but the lack of resources made things still worse.

On the last point, finally, it has to be said that the economy of the new German **Länder** is in deep crisis. The former GDR is showing huge gaps in its structure, not only in respect of environmental protection but in its entire economy, and this has dramatically worsened environmental problems. The ecological damage from pollution, specifically because of processes in the energy economy and heavy industry, the over-exploitation of resources and wastage of energy is enormous: calculations by the former GDR government show that the losses to the national economy from environmental and health damage amount to 30 billion Marks annually, corresponding to 10% of national income. The GDR's direct environmental investment amounted to only 1 billion Marks, corresponding to 0.4% of gross domestic product.

3. Prospects for environmental development in the new *Länder*

One model for rehabilitating the new German **Länder** calls for the setting-up of an ecologically-oriented social market economy.[7] The ecological renewal of the industrial society in these states, which constitutes a central point of economic policy, calls for enormous capital expenditure. For this, the new **Länder** are dependent on help from the Bonn government. This aid is also justified because Federal policies to maintain employment and protect the environment will together have very positive economic repercussions for other parts of Germany, since environmental technology has in the main been supplied by the Federal Republic. There are a number of areas in which guided investment in environmental protection can have positive effects not only for employment but also for environment policy, for instance in the case of air and water pollution from the new **Länder** to the other parts of Germany.

One, **energy saving**. The former GDR had the third highest per capita energy consumption worldwide. In future, the rational and economical use of energy should have top priority. With the methods mentioned above, and additional ones, say in construction techniques, for energy saving, this area too could be decisively eased. The costs of a modern environment-friendly energy-supply structure amount to some 200,000 million DM.[8]

Of these some 40-50 billion are accounted for by the renovation of power stations, including district heating schemes; 100 billion are for energy saving for homes and workplaces; and about 50 billion in the industrial sector. In this ecological renewal, nevertheless, it would be a mistake to extend the use of nuclear power. Simple calculation shows that alternative use of the money it takes to set up a 1000-MW nuclear power station (5-7 billion DM in construction costs) could give three or four times the amount in energy saving, for instance by insulating dwellings and making technical improvements to improve efficiency rates.

Two, **clean air**. The union of the two German states, by Article 16 of the State Treaty, establishes the Federal Republic's major environmental provisions as the law in force throughout Germany (of interest here is the ordinance on large incinerators and technical installations for clean air). Equipment to remove nitrogen oxide, sulphur and dust for some 5000 MW of old lignite power stations means an investment cost of 5 billion DM. There is a great opportunity here to lower emission rates.

Three, **water protection and drinking-water supplies**. The same applies to this environmental sector as to clean air. Only FRG standards (including implemented Community directives) will be made law. Representatives of the Federal Office for the Environment estimate total expenditure needs for rehabilitating polluted waters in the new German **Länder** at 100 billion DM. A programme should also be drawn up for the economical use of water on the basis of prices that cover costs (such as water meters).

Four, **refuse**. In the new German **Länder** there is a great need for investment in refuse-avoiding technologies such as sorting, recycling or composting; for setting up environment- friendly means of disposing of hazardous waste and household refuse along with landfill and incinerators; and in the rehabilitation of problems left over from the past. The costs are estimated at some 4-5 billion DM annually over the next fifteen years. Prior construction work alone will absorb two-thirds of all investment here.

Five, **ecological transport policy.** This point seems very difficult in view of present developments. The backward rail and road networks need an investment of some 200 billion DM (modernising the Reichsbahn, extension and modernisation of public transport, traffic noise-reduction in towns, rehabilitation of the road network, noise protection, extension of East-West traffic with regard for the protection of nature).

Six, **the "environment industry".** By expanding their environment industry, the new German **Länder** can help themselves in employment terms. To extend this industry, joint ventures with West German firms suggest themselves (know-how and technology transfer).

Seven, **ecological renewal of the chemical industry.** One of the most important branches of industry in the new German **Länder** is the chemical industry, but it is also one of the most burdensome in terms of energy and the environment. Maintenance is in many cases possible only at risk to life; almost all plants are technically and economically outworn. Reconstruction and environmentally-friendly new construction will have positive effects on both the environment and employment policy.

Eight, **environmental measuring systems.** For industrial firms, independent environmental institutes and state control agencies, there is scarcely any possibility of determining the environmental impact comprehensively and adequately. The most urgent need would be 2 million DM per plant or institute. The cost would be around 500 million DM.

There are undoubtedly grounds for confidence that the environmental situation will improve. Particularly as far as the sphere of mass emissions is concerned, successes may become visible in a relatively short period. However, one should not allow oneself to be lulled into a sense of false security by these gigantic investments. In our view, a number of environmental stresses, particularly from private-vehicle traffic, are still likely to affect the new German **Länder.**

The decisive thing here will be how citizens' environmental consciousness develops. It is doubtful whether the Green movement (a force that played a part in bringing about a peaceful revolution in political circumstances) can play its part in the present climate; and materialist, as opposed to ideological Green motivations may endanger the process at its very heart.

References

1. Institut für Umweltschutz, **Umweltbericht der DDR**, Berlin 15 February 1990, p. 24.

2. **Ibid.**, p. 28.

3 Because of the careless exploitation of agricultural land, over half the 4% land loss is accounted for by dereliction of agricultural land.

4.TCE = tonnes coal equivalent.

5. 29 June 1990, p.23.

6. See also Environment Sector Clean Air above.

7. Sozialdemokratischer Informationsdienst, **Umweltpolitik: Arbeit und Umwelt in der DDR** , no. 2/90, Bonn 1990.

8. **Ibid.**

Demographic and social trends in a united Germany

Charlotte Höhn

1. The mechanisms of demographic and social change

The outstanding feature of demographic change is its almost pitiless inertia. What has happened to fertility and mortality in the past determines the demographic future. Long-term fertility and mortality decline inevitably induce demographic ageing and eventually population decline. Both fertility and mortality are closely interrelated to social and ecnomic change. Migration is important too for demographic change, but it is more capricious and less predictable. In the past, migration has had little to do with demographic change in a given country. It was rather determined by socio-political and, more important, economic change.

Social change, like demographic change, is fairly slow, and escapes immediate political influence. There is, however, a long-term interrelation between policies and both social and demographic change. Economic policies produce business cycles ideally fluctuating around a positive trend of economic growth. One of the possible effects is the recruitment of migrant workers in times of native labour shortage during phases of economic boom. But economic prosperity as such attracts immigration from poor countries even in times of economic recession. Both unsolicited and recruited immigration have demographic and social effects.

2. Demographic trends as social indicators

Towards the end of the 19th century fertility began to fall in central and northern Europe. This was caused by a set of social and economic factors and processes, namely rapid industrialisation, urbanisation and secularisation (see Coale and Watkins, 1986). These processes changed the economic role of children, the meaning of the family and the position of women. Formerly many children were necessary (and therefore desired) as helpers for their parents on the farm, in business and, as long as child labour was legal, as additional earners. For the family children were an asset as they were expected to care for sick and frail relatives. Thus a private, family-based system of social security prevailed. Women were integral parts of this system as mothers and kinkeepers. The move from family-based production and security to market production with quickly-spreading social security systems reduced the economic attractions of large families. Compulsory schooling withdrew children from the family and even made them a cost factor. Mass education also increased rational analysis, leading to the slackening influence of religion, a growing desire for upward social mobility and women's emancipation. The dogma of the church (be fertile!) was no longer generally obeyed, upward social mobility was easier to achieve with fewer children, and women sought to be economically active outside the home (see Höhn and Mackensen, 1982). Living in small city apartments, moreover, was not easily combined with an extended family. Knowledge of contraception and easier access to abortion (including its acceptability) facilitated the planning of the family's size.

In Germany the completed family size dropped from 5 children in marriages contracted towards the end of the 19th century to 2.2 children in marriages contracted in the 1920's. It cannot be strictly proven that the early introduction of a compulsory old age pension system by Bismarck (1889) and the fairly liberal birth-control movement during the Weimar Republic account for the dramatic fertility decline and the rapid fall to (sub)replacement level of fertility in Germany. (Replacement fertility means a level of births sufficient to maintain the general age and size of the population). However, this early and particularly fast decline to replacement fertility has determined the ageing process and population decline of 50 years on in the two Germanies.

As for the newer and more "popular" fertility decline since the mid-1960's, it is fascinating to note that this trend began simultaneously in almost all European and other Western countries (Van de Kaa, 1988). The common determinants are trends to greater emphasis on the individual, new consumption patterns, and female emancipation. A careful analysis of such social trends, however, reveals that there is no distinct turn in the relevant trends around 1965; they develop and gain speed only in the 1970's. A new and plausible determinant seems to be the introduction of hormonal contraceptives in the early 1960's. For 20 years demographers considered the explanation of the fertility decline by the "pill" as naive and typical of journalists. Today this attitude has changed (Calot, 1988). The argument is that a technical revolution made it possible to decide on the number of children. Comparisons between desired and achieved family size for the 1950's and 60's show a discrepancy, a surplus of "undesired" fertility. The new and effective methods of contraception made it possible for a couple to assess all the advantages and disadvantages of having a child. Would the woman have to give up her career or merely interrupt it for a few years? Would the family have enough money? Would they still be able to travel, to go to parties, to practise sport? A calculating spirit was able to spread. Also the decision process was reversed: in the past a couple had to decide against a baby, whereas today one has to plan well in advance, with the possibility of **revising** the plan. All spontaneity has disappeared in a perfect contraceptive society.

Behind the almost uniform fertility decline in Europe we find more remarkable variations in more refined fertility indicators. Here East and West Germany provide a fine example of how social and economic conditions shape fertility (Höhn, Mammey, Wendt, 1990). While the Federal Republic of Germany has followed the pattern of delaying family formation, in the former GDR women still have a fairly low age at birth and short intervals between births (as in other socialist and former socialist countries). Free-market economies allow couples first to pursue a career and to enjoy consumption and leisure before forming a family; couples in the East have been expected to function for the state economy and the socialist society, with much less choice and consumptive temptations. The family has been a realm of independence both from parental households and from working life. For these reasons it has been a desirable and socially-approved strategy to have children early. No doubt this strategy will crumble under the new economic and social system of a united Germany.

Another surprising aspect is the difference in illegitimate fertility. While the Federal Republic still has a fairly low illegitimacy ratio (10%) in comparison to other western countries, thus maintaining the German tradition of avoiding children out of wedlock, the former GDR witnessed a sharp rise in illegitimacy, to one third of all births, after 1976. This year marked the beginning of a generous pro-natalist policy, favouring single mothers over married ones. We will discuss this aspect of political action later in more detail.

The marriage system in Europe has undergone considerable change since the early 1960's. Western countries have experienced a sharp decline in the propensity to first marriage, an increase in divorce, a decline in remarriage and a more or less pronounced tendency to form informal unions or to live in a one-person household. In Eastern Europe, marriage is still very popular. People marry young, and remarriage remains high. A common European feature is increasing divorce. Indeed, some East European countries have a higher divorce rate than West European countries. The reasons for this are similar to the determinants of fertility decline. Perhaps the increasing economic independence of women makes marriage less attractive to them.

In the West, individualism and self-fulfilment in young men and women can flourish through a broad variety of life-styles. People may stay with their family while studying or leave. If they leave the parental household, they may live alone, cohabit or marry. A sequence of such living arrangements is in fact feasible, since both large and small apartments are available, particularly to young professionals but also to students. Living in a network of friends seems to be of a different quality from the commitment of belonging to an isolated nuclear family. It goes without saying that many children are an obstacle to such a sequence of living arrangements. Indeed, the changing family system is concomitant with fertility decline (Schmid, 1984). For the Federal Republic of Germany 40% of the fertility decline since 1965 can be attributed to the changing nuptiality pattern.

In the former GDR the situation of young people has been less liberal. Due to the housing shortage, the social "rules" and the administrative allocation of flats to married couples only, young people have had to marry to obtain independence from their parents. They could not choose to live alone. Though no household statistics were published, it can be safely assumed that the vast majority of households today contain married couples or widow/widowers. It seems that even a divorced partner has sometimes to share a flat with the rest of the family until he or she remarries. There is also no information on how many couples live in an informal union. The high illegitimacy ratio and the fact that age at first marriage is higher than age at first birth suggest that such unions do exist. Perhaps these young unmarried couples are "living apart together". While this is a very modern and liberal living arrangement in the West, it seems to have been forced on couples by social and political circumstances in the East. Once this political pressure has been removed and sufficient housing has been constructed in a united Germany, young people will deliberately choose between different life-styles. Attitudes towards marriage and non-marriage already seem to be the same.

Mortality belongs to the generally-recognised social indicators. Life expectancy at birth (or at any other age) and the infant mortality rate reflect standards of living, the quality of medical services and infrastructure, and to some extent the quality of the environment. While life expectancy has been increasing for men and women and infant mortality converging at very low rates in the West, some East European countries have experienced a decreasing life expectancy or at least a temporary increase in adult mortality. Infant mortality, however, always belonged to the very cherished fields of political support in Eastern Europe, so in that respect decreases have been reported everywhere (Van de Kaa, 1988). A comparison of life expectancy between the two Germanies shows that in both countries there have been only increases. However, since the early 1970's life expectancy has increased much faster in West Germany. Before, the difference was a half to one year but in 1986 it is nearly three years for females and 2.3 years for males in favour of West Germany's population. From 1966 to 1980 infant mortality in the former GDR was lower than in West Germany. Since then the Federal Republic of Germany has pulled ahead here too (Höhn, Mammey, Wendt, 1990).

From the late 1970's onwards the GDR authorities ceased to publish "sensitive" rates of mortality due to such causes as suicide, cirrhosis of the liver, and work accidents. These causes of death were merged into a very mixed grouping of causes, very probably because they showed undesirable increases, as elsewhere in Eastern Europe (Höhn and Pollard, 1990). Individual frustration and a loss of hope in the future may lead to an increase in the number of suicides and alcohol abuse. Alcoholism may induce cirrhosis of the liver and cause accidents. In addition, health and safety measures in East German industry were deplorable. Future research will doubtless reveal the true mortality data and demonstrate the toll which the system took. Observing mortality trends in a united Germany by region will also make it possible to assess progress in improving the quality of life in the former GDR.

In addition, in future foreigners will move to live and work in the former GDR and some other East European countries, as they have done in other parts of Europe. The socialist countries allowed neither immigration nor emigration, closing their borders to prevent undesired foreign (capitalist) infiltration of their populations. Furthermore, because of the call for women in the labour force, there never was a true shortage of native labour.

The right (or rather duty) to work led to the hiding of unemployment and a very low labour productivity. Official propaganda, meanwhile, proclaimed a shortage of labour with the aim of absorbing all the adult population in the organised work-force as a way of making party and state omnipresent. Had there been a real shortage, as in West European countries, the recruitment of foreign labour would have been the logical consequence. It is, I believe, only for ideological reasons that women and mothers were induced to be economically active despite the possible negative effects on fertility. To counterbalance the latter a pro-natalist policy was launched in most socialist countries. The example of the former GDR, including an assessment of the policy's efficacy, will be provided later in this essay.

Until now, very few foreigners have been working in East European countries. Even commuters from neighbouring socialist countries were not numerous. There are, however, ethnic minorities with their traditional rivalries in Yugoslavia, Romania, Bulgaria and Hungary. East Germany has had practically no experience either of foreign labour or of ethnic minorities. Confronted with the foreigner issue the former GDR's population has begun to show serious signs of hostility.

The demographic trends outlined in this section are indicators of two different German societies. In West Germany, fertility and nuptiality reveal an individualistic pattern while in the East a rigid demographic regime reflects social pressure and control. Mortality decreased much more rapidly in West Germany, indicating an improving quality of life, while many hazards (accidents, pollution, meagre quality of food) have acted as a brake on the improvement of East German life expectancy. A fairly long tradition of immigration has contributed to the development of a multi-cultural society in the West, while East Germany has still a long way to go until its values and attitudes are as liberal as in the West. Demographic measurements will be a good way of monitoring such adaptations.

3. Political action and demographic change

The conviction has been growing among social scientists and demographers that there are complex interrelations between political action and demographic change. This seems to be obvious where population policies are concerned, but also applies to many other policies (Demeny, 1986; Birg and Mackensen, 1990). We will discuss "population-related" policies, that encompass "indirect" and "direct" policies. "Indirect" policies have no demographic component, but completely other objectives; nevertheless they have (unintended) demographic effects. In addition there are direct policies (pro-natalist and/or family policy) and "mixed" measures like income taxation. A closer examination of pro-natalist policies shows that they are less powerful and effective than usually intended. This insight has induced some researchers to investigate the reasons for the limited success of pro-natalist measures. The main reasons appear to be conditions which are also shaped by indirect political action (Höhn, 1987 and 1989a).

Since the two Germanies were exposed to two different political systems for 40 years, the possible effects of political action on demographic change can be studied fairly accurately. In this section we start with the effects of indirect policies.

One of the key determinants of fertility decline in developing countries is the status of women. The usual suggestion made by international organisations to governments interested in reducing fertility in their countries is the launch of an emancipation policy. In developing countries an emancipation policy has long since had its place and intrinsic value: when women vote they also claim their fair share of the world. And what is this fair share? Equal chances in education, equal career opportunities and equal pay. Equal access to education for boys and girls has balanced the educational level among the younger adult population. But significant differences remain, particularly concerning technical education and natural science. East Germany, which followed the Soviet ideological goals of erasing gender differences and praising the female engineer, bricklayer and tractor-driver in art and propaganda, has a conspicuous under-representation of females in the technically-qualified population and hence technical jobs, though they perform better than West Germany where such programmes are more discreet. The objectives also seem to be different. While the Western government has invited females to enter well-paid occupations and thus reduce income disparities with men, the Eastern government has sought simply to close the technological gap with the West.

In socialist countries, according to their propaganda, there have been no income gaps between men and women. In reality such differences do exist. Perhaps, with the less differentiated income distribution of a country like the GDR, one would expect the gap to be smaller. An unpublished study (because the results did not appeal to the authorities) demonstrates the gap to be as big as elsewhere (Roloff). The reasons are also the same: women until recently had a lower education, they tended to interrupt their occupations while rearing children, and because of their family duties they often worked part-time. These facts amount to reduced chances of a career and an income comparable to that of men.

It is true that the West German mother has poor child-care facilities, having to interrupt her work until children are 3 years old and admitted to the kindergarten, unless she has her mother or another person to mind the child. The East German mother has been able to deliver her child to collective care and socialisation very early. But she has not only been expected to do so; she has also needed the second income. Moreover, despite the short career interruption, East German women have rarely climbed to higher posts. Making a career always requires much time, means giving any leisure and "family" time. If women are still responsible for family duties, and in countries like the GDR this has also included time-consuming queuing, men have enjoyed a career advantage, including in East Germany being active in the Communist party. Only "child-free" and unmarried women seem to have enjoyed equal chances. This is the decisive goal conflict between an emancipation policy (enhancing female independence, typically via a professional career) and a pro-natalist policy. In addition emancipation means more education and, with that, more rationality. This rationality will penetrate all spheres of life, including reproductive decisions. If children are no longer an economic necessity but rather a cost factor, why should one have many?

Economic policies are aimed at supporting economic growth, international competitiveness, full employment and the like. They seem to be neutral to a family background. A man or a woman is paid or makes a profit according to his or her individual performance, irrespective of how many dependents they have. However, even after redistribution, taking into account marital status and number of children, as a rule a single person or a DINK (double income-no kids)-couple enjoy a higher per capita income than a family with father, mother and children. In addition the unattached are also less constrained by time, they are free from the operating hours of schools, kindergartens and the like. They are also more mobile to look for the best jobs or opportunities. The economy therefore is not neutral, it is blind or even ruthless to the family.

In principle this assertion applies both to socialist and market economies. But socialist countries very often limit mobility, both professional and private, to such a degree that the differences between the family-attached and family-free workers are blurred. More important, the socialist state and party constitue a monopolistic employer that easily can, and indeed often does, decide to reconcile societal and family needs. If the state holds that higher fertility is desirable for overall development, it can introduce measures concerning working conditions (paid maternity leave, family-friendly working hours, longer vacations for parents - typically mothers - and firm nurseries) that support individual decisions to have a/another child. The GDR authorities made such measures part of their pro-natalistic programme.

Certainly, a Western government too can include such elements in its policy. The organised employers and the trade unions will, however, block legislation increasing either private costs or the risk of unemployment. The measures mentioned above are usually not part of general economic policy in the context of free-market economics. Some big private firms have introduced such measures voluntarily, as in the "patronage policy" of French corporations like Michelin (Schultheis, 1990), or in West Germany (Siemens, Bayer-Leverkusen, Hoechst and Mercedes-Benz now offer prolonged maternity leave with a re-employment guarantee). In this respect the state too can act like an entrepreneur. West German civil servants, for instance, enjoy additional, family-related elements of income, a higher refund of health expenditures to families, better conditions for part-time work and unpaid longer leave (up to 12 years). It can also provide (as more and more private firms do) day-care facilities. But if a Western government wants to introduce such measures generally, the state has to pay. Then such measures are part of a pro-natalist or family or social policy, but not economic policies.

Economic conditions have another impact on the family and the individual because they offer other options. The market economy created welfare for everybody, expanding the choice between many ways of consumption and leisure. Very often these options strongly compete with the decisions to form a family or to increase family-size. The socialist system certainly also aimed at economic growth and satisfaction of needs. In practice, however, it failed to achieve these objectives, creating instead rather restricted economic conditions and options that competed with, rather enhancing, family life. Thus the higher fertility in the former GDR was (also) indirectly supported by a less successful economic policy.

Also important for family life and well-being are adequate housing, a safe environment and a sound infrastructure. In that respect cities everywhere in Europe have become hostile to children and young people. In the West, apartments are either too small or too expensive for families. In the socialist countries, there is a chronic shortage of accommodation. Rents are cheap but there is no free housing market, and the few available flats are allocated by an oppressive and clumsy administration. Private houses are few or non-existent, while in West Germany real estate and construction costs (owing to high salaries) have become prohibitively high for familes to build their own house.

Everywhere in Germany playgrounds are scarce and the streets very dangerous. Distances to schools, day-care facilities and to the work-places of the parents are long. This infrastructure has been designed for a mobile society - but not for families, and since infrastructure represents a long-term state investment it is not easy to change in order to make it more congenial to families.

The most powerful political impact on families, and hence fertility, stems from an important area of social policy, i.e. compulsory old age and health insurance. Germany was the first country to introduce a system of social security in 1889. No doubt it was not Bismarck's intention to weaken the family system or reduce the value of children (and hence fertility). Rather, he aimed at fighting the poverty of the working class (and their revolutionary potential). But he replaced family functions by state provision. This political action is now 100 years old. Its influence is still valid, the two political systems have not touched it (though pensions were very low in the GDR) and indeed nobody would dream of abolishing this most important feature of a welfare state. Remarkably enough - and to illustrate the goal conflict - in order to reduce fertility in developing countries international agencies have suggested that governments guarantee a pension, as part of the development of a social security system.

Last but not least, let us look at the direct intervention of the state, at population policy. Governments in West Germany have always maintained that they pursue not a population policy but only a family policy, and that such a policy does not require a pro-natalist justification. Elements of this family policy are child allowances (since 1955), child rebates in income taxation (1950-1974 and since 1983), single-parent rebate (since 1977), income-tax splitting for spouses (since 1958), paid maternity leave (since 1980; since 1986 extended to all mothers, whether economically active or not), and a "baby year" considered as an active year for pension (since 1986). All these measures indeed have no pro-natalist dimension, being much too low to cover a substantial part of a child's cost. In addition day-care facilities for children below the age of 3 years and for school children (who go to school only in the morning) are virtually non-existent. Kindergartens are in reasonably good supply (Höhn, 1989b). As for alleviating either the financial or the time constraints of having children, the West German political and organisational measures of family policy have been far from pro-natalist: they are neither generous nor consistent. They rightly do not claim to be pro-natalist.

In the 1970's the GDR authorities launched a broad programme of measures within a consistent population and social policy "to enable the realisation of the desired number of children." These measures encompassed a family formation credit, a birth grant, child allowances, paid maternity leave, reduction of working hours and days off to nurse sick children, and longer holidays. There was also a fairly good supply of day-care facilities, full-day school and holiday camps for pupils. A preference for single mothers for a day-care place and other privileges made the illegitimacy ratio jump to one-third of all births. The total fertility rate rose spontaneously from 1.5 in 1975 to 1.9 in the late 1970's but then fell again. The generous programme was too expensive, however, to be increased in order to remain attractive. Also the desired number of children was not very high (2.1), and the average number of children actually born (1.9) is the realistic equivalent, taking into account primary and secondary sterility, the high incidence of divorce, and, perhaps, the discouraging shortage of housing. So, except for short-term, "windfall profit" effects, the effective increase in final family size was not even 0.1 children per younger female generation (Monnier, 1989).

The more powerful "indirect" (but population-relevant) policies are the great enemies of a successful pro-natalist policy. This is true for free-market economies but also, and perhaps even more so, for socialist countries. The ideals of the emancipation of women, economic growth and welfare are important goals that conflict with the ideal of a large family. The prevailing desired number of children of around two reflects economic and social conditions and the value placed on children in advanced societies. If a government wishes to remove all barriers in order to regain replacement fertility, the direct population policy has to be generous and increased at regular intervals (at least to inflation levels and to meet rising standards of living). It is more likely that replacement fertility will not be achieved.

4. The social and economic consequences of demographic change

The main consequence of sub-replacement fertility is demographic ageing and, after approximately 50 years, population decline. Germany (including its two post-war systems) is a pioneer country is this respect. Since the 1920's Germany has had a slight sub-replacement fertility, which became more pronounced from the mid-1960's on.

20 plus 50 is 70. About 1970 the German population started to decline, both in the GDR, since 1969, and in the Federal Republic of Germany, since 1972. Ageing, of course, started earlier. When the German Reich was founded (1871), just 4.6% of the population was older than 65. At the beginning of World War II, i.e. 68 years later, it was 7.8%. Only 21 years later, 9.4% of the West German population was 65 years and older.

Table 2 shows that in 1950 the GDR's population was demographically older than the West German. This continued until 1970, when the GDR seemed to rejuvenate. This is, however, a misguided interpretation of the data. The GDR data also show that the GDR's population has declined ever since 1950. The reason is emigration. The GDR continually lost population to West Germany - up to 1961 these were mainly young people. When in 1961 the Berlin Wall was built and the Iron Curtain came down (the most remarkable measure intended to stop migration) the GDR started to develop "naturally": then its population stagnated and aged. Birth deficits started in 1969 and the population declined "naturally". In the 1970's GDR pensioners were allowed to leave for the West. The GDR then had fewer old people to feed, since the West German authorities paid the émigrés' pensions. This seemed to stop ageing in the GDR after 1970.

All these migratory, political turbulences disappear, however, when we combine the two parts of Germany. The inevitable demographic ageing is disclosed. From 1970 to 1985, this process is still blurred: firstly, by the immigration of (young) foreigners to the Federal Republic of Germany, and secondly, by the war-losses of men (since 1980 most of them have been 60 years old). But even these additional factors make the total "united" population decline after 1980.

Up to 1985, foreigners were included in the West German population statistics. After 1985 no immigration is considered. In these UN projections (1989) only declining mortality and, interestingly, converging low fertility are considered. Inbuilt demographic mechanisms will lead to the increasing decline of the German population in a united Germany and accelerating ageing. As early as the mid-1970's, when for the first time FRG population projections indicated a decline of the German population, an interministerial working group started to assess the possible economic and social consequences of these new demographic trends. Two government reports were published, one on the trends and their determinants (Bundestagsdrucksache, 1980), the other on their consequences (Bundestagsdrucksache, 1984). Since past and future demographic trends are the same for a united Germany, the consequences will apply too.

West Germany is a pioneer country, demographically and in its reaction to population decline and ageing. But other European countries will soon folllow. If fertility remains below replacement and excluding immigration, Europe's population as a whole (including the Soviet Union) will cease to grow by the year 2000 (table 1; Macura and Malacic, 1987). Only the Soviet Union (mainly due to the Asian population groups) will continue to grow. All the other European countries will demographically decline. In this perspective other European countries can usefully study the assessments of demographic change in the Federal Republic of Germany and the political reactions. These political remedies will also apply to a united Germany because the demographically-induced issues remain the same.

What are these issues (Höhn, 1989a)? The most relevant is the adaptation of the social security sytem, pensions and health insurance, to the increasing weight of old age. A first big reform has already been implemented. From 1992 the adjustment of pensions will be shifted from average gross to net incomes in the active population, with a much slower increase in pensions as a result. In addition the age of retirement will be gradually increased to 65 years for both men and women. Any incentive to retire early, seen from today's perspective, disappears. Those who wish to work even longer will be encouraged to do so. Persioners will have to pay income tax and health insurance, without special privileges (as in former times). This will increase contribution rates up to 2010 much less than if there had been government intervention.

An unsolved but recognised problem is who will nurse the frail aged. It seems quite out of the question to expand institutional care. This has already become very expensive. Today family members (typically middle-aged women) care for the old, and receive no financial compensation from the state. This family care system should be maintained and supported by, for instance, tax relief. One should also bear in mind that kinship size will become smaller. Those without children in particular should be encouraged to insure themselves. Nursing costs usually exceed average pensions.

As to all the other consequences the government report and other experts express a confident view. The shrinking labour force will first reduce unemployment, then, well after 2000, it will be possible to further rationalise the production of goods and services. Already a considerable share of unemployment is structural. Computerisation and automation allow, indeed require, a smaller labour force.

This labour force needs to be highly qualified. Since a shrinking labour force is also demographically ageing, the turn-over of active persons will be slower. To maintain innovation and productivity, the labour force has not only to be well edu-cated, but also frequently retrained. Life-long learning will be a feature of future life for everybody under 60 years or so. Both the official sector and business will develop strategies to retain population of workable age. This will lead to restructuring of the education sector. In the past decade quite a number of West German teachers-to-be have had to face unemployment because pupil-cohorts became smaller and smaller. The "baby boom" generation is now in the university sector. Soon there will be a bust too. Any free capacities should be used for retraining mid-career people to new technological developments.

Concerning the environmental issue, it would be a mistake to believe that a declining population automatically leads to less pollution and less environmental deterioration. To support the old-age social security provision in a declining and ageing popu-lation, economic growth is definitely required. The protectic of the environment under the double condition of population de-cline and economic growth has to be guaranteed by environmen-tally-friendly technology and consumption patterns.

Could immigration counterbalance population decline and its consequences? The answer is that only considerable and se-lect immigration could help. But these immigrants would come from distant countries and other cultures, since population de-cline will soon affect all European countries (see table 1). The cultural separateness of a huge proportion of immigrants, typi-cally living in urban areas, would aggravate the problems of inte-gration and increase social tension. Do we have a choice? It seems quite clear that immigrants are not attracted by a demo-graphic vacuum; they are not guided by any reading of popula-tion statistics. People from poor countries try to come to rich ones for economic reasons, in the hope of a better life. They are not discouraged by unemployment. As long as European countries are so much richer than Third World countries (or Eastern Europe) migrants will try to enter Europe. Should we in the future need immigrants for demographic reasons therefore, we will have ample choice to recruit (or legitimise) those we want. Then immigration policy will become part of adaptation policies to overcome the undesired consequences of demographic change. It is a social policy. It might, however, be wise to include foreigners' issues into general education and TV programmes, to avoid xenophobia today, and thus be better prepared for the future.

Finally, do we need a new population policy? A pro-natalist policy can only be successful and avoid ageing, if it is very generous and comprehensive, and if it is started early enough. France is a good example of the good start of a population policy, i.e. when cohort fertility is still above or close to replacement. The effect of slowing down fertility decline is difficult to demonstrate (but see the example of Hungary; Andorka and Vukovich, 1985), but very plausible. However, once fertility is well below replacement and demographic ageing is in progress, pro-natalist policies miss the adequate "ambiguous" motivation of couples concerned, and they get a rival in public expenditures: ageing itself. The obligation to pay pensions to voters outweighs the possibilities of supporting babies, who of course have no vote. Here the GDR's case provides a convincing warning that even enormous efforts will not redress fertility from a very low level to long-term replacement.

Zero population growth or a very slow population decline might seem desirable and preferable to a much faster process of population decline, such as the two Germanies are experiencing. But the West German reaction was and still is to keep one's nerve. None of the West German political parties advocates a pro-natalist policy. Past and present Federal German governments maintain the assertion that a family policy needs no pro-natalist justification. But perhaps families deserve a more generous family policy and much better child-care facilities; in this respect the GDR's experience should provide inspiration.

To summarise, it is not population size that counts, but age structure. Demographic ageing is inevitable for advanced societies in Europe. Germany was and is just a forerunner. The "demographic" lesson which Germans can offer to their European neighbours is that coping with demographic ageing means a timely adaptation policy and fostering the integration of foreigners. The problematic consequences of demographic change are manageable if an appropriate policy of adaptation is launched early enough.

Table 1: **Population projections, 1980-2035**
(millions)

	1980	2000	2010	2020	2025	2035
Europe	484.5	512.3	507.3	493.7	483.0	450.9
East	109.3	120.3	**123.5**	123.4	122.4	117.7
North	82.1	**83.7**	81.9	79.1	76.9	70.7
South	139.5	152.3	**152.9**	150.7	148.8	141.7
West	153.5	**156.0**	149.2	140.5	134.9	120.8
Poland	35.5	40.8	42.9	43.9	**44.0**	43.4
Yugoslavia	22.2	25.2	**25.7**	25.4	25.0	23.0
Hungary	**10.7**	**10.7**	10.5	10.2	9.9	9.2
Sweden	**8.3**	8.1	7.6	7.1	6.7	6.0
Netherlands	14.1	**15.0**	14.5	13.7	13.1	11.6
Italy	57.0	**58.6**	55.4	53.4	51.6	46.7
Spain	37.4	42.2	43.3	**43.5**	**43.5**	42.6
France	53.7	**57.1**	55.9	53.9	52.4	48.0
UK	55.9	**56.3**	55.0	53.1	51.9	47.5
USSR	265.9	314.7	336.9	351.5	355.8	359.1

Source: Macura and Malacic, 1987. Bold type shows maximum population size.

Table 2: **Population development in the two Germanies, 1950-85, and in a united Germany to 2025**

	1950	1960	1970	1980	1985
Population (millions)					
Federal Republic of Germany	50.0	55.4	60.7	61.6	61.0
GDR	18.4	17.2	17.1	16.7	16.6
together	68.4	72.6	77.8	78.3	77.6
Percent 60 years and over					
Federal Republic of Germany	14.0	16.4	19.3	19.3	20.2
GDR	16.2	20.2	22.1	19.2	18.3
together	14.6	17.3	19.9	19.3	19.8

Projected* population (millions)	1995	2000	2010	2020	2025
Federal Republic of Germany	60.0	59.3	56.6	52.9	50.8
GDR	16.5	16.4	16.1	15.4	15.0
United	76.5	75.7	72.7	68.3	65.8
Percent 60 years and over					
Federal Republic of Germany	21.6	24.0	27.1	31.7	34.6
GDR	19.0	21.4	22.8	27.1	30.3
United	21.0	23.4	26.2	30.2	33.6

* low variant, no migration; total fertility rate: Federal Republic of Germany 1.4, GDR 1.6 falling to 1.5.
Source: UN, 1989.

References

Rudolf Andorka and György Vukovich, "The impact of population policy on fertility in Hungary, 1960-1980", in **International Population Conference Florence 1985**, Vol. 3 (Liège: IUSSP, 1985), 404-412.

Herwig Birg and Rainer Mackensen eds., **Demographische Wirkungen politischen Handelns** (Frankfurt/New York: Campus, 1990).

Bundestagsdrucksache 8/4437, **Bericht über die Bevölkerungsentwicklung in der Bundesrepublik Deutschland, 1. Teil** (Bonn: Der Bundesminister des Innern, 1980).

Bundestagsdrucksache 10/863, **Bericht über die Bevölkerungsentwicklung in der Bundesrepublik Deutschland, 2. Teil** (Bonn: Der Bundesminister des Innern, 1984).

Gérard Calot, "La fécondité en Europe: évolutions passées et perspectives d'avenir", paper submitted to Symposium on Population Change and European Society, Florence 1988.

Ansley Coale and Susan Watkins eds., **The Decline of Fertility in Europe** (Princeton: Princeton University Press, 1986).

Paul Demeny, "Population and the invisible hand", **Demography** 23(4), 1986, 473-487.

J.G. Farrell and Miklos Jakesz eds., **Population Trends 1960-90** (London: Viking, 1991).

Charlotte Höhn, "Population policies in advanced societies: pro-natalist and migration strategies", **European Journal of Population** 3(3/4), 1987, 459-481.

Charlotte Höhn, "Zum Konzept bevölkerungsrelevanter Politiken auf dem Hintergrund eines Bevölkerungsrückgangs", **Zeitschrift für Bevölkerungswissenschaft** 15(3), 1989, 211-220.

Charlotte Höhn, "Country Report: Federal Republic of Germany", in W. Dumon ed., **Family Policy in EEC Countries** (Leuven: Katholieke Universiteit Leuven, 1989) 79-102.

Charlotte Höhn and Rainer Mackensen eds., **Determinants of Fertility Trends: Theories Re-examined** (Liège: Ordina, 1982).

Charlotte Höhn, Ulrich Mammey and Hartmut Wendt, "Bericht 1990 zur demographischen Lage", **Zeitschrift für Bevölkerungswissenschaft** 16(2), 1990.

Charlotte Höhn and Janez Malacic, "Population prospects for Europe", in **European Population Conference 1987** (Helsinki: IUSSP/EAPS/FINNCO, 1987), 1-45.

Alain Monnier, "Bilan de la politique familiale en République Démocratique allemande: un réexamen", **Population** 44(2), 1989, 379-393.

Juliane Roloff, "Die Differenzierung der Arbeitseinkommen zwischen Mann und Frau und Probleme der Frauenberufstätigkeit" (unpublished manuscript, 1990).

Josef Schmid, "The background of recent fertility trends in the member states of the Council of Europe", **Population Studies** No. 15 (Strasbourg: Council of Europe, 1984).

Franz Schultheis, "Die pronatalische Bevölkerungspolitik in Frankreich", in Birg and Mackensen eds., op. cit. 303-355.

United Nations, **World Population Prospects 1988** (New York: UN, 1989).

Dirk Van de Kaa, "The second demographic transition revisited: theories and expectations", **Werkstukken** No. 109 (Amsterdam: Planologisch Demographisch Institut, Universiteit Amsterdam, 1988).

Adapting East German agriculture to the EC agricultural market

Horst Schilling

This seems a particularly appropriate time to discuss the problems arising for agriculture in Eastern Germany, the territory of the former GDR, in connection with German unification and the associated integration into the EC agricultural market.

On the one hand, now that the upheavals which resulted directly from the introduction of the Economic and Monetary Union between the Federal Republic and the GDR are beginning to subside, the real structural, economic and social problems are becoming more and more apparent, as are those connected with regulatory policy and legal adaptation. The extent and complexity of the consequences of adapting to market-economy demands and to the European Common Agricultural Policy are affecting pre-existing ideas and fears in many ways.

On the other hand, some very important decisions have to be made in the next few months within this agriculture and on its behalf - both by the people currently employed in it and by the politicians responsible for it at all three levels: **Land**, national and European Community. These decisions will not only be of major importance for the population of over 800,000 employed in agriculture in the former GDR and their families, but may also affect farmers in the remainder of Germany, and even throughout the Community.

1. The initial situation

For four decades the former GDR's agricultural policy was aimed at maximising production; its objective was to achieve the highest possible level of self-sufficiency and to create surpluses for export. From a market-economy viewpoint, the expenditure on labour and capital incurred to this end was unacceptably high, added to which land with an extremely low productivity was farmed. The results were exorbitant production costs and excessive environmental pollution. The production dictated to farms by the Plan, which was often inappropriate for the location and too expensive overall, made it necessary to pay high producer prices. However, in order at the same time to maintain the (politically-motivated) low consumer-price level for basic foodstuffs, high state subsidies had to be paid (about 33 billion Marks in 1989). This system was a major cause of the increasing disproportions and general ineffectiveness prevailing in the agricultural and food sector. With the transition to a market economy and the abolition of subsidies, they became fully apparent.

The introduction of German Economic and Monetary Union on 1 July 1990 provided for the adjustment of prices to agricultural producers and for means of production to the level of the Federal Republic (crop products 49%, animal products 66%, industrial inputs 31%). This would have meant a computed cutback in income of over DM 25 billion per annum, or an average of DM 2 billion per month, for agriculture in the former GDR. The actual direct loss of income was, however, much higher in the first few months, as initially there was an almost complete collapse of sales. Even today, farms in the five new Federal **Länder** often receive much lower prices than the farmers of the former FRG, even for products of equivalent quality.

Dairies, for example, often pay only 50 to 55 Pfennigs a litre for milk, while farmers in the FRG receive 10 to 15 Pfennigs more, even with a milk yield a good 20% below that of the previous year. The low prices paid by dairies are understandable in view of the fact that they have lost a considerable proportion of their liquid milk sales to long-life and fresh milk from the western Federal **Länder**. Butter production has fallen by over 30% compared with the previous year and cheese production by as much as 80% (figures for the first week in December 1990). Out of over 264 milk-processing firms in the former GDR, more than 120 have had to close down.

The prices for beef are even worse than for milk. On the other hand, there have been reports of certain trends towards an adjustment of prices for cereals and pig meat. However, in the case of cereals one must take into account that in the past East German farms usually had no storage facilities and hence had to sell almost the whole of their harvests directly from the field, at a time when prices were extremely low. There was often no market at all for some products.

In view of the situation described, the payment of liquidity grants and other equalisation and development aid to farms in the territory of the former GDR, in accordance with the agreements contained in the two state treaties, was and is vital. These payments enabled the initial shock of incorporation, without advance preparation, into the Economic and Monetary Area of the Federal Republic of Germany, and hence the EC agricultural market, to be somewhat mitigated. They could not, however, fully compensate for the income losses, nor should they do so, in order for the necessary pressure for reorganisation and adaptation to be maintained.

In this respect, it should be pointed out that the cessation of all equalisation payments to agricultural workers' co-operatives suddenly and unexpectedly announced by Bonn in December 1990, would probably have devastating effects, namely the virtually complete bankruptcy of all these farms. This would be neither in the interest of the people directly affected, nor sensible from the viewpoint of the national economy. This had already been pointed out by experts from Western Germany. Volkmar Nies of the Rhineland Chamber of Agriculture in Bonn remarked at a specialist conference of the Konrad Adenauer Foundation in November 1990:

> The bankruptcy of agriculture in the former GDR wished for by some is resulting in the destruction of asset values and hence, from an economic and national viewpoint, is the worst possible method of structural adaptation. Even though in many cases such a destruction is seen as a chance to build up family farms, the political priority must be to bring about socially-acceptable agricultural reform.

In response to the massive protest which arose in both East and West upon the termination of equalisation payments, it was stated that this was only a temporary measure, until new allocation guidelines could be laid down at the end of January. Yet steps such as these, which unfortunately are not an isolated case, considerably increase the uncertainty among East German farmers. They do not even increase the pressure to adapt, and the confusion they cause impedes and considerably delays those decisions which have to be taken in the interests of adaptation and farm reform.

Pressure to adapt is being exerted in three main directions: i) towards a marked reduction in the agricultural factors of production, labour and land, with the aim of limiting and even reducing the production volume; ii) towards a basic reorganisation of the production structure with a view to making it more suited to the market and location and hence organised in a more efficient and environment-friendly way overall; iii) towards a complete reform of the farm structure with regard to the size of farms and their adaptation to the economic climate, and to increasing their efficiency and environmental compatibility.

2. Reducing and reorganising production

The five new Federal **Länder** have more than twice as much arable land available per head of the population as the other **Länder** of the Federal Republic. In the former GDR, the production per inhabitant of potatoes was 8 times, sheep-farming 7 times, poultry-farming 2.5 times, pig-farming 2 times and cattle-farming 1.5 times as high as in the Federal Republic. This means that agricultural production in the five new Federal **Länder** must be cut back considerably for many products, if the problem of EC surpluses is not to be even further aggravated. In crop production this will initially affect potatoes and rye in particular. In animal production, cut-backs of 30% and more are considered necessary for pig, poultry and egg production. In the case of cattle-farming, one must assume that future milk quotas will be 20% below the previous production volume. On the other hand, it is anticipated that the average milk output per cow will rise from just under 4000 to around 6000 litres per year, so that in the foreseeable future 1.2 million dairy cows will be sufficient to cover the milk quota, instead of the present 2 million. The cut-back in livestock numbers will in turn mean a further marked reduction in field-forage growing; the resulting reallocation of these areas as well as part of the potato-growing areas means that cereal production is likely to increase to the 66% already accounted for by arable land in the Federal Republic. This would then cause another surplus problem, even with only a small amount of cereal substitutes being used as fodder.

Thus agriculture in the East German **Länder** cannot achieve economic efficiency in the future by using excessive quantities of chemicals and outside energy to produce surpluses. This is even less true in the medium and long term, since such intensive farming causes an excessive burden on the soil in addition to polluting the air and groundwater.

In the former GDR, the level of costs in agriculture was 30 to 50% higher than in the Federal Republic for crop production and more than double for animal production. The reasons for this lay in the differing level of physical consumption of individual factors of production as well as the differing valuation level (prices) of these factors. A higher labour input, as well as lower yields, per hectare and per animal meant that the productivity of labour in East German agriculture was considerably lower than in the agriculture of the Federal Republic and other Western European countries. This is still the case. With freedom from the fetters of a centrally-planned economy, the change-over to production more appropriate to the location, the availability of modern, cheaper means of production and some of the benefits of the local farm size structure, it should be possible to reduce the differences in productivity levels relatively quickly, even if they cannot be completely equalised. The consequence would, however, be a further considerable increase in the production volume, and as already noted this would conflict with both real market conditions and specific EC stipulations.

The path towards an agriculture in the five new Federal **Länder** which is economically profitable and whose existence is assured in the long term cannot, then, consist in repeating all those intensification processes undergone by the agriculture of Western Europe in the course of the last three decades. This is all the more true in that this agriculture itself is already coming up against increasingly more marked economic and ecological limits, making a shift of direction for agricultural policy in the EC ever more urgent. All structural decisions in the agriculture of the five new Federal **Länder** should therefore be based on the assumption that, in future, pressure on agricultural-producer prices will increase further, while at the same time a Community-wide price increase for means of production which increase yield and pollute the environment will become more urgent and also more probable.

The need to considerably reduce agricultural production in the territory of the former GDR requires that the agricultural area be reduced. This should be achieved by set-aside and reallocation primarily of land with a low yield, but also of highly polluted or otherwise damaged land. The extent to which farmers in the East German **Länder** had already accepted the set-aside programme in 1990 is shown by the following figures. Up to the middle of October applications had been made for over 600,000 hectares to be set aside, or 13% of the total arable land. This set-aside rate is more than three times that of the old Federal **Länder**, where the programme has already been running for several years, but has so far resulted in the setting aside of only 4% of the area.

The areas set aside differ in their distribution over the territory of the East German **Länder**. The highest percentage is of course in those areas with the poorest soils. In the **Land** of Brandenburg, for example, it is almost 20%. A total of 624 applications have been submitted there, covering an area of 207,000 hectares. Of this, 56% would be converted to permanent fallow and 40% to rotation fallow. Extensive use of a further 3% as grazing land is planned and around 800 hectares is to be afforested. In line with the size of farms in the East German **Länder**, applications have been received to set aside an average of 332 hectares per farm in Brandenburg, for example. The set-aside subsidies will amount to an average of just under 500 DM per hectare. Thus they amount to around half the average rate for the former Federal Republic.

However, for reasons of economic efficiency, social policy and regional planning, as well as ecological reasons, the size of the areas which can be taken completely out of agricultural use is not unlimited. This means that there should be, at the same time, a large-scale transition to extensive forms of use. It is precisely in the former GDR that the promotion of and financial support for ecological farming and land cultivation of limited intensity is particularly appropriate. In many places this policy is preferable to complete set-aside.

3. Changes in farm structure

While it is already possible to make some very clear statements on the hoped-for and anticipated changes in the production structure of agriculture in the five new Federal **Länder**, this is much less true of changes in the farm structure. Nobody disputes that, firstly, the unnatural separation between animal and crop production must be reversed and, secondly, excessively large farms must be reduced to an economically viable size.

This process is already under way in many places, in that the big agricultural producers' co-operatives in crop production, covering up to 6000 hectares, have broken up, and the smaller units being formed from them (usually with boundaries identical to those of a local community) are uniting with the corresponding farms or parts of farms raising animals. As a rule, the resultant new farms have the legal form of an agricultural producers' co-operative, that is a registered co-operative, or of the GmbH (private limited company). The motivation of the farmers involved varies as regards the question of which of these two forms of farm they should decide upon. At present, however, there are generally two deciding factors: tax and personal liability. While for those deciding on the co-operative form the prime consideration is the related tax advantages, for those preferring the GmbH, the limited personal liability is the decisive factor. With the new farms' economic future still very uncertain, many farmers shrink from full liability as a member of a registered co-operative.

The number of farmers who have taken or want to take the step to sole proprietorship of an individual farm is still very small, despite the aid made available for this. In all five new Federal **Länder** it represents well under 1% of the total number of those employed in agriculture. By the start of December 1990, in Saxony around 1650 farmers had applied to take over the sole proprietorship of a farm or market garden. In Thuringia the number was just under 800, Saxony-Anhalt and Mecklenburg/Western Pomerania each numbered around 600, and in Brandenburg the figure was as low as 360. Thus, of the 800,000+ persons formerly employed in agriculture, so far fewer than 0.5% have decided to farm on an individual basis.

The reasons for this are very varied. First of all there is the large number of former farmers and farm workers from the agricultural producers' co-operatives who had no land of their own, or very little, and who - at least in order to farm full-time - would thus have to rent or buy a considerable amount of land. While the latter do not have the resources, the former are uncertain as to whether they can even earn the farm rent. Even those farmers who have contributed large areas to the agricultural producers' co-operatives themselves, or whose parents did so - areas which they are now free to use as they wish - would have to make sizeable investments in livestock, machinery, equipment and buildings, which they could finance only with the help of loans. Most of them are very reluctant to do so. This is quite understandable, as many of them are already advanced in years and can see, moreover, from the example of the old FRG, how difficult it is to maintain a farm with a high debt level under the conditions there.

It is quite clear that the situation of many family farms in Western Germany is far from encouraging farmers in the new Federal **Länder** to start again as individual farmers. Added to this is the fact that, as a result of their previous specialised training on the big farms, even young people are often doubtful of their own ability to manage a farm independently under completely changed economic and social conditions.

Finally, it is also true that many of these people, again particularly the young people, who have grown up on big farms, do not want to give up certain advantages of joint farming - such as shorter and relatively regular working hours, guaranteed holidays and work in a community. They are also asking themselves whether bigger farms do not have better economic prospects in the EC as well.

A lively and extremely argumentative debate has broken out on all these questions, both among those directly involved and among agronomists and agricultural politicians; this is understandably not free of emotion or of ideological and political prejudices and reservations - a debate which, for the moment, is further increasing the uncertainty felt by many of those employed in agriculture. Yet irrespective of how one evaluates the extremely contradictory views expressed in the debate, some based primarily on economic arguments, some more strongly on considerations of social and regulative policy, it must be assumed that farm structures will be very varied and highly differentiated in the five new Federal **Länder** for the foreseeable future. This applies both to farm size and also to farm types and their legal forms and forms of ownership.

Nor should anyone be surprised if farmers whose sense of responsibility conditions their thoughts and actions require a little time for consideration, in the face of a situation which is completely new to them and is in many respects difficult to understand, before they decide to embark on farming as individuals. They will, however, have this time for reflection only if their present farms do not collapse over the next few weeks and months. The successful reorganisation of these farms into efficient and competitive units, which are hence viable in the immediate future, does not by any means conflict with the creation of family farms.

There is a lot to be said for giving all types of farms and forms of ownership the same chances as far as possible, so that in each specific individual case the solution which best meets the relevant natural, economic and personal circumstances and thus is most economically effective can be implemented. Objectivity and a sense of reality do, however, require it to be stated that this will be a complicated and, for many of those involved, a difficult and painful process.

The main problem stems from the way in which ownership of land and the agricultural stock have developed in the course of the last four decades. This is such a complicated question that only a few problems can be mentioned here: in many of the agricultural producers' co-operatives up to half the present members neither contributed land or stock nor took over those of their parents when entering the co-operative. They have, however, worked, often for decades, on increasing the property of the co-operative. When the co-operatives are dissolved, or when the members leave them, not only do they have no land, but there is also the question of what share they should receive from the co-operative's assets, especially if it has gone bankrupt.

On the other hand, there are many co-operatives in which less than half the land farmed by them is owned by members of the co-operative. The remaining land is either owned by the state or by local authorities - in the past it was handed over to the co-operatives free of charge for them to farm, for the co-operatives did not purchase land - or it is owned by private individuals who are not working or are no longer working, in farming. If this land is no longer available to the co-operatives, because the owners (in the case of state ownership, for example, in the

form of the Trusteeship Agency) decide otherwise, their continued existence will not, as a rule, be possible.

In the case of land owned by the state, as a rule the co-operatives have applied for assignment in accordance with a law enacted by the last GDR government. However, as this regulation
was not incorporated in the Unification Treaty, no decisions have
yet been made. In the case of private land, the co-operatives are
trying to sign lease agreements with the owners. Here, however,
they are often coming up against serious difficulties. Increasingly, farmers or companies with share capital not resident in the
territory of the former GDR are seeking to purchase or rent land,
not only in the regions in the vicinity of the former border, but
above all in the places with the best land. It is not usually hard
for them to outbid the co-operatives or local individual farmers
on the rent or sales prices.

In my view this development is very questionable, if highly-
mechanised and intensively-run large farms with extremely small
labour forces are to be created in areas acquired in this way. This
conflicts with the interest of safeguarding jobs for the people resident there and would contravene the objectives of EC agricultural policy. On the other hand, in view of the economic situation
in the new Federal **Länder** it is not surprising that landowners
accept such offers, which appear extremely lucrative to them.
This applies in particular to older people, even when they themselves are at present still working in farming as members of a
co-operative.

It seems to me that there is an urgent need for a statutory
regulation, without delay, covering transactions in farmland in
the five new Federal **Länder**, in order to prevent developments
which are undesirable from the point of view of both agrarian
policy and social considerations.

4. The demands of integrated regional development

This all shows that one of the central problems, if not the central problem, is the adaptation of the excessively-large agricultural labour force in the territory of the former GDR to the conditions of a market economy and the EC agricultural market. Overmanning threatens the very existence of most of the present farms. At the same time, the lack of alternative employment is one of the main obstacles to swift implementation of the necessary structural change. This applies in particular to the agricultural producers' co-operatives, for it hinders their dissolution and reorganisation into smaller, more efficient economic units.

On the basis of the possible volume of agricultural production in the five new Federal **Länder** as well as the objective of the adjustment of farm incomes to those of the old Federal **Länder**, the number of workers in East German agriculture must be cut within a few years by at least half, to between 350,000 and 400,000 full-time workers. According to provisional estimates, around 100,000 workers had already left farming in 1990. Some of these were employees in the trade and services sectors who had previously worked on farms and have now been classified separately. This does not, therefore, mean a real reduction in the agricultural workforce. The majority of those leaving the land are people who have already passed retirement age or have taken early retirement.

The possibilities for separate classification of occupational groups not typical of farming have now been largely exhausted. This is also more or less true of those taking early retirement. This means that at least 300,000 alternative jobs have to be found in order to achieve a further reduction in surplus labour on the farms. In view of the high and, at present, rapidly-increasing level of unemployment in the towns, and in order to avoid mass migration from the countryside, these new jobs should be located in the rural areas themselves as far as possible.

In theory, new jobs for the workforce released from former agricultural production can be brought into being in a number of areas. Firstly, within farming itself, this can be done by expanding the existing range of production (e.g. in the non-food sector) and extending the range of economic activities of individual farms (e.g. by processing on the farm, direct marketing and farm-related tourism). Secondly, the production and services sector upstream and downstream of farming can be developed and reconstructed (in addition, for example, to efficient processing works, machinery repair and contracting firms). Thirdly, in the rural infrastructure, appropriate small and medium-sized firms may be created and the corresponding local sector extended. Fourthly, in industry, specific industries could be established in suitable rural locations, with small and medium-sized industrial firms playing a particular part.

This makes it clear that the restructuring of agriculture in East Germany, especially in the problem areas there, will present problems which cannot be solved either by the farms themselves or by agrarian policy alone. There is a need for a regional structural and development policy which will take into account all the economic, social, regional-planning and ecological aspects and will stimulate and bring together both internal and external development potential. This involves integrated regional development, in which the necessary restructuring, the creation of new jobs and measures for qualification and retraining take place, as far as possible, on the same time-scale. To achieve this, reliance must be placed on the experience acquired to date in regional development programmes in the old Federal Republic and in the EC as a whole, even though the conditions in Eastern Germany are, in many respects, new and unique.

Conclusion

The integration of the agriculture of the five new Federal German **Länder** into the EC market is posing unprecedented problems in the history of the development of the European Community. This is not only, and not even primarily, a question of adaptation to EC agricultural-market regulations, although, as previous enlargements of the EC have shown, this in itself can be an extremely complicated and difficult process. In the case of the East German **Länder**, it is a matter of effecting the transition from a socialist planned and controlled economy to a capitalist free-market one. While it is true that this applies to all sectors of the economy in this region, it does not reduce the problems of agriculture - on the contrary, it increases them still further. One has only to think of the disruption to the economic sectors directly upstream and downstream of agriculture and, above all, of the disastrous situation in the labour market. Added to this is the fact that, in the last few decades, the living and working conditions of the population have probably changed more drastically in agriculture than in any other economic sector of the former GDR. For an industrial worker, an office worker or a craftsman, the transition to a market economy - even in the case of temporary unemployment - will in general be accompanied by far fewer problems than for former co-operative farmers.

The demands for special transitional regulations and relief action, therefore, to provide aid, support and social safeguards for the necessary restructuring and adaptation in the agricultural sector in the five new Federal **Länder** do not in any way stem purely from professional egoism, but are genuinely justified.

The new **Land** authorities, as well as the Federal Government, will face weighty and complicated tasks. However, the EC authorities are also faced with a challenge, for ultimately it is not only the fate of those directly involved in East German agriculture which is at stake. Future economic and social development in those rural regions will have a decisive influence on the German unification process and on the development of Europe as a whole. The success achieved in overcoming the consequences of the inappropriate agricultural policy of the former GDR and giving it new prospects within the framework of the European agricultural market could ultimately also serve as a signal to the reform movements in East European countries, themselves highly dependent on agriculture.

Intra-Community trade: problems of transition and adjustment

Rudolf Brauer[1]

1. German unification and potential European economic growth

With the accession of the German Democratic Republic to the Federal Republic of Germany pursuant to Article 23 of the latter's Basic Law, the former GDR became an integral part of the European Communities with effect from 3 October 1990. This brings about an unprecedented situation for the EC.

Accession enlarges the Community market and the market of one of the founder members, the Federal Republic of Germany, by 16 million people. The market of the united Germany now covers some 80 million consumers, and the future EC internal market around 340 million. The latter is accordingly bigger than the internal markets of the US or Japan. Germany's competitive position in the EC and in the world economy in general is thus still further strengthened. At the same time, the Federal Republic's traditional Western trading partners will also benefit. The market of the ex-GDR is opening up for them too. The flow of goods from the old Federal Republic to the newly-acceded territory will lead to a relative weakening of German exports to other Western countries and an increase in German imports, with positive effects on trade and payment balances. The Danish Finance Minister recently estimated the effects for his country as an improvement in balance of the payments of some 5bn Danish crowns and the creation of 40,000 jobs. Dutch exporters have since November 1990 been able to increase their exports of fruit and vegetables to the East German territories from zero to tens of thousands of tons. France is expecting a lasting levelling of its foreign trade balance with Germany.

The Institute for Economic Research in Hamburg expects an increase in German imports by mid-1991 amounting to 20-25bn DM. Experts foresee a halving of the German surplus on the current-account balance in three to four years. The growth and equilibrium of international trade, particularly in Western Europe, should derive great benefit from the enormous backlog of demand in the former GDR for investment and consumer goods. To that extent, German unification is supporting growth in the world economy.

With the GDR's accession to the Federal Republic of Germany, for the first time since the existence of the EC a former state-trading country is being admitted into the Community, and without a prolonged transition or adjustment period. For decades the former GDR's economy has been tied into a dense network of trading and co-operative relationships with the USSR and other CMEA member states. This network now threatens to abruptly disappear. The state treaty (**Staatsvertrag**) between the GDR and the Federal Republic on economic, monetary and social union, and the unification treaty (**Einigungsvertrag**), do guarantee protection of trust in these relationships; but the introduction of the DM as the contractual currency in East German trade, and the general economic situation of all CMEA countries, has sent the traditional pattern of exports and imports in Eastern Europe into headlong decline.. Economic and social crisis, particularly in the smaller CMEA countries, is intensifying. It is already becoming apparent that in consequence, high demands for compensation for damages may come from the former GDR's East European and overseas trading partners. For instance, the former GDR was one of Poland's favoured economic partners in the area of finished and semi-finished products in vehicle construction, electronics, chemicals and paper. The Polish government is now claiming losses of some 50m roubles, plus 70m DM, as a result of the turning down of import contracts by firms in the new German **Länder**. Since many Polish firms have continued to import from East Germany, the Polish negative balance of trade already amounted to 408 million transfer roubles by early October 1990 (equivalent to about one thousand million DM), further increasing Poland's debts in convertible currency.

These relationships are seen in Poland as vital. In 1989 trade between Poland and East Germany amounted to 6,900 million Marks. The de facto loss of the East German market means a bitter blow to the economic rehabilitation of Poland's economy. The emerging situation is similarly assessed in Hungary and Czechoslovakia. Hungarian Prime Minister Antall foresaw losses amounting to 500-800 million DM for Hungary in 1990.

The former GDR's trade with its CMEA partners was expected to show very heavy surpluses at the end of 1990, which would have to be paid for by the partners in convertible currency. A serious commercial conflict is therefore brewing between united Germany and East European states. It is in the interest of both Germany and the EC to maintain and extend the market positions of the East German economy in the USSR and Eastern and South-Eastern Europe that have grown up over decades. It would also be an important contribution to the economic relinking of these countries with Western Europe. Thus the East German economy could be a bridge for the economic integration of East and West. The large open market of 340 million people that will be completed in 1992-3 could give rise to a market of some 700 million people. The alternative to this would be economic barriers along Germany's eastern frontier and a de-coupling or even exclusion of the Soviet republics, Poland, Czechoslovakia, Hungary and the other European CMEA countries from European unification, with negative political and economic consequences for all states of Europe.

If the East German economy's strong positions in Eastern Europe are actively exploited, the united Germany's international competitive position on these markets will be greatly improved. In the medium term these markets will, particularly if the processes of transition to a market economy that have begun there develop successfully, prove to be expanding markets for the future. New possibilities could open up for firms from other Western industrial countries too, if they acquire firms from the ex-GDR with good market positions in Eastern Europe as bases. In this way all EC states could increase their growth potential in coming years and become the economic growth centre of the 1990's.

With the creation of economic, monetary and social union and the concomitant opening-up of the former GDR's market, firms in East Germany have simultaneously lost three existing preferential markets - their own internal market, German-German trade and trade with CMEA countries. This has led to considerable problems in manufacture, sales and employment, in both industry and agriculture. In EC professional circles, the talk is therefore already of an "economic region in decline". It is in the interest of both Germany and the European Communities to avoid a collapse of the economy in the former GDR, with lasting mass unemployment and drastic social conflict. The united Germany and the EC both have the necessary resources and suitable machinery.

2. Adapting the trade relations of the former GDR

In 1989, the GDR had trading relationships with some 100 countries. Foreign trade turnover was worth around 66bn DM. A good half of this was with OECD countries (including the old Federal Republic of Germany), and more than 40% with CMEA countries, of which almost a quarter with the Soviet Union. German-German trade (including services) similarly took up almost a quarter. The rest of the EEC countries accounted for about one-tenth of GDR foreign trade. A bare 5% was with developing countries.

The GDR's accession to the Federal Republic of Germany and the increasing integration of the East German economy with the European Communities are leading to new conditions for the external economic relations of all countries concerned. A de facto customs union was already in place by 1 July 1990 between the EC countries and the GDR. On 1 August 1990 a de facto agricultural union between the EC and the GDR entered into force. With the coming into effect of the customs union, the late GDR government undertook to apply the EC Common Customs Tariff (TARIC) in trade with non-EEC countries. It was agreed - initially until the end of 1990 - not to apply the EC external customs tariff in GDR trade with CMEA countries.

For the USSR and the other CMEA countries, trade with the former GDR is of considerable economic importance. The GDR share in total USSR external trade was approximately 11% in 1988; the figure for Czech foreign trade was around 10%, 8% for Poland, 6% for Hungary and Bulgaria and 7% for Romania.

Internal CMEA trade provided many people with employment and with imports of important raw materials as well as consumer and investment goods. This trade, until now based on governmental or ministerial agreements by way of commercial contracts between national foreign-trade agencies or export agencies and at essentially uniform terms (pricing, clearing, terms of delivery, immediate collection), is now undergoing fundamental change. The state agreements governing existing terms of export and import mostly ended in 1990. New agreements at government level, for instance with the USSR, have been set up on new bases. Adaptation to customary usage in international trade is advancing rapidly.

At present, East German firms have foreign-trade agreements of both the old and the new type with CMEA countries. For consignments on the terms customary to date, export firms can on application and on proof of necessity still secure subsidies from the national budget. For contracts of the new type, concluded on international market terms, this is not provided for. Commercial contracts on existing CMEA terms extending beyond the year 1990, in connection, for instance, with investment in the USSR, continue to come under special provisions.

There is marked interest on the part of the USSR and other CMEA countries in continuing their extensive trade and economic relations with firms in East Germany under the changed conditions. There are, however, serious problems. In the course of 1990, GDR firms cancelled a considerable proportion of supply contracts with partners in CMEA countries. It is to be expected that trade with these countries will - at least temporarily - fall markedly, since they have considerable difficulties in securing the foreign currency necessary for the imports they urgently need.

In my view, the future shaping of the European Community's trading and economic relations with the countries of eastern and south-eastern Europe to take account of the positions secured by the former GDR economy in those markets offers a great opportunity to make German unification and pan-European developments interact fruitfully. A declaration in favour of the association of CMEA states with the European Communities would be desirable.

The initiative by the European Commission in adopting, on 1 August 1990, a report containing new ideas on economic and political co-operation with eastern and south-eastern Europe is welcome. According to this, new "European agreements" could lead to an "extended free-trade area" in Europe.

3. Reforming internal German trade

German-German trade, including the exchange of services, had a volume of over 15bn DM in 1989. This was over 70% of the GDR's total trade with EC states. The legal basis for trade between the German Democratic Republic and the Federal Republic of Germany was the "Agreement on trade between the monetary territories of the German Mark (DM West) and the monetary territories of the German Notenbank mark (DM East)" (Berlin Agreement) of 20 September 1951. The status of German internal trade was not affected by the Federal Republic's membership of the EC. The "Protocol on German internal trade and related questions" attached to the EEC Treaty laid this down explicitly. Until the entry into force of the treaty on German economic, monetary and social union on 1 July 1990, German internal trade was based on exclusively bilateral clearing transactions. Among the features of the special status was that no duties were charged on trade in either direction, and imports from the GDR were fiscally privileged.

Article 12 of the treaty creating a monetary, economic and social union between the two German states of 18 May 1990 made an agreed adjustment of the Berlin Agreement to the present situation. With GDR accession to the Federal Republic of Germany, the special status of German-German trade, which in the past had led Eastern and Western partners of both German states to speak of the GDR as the "secret 13th member of the EC", has come to an end. It was indeed true that the additional protocol to the Rome Treaties on German internal trade gave firms from both German states a special preference on each other's market.

4. Accommodating the Community's trade régime

The EC and Federal Republic made a joint declaration to the GATT Council in July 1990 on de facto incorporation of the GDR into the EC customs area, which was accepted without opposition. In practice, the GDR had long been granted most-favoured-nation status in respect of customs by most OECD countries - including all EC and EFTA member states - even though this had not been legally sanctioned in the GATT. The economic area of the former GDR has now also been included in the free-trade area arrangements for industrial goods between the EC and the individual EFTA countries (except Iceland), so that duty-free status exists in these relations too.

The procedural rules on the inclusion of the economic area of the former GDR in the EC customs union were laid down for the industrial goods sector in Regulation (EEC) no. 1794/90 of the Council of 28 June 1990 on transitional measures for trade with the German Democratic Republic.[2] The most important provisions of this Regulation are as follows.

In EC trade with the territory of the former GDR, duties and charges of equivalent effect and quantity restrictions and restrictive measures in connection with the machinery of EC common commercial policy were "suspended", i.e. abolished. For Spain and Portugal particular exceptions would continue to apply for some time. Secondly, the former GDR adopted the common customs tariff and Community customs law in its trade with third countries, as well as the measures of the common commercial policy. Thirdly, a protective clause gave both sides the possibility of warding off particular disruptions of markets. Thus, Article 3(2) of the Regulation allowed the former GDR - and therefore now the Federal Government - the possibility to "take protective measures to prevent free access for Community goods to its market from leading to serious economic difficulties for any of its industries". (Whether this theoretical option is still applicable after the GDR's accession to the Federal Republic, however, it is too soon to say.)

To supplement Council Regulation No. 1794/90, Commission Regulation (EEC) No. 1795/90 of 29 June 1990 on implementing measures was adopted.[3] It stressed that trade between the former GDR and third countries would from 1 July 1990 would be treated "in respect of all goods with the exception of the agricultural sphere in accordance with the same rules and tariffs as trade between the Federal Republic of Germany and third countries". This Regulation lays down that in commodity trade between the EC and the economic area of the former GDR, Community internal dispatch practice will be applied. The customs and statistical instrument is the unitary EC document.

Duty-free trade between the former GDR and the European CMEA countries will probably be retained at least until the end of 1991 - possibly even 1992. A binding decision on this has not, however, been taken yet by the EC institutions. By a Decision of 27 September 1990, the Commission empowered the Federal Republic of Germany to suspend common customs tariff duties and all measures of equal effect except for anti-dumping duties for goods originating in the European CMEA countries and Yugoslavia. The condition is that the goods concerned be imported into the accession territory (former GDR) under bilateral agreements or protocols between the former GDR and the countries mentioned and marketed and consumed there. Instead of consumption there may also be processing or transformation in the accession territory, which confers the status of Community-originated goods on the imported commodities. The German government will apply to GATT for the appropriate waiver to suspend the duties.

Provisionally, a few exceptions still apply to the economic area of the former GDR in connection with the customs union with CMEA countries. This concerns, for instance, the common EC import restrictions on third countries, affecting particularly such sensitive areas as textiles, metallurgy and glass/ceramics. The economic area of the former GDR was not involved in the annual apportionment of established quantity or value quotas to the individual EC countries by the Commission in the second half of 1990. However, the former GDR had already enacted implementing provisions to bring the common EC import-regulations vis-à-vis third countries into operation through its new "Act on external trade, capital movements and payments". This made the import of particular goods (particularly textiles and clothing products) subject to authorisation as from 1 July 1990; for other goods, origin must be proved.

The inclusion of coal-mining and steel products in the customs union was, as with the regulations for other industrial goods, undertaken through Commission Decision No. 1796/90/ECSC of 29 June 1990 suspending customs duty and quantity restrictions for products from the German Democratic Republic coming under the ECSC Treaty.

5. Agriculture

Since 1 August 1990 the GDR has de facto belonged to the EC agricultural union. This means that in bilateral trade in agricultural products, import levies (representing a sort of variable duty), export refunds and existing quantitative restrictions have been abolished. Agricultural union also means taking over the EC intervention arrangements, that is, state take-up of surplus production, for instance of grain or butter, at set EC-wide unitary minimum prices. The stored surpluses ought in principle to be exported as quickly as possible in order not to bring about any additional price pressure on the EC internal market. It is assumed on the basis of the good harvest for 1990 that some 3.5 million tons of grain will come into consideration.

For the East German agricultural economy, which is in an extremely difficult sales position because of the total opening-up of the market to the Federal Republic and the other EC states, the improved sales possibilities in the western part of Germany and other EC countries mean some relief. To be able to exploit this more fully, however, it is necessary to give quick state assistance in reconstructing and modernising dairies and slaughterhouses and for plants in the confectionery, beverage and margarine industries. To date, only two slaughterhouses in the GDR meet the criteria applying in EC countries. Whether temporary exceptional provisions can be arrived at in order to allow export or consignment from a plant that does not yet meet EC requirements has not yet been clarified. It ought to be considered whether low-interest loans from the EC countries' European Investment Bank (EIB) to finance such reconstruction projects could be claimed.

Incorporation into the EC agricultural union means for the East German farm economy and foodstuffs industries a considerable intensification of competition on the sales markets in the territory hitherto reserved for them. For all other states that have acceded to the EC, most recently Spain and Portugal in 1986, transitional periods of several years have been agreed for agriculture in particular.

For East German farm producers, the adoption of the EC producer-price level means a reduction, differing according to product but mostly considerable, from the level that applied in 1989, and thus a reduction of profit. On the other hand it allows stabilisation by comparison with the particularly severe price collapse that occurred immediately upon introduction of the DM to the GDR market. In these circumstances of enhanced pressure to adapt, various measures were adopted for a transitional period, including buying up grain and butter and state-subsidised exports of butter and meat to countries of Eastern Europe.

6. CoCom, high-technology transfers and standardisation

After 1 July 1990, in connection with the economic union then formed between the GDR and the Federal Republic of Germany and the de facto customs union with the EC, the CoCom provisions were largely relaxed in respect of the former GDR. At CoCom (the Western industrialised countries' Coordinating Committee for East-West trade policy), the US also ultimately agreed to make it possible for firms in the economic area of the former GDR to import and manufacture high technology appearing on the CoCom list of prohibited exports. As a counterpart, the then GDR government gave an undertaking to all CoCom member countries that goods and technologies graded as "requiring supervision" in the West would be used in the GDR exclusively for peaceful purposes and not passed on to third parties (i.e. re-exported) without agreement by the governments of the suppliers, not even as components of goods manufactured in the GDR. This means in particular a possible restriction on consignments from the economic area of the former GDR to the USSR and other CMEA countries. A so-called CoCom core list with explicitly military goods has continued in force.

The integration of the economic area of the former GDR into the EC should be largely completed by the end of 1992, the date for planned completion of the EC internal market. To take account of the date of 3 October 1990 for accession of the GDR to the Federal Republic, the Commission speeded up its work on a total package of further draft enactments and adjusting rules, taking a decision in principle on it on 21 August 1990. The package of measures was to be discussed by the EC Council of Ministers and the European Parliament, with definitive decisions to be made by the end of 1990 containing very detailed provisions.

Prior to that, provisional measures valid until 31 December 1990 were decided, to be applied after the date of accession. According to statements by EC Commissioner Martin Bangemann, around four-fifths of the legal acts for the planned internal market are immediately applicable to the territory of the former GDR. Transitional arrangements are provided in particular for the foodstuffs sector, chemicals including medicaments and cosmetics, and agriculture and fisheries. These are to give firms in the economic area of the GDR a chance to come up to the West European level for products and operating plants within set periods before the Community requirements apply to them in full. This relates, for instance, to technical measures, safety provisions and environmental requirements. Most transitional arrangements are planned to run until the end of 1992. In environmental protection the time is to be extended until the end of 1995 (regulations on water and air quality and legislation on waste), and in individual cases (provisions on sulphur dioxide content) even further.

Products in the industries mentioned above manufactured by firms in the former GDR territory, but not yet meeting Community requirements, are as a rule to be permitted until the end of 1992 for sale in that territory but not in the rest of the EC, not even on previously Federal territory. This will lead to great pressure on firms in the territory of the former GDR to adapt rapidly to West German and West European levels of technical standards and environmental protection regulations.

One of the measures accompanying the State Treaty between the GDR and the Federal Republic of Germany was the decision of 4 July 1990 by the GDR government to set up a standards union with the Federal Republic. This states that on the then GDR territory, its own activity in the area of technical standards and standardisation would be suspended on 30 September 1990, with a few special areas (health, work safety and fire protection and military standardisation) being for the moment excluded.

The German Institute for Standardisation (DIN) in Berlin (West) has extended its area of operation to the territory of the former GDR. Firms in the economic area of the former GDR must now on their own responsibility push forward broad-scale application of DIN standards and collaboration on DIN bodies. DIN and ASMW, the agency competent in the former GDR for standardisation, are to verify jointly which national standards of the former GDR can be taken over in whole or in part into the DIN set of standards. The work carried out in the new German **Länder** to conform with that of the West European standard-setting bodies, CEN and CENELEC, will undoubtedly have positive effects on trade with EC and EFTA countries.

In the area of competition (anti-trust) policy likewise, the economy of the former GDR is rapidly coming closer to the corresponding provisions of the Federal Republic of Germany and the EC. Among the laws already introduced in connection with the German-German economic union on 1 July 1990 is the Act against restraints of competition, largely identical with the corresponding statute for the Federal Republic.

In talks in July 1990 between the European Commission Vice-President responsible for competition policy, Sir Leon Brittan, and the GDR government, willingness was declared to apply the competition provisions of the Rome Treaties even now; this would apply in particular to merger control. Sir Leon expressed the criticism of the Federal Republic's EC partners to the effect that Federal German firms in particular were setting aside the rules of fair play in the former GDR. Part of this was putting foreign firms at a disadvantage by comparison with Federal German ones. This was also true of the work of the **Treuhandanstalt**. The Chairman of the **Treuhandanstalt** board, Detlev Rohwedder, suggested to Sir Leon that representatives from EC countries be brought into auxiliary positions in the **Treuhandanstalt**.[4]

7. Relations with developing countries

A new situation also exists in respect of the former GDR's commercial relationships with countries outside the EC and EFTA areas, that is, with both the CMEA countries and developing countries. While intensive negotiations were already carried out during 1990 on the future shape of relations with the USSR and the other CMEA countries - until then the main trading partners for the GDR - with very active involvement by the West German government, the continuation of relations with CMEA countries became an object of intensive discussion only very recently.

The 'Treaty between the German Democratic Republic and the Federal Republic of Germany on the creation of the unity of Germany - Unification Treaty" states in this connection: "The external economic relationships of the German Democratic Republic that have grown up, in particular the existing Treaty obligations to countries of the Council for Mutual Economic Assistance, shall enjoy protection of trust. They will be further developed and extended taking into account the interests of all involved and having regard to market-economy principles and the powers of the European Communities."

With its accession to the Federal Republic of Germany and the EC, the GDR territory is also committed to taking over the commercial agreements concluded by the EC with third countries; the possibility should exist of agreeing time-limited adaptation measures on particular individual issues. Regarding developing countries, this concerns the ACP Agreement with a total of 69 developing countries in Africa, the Caribbean and the Pacific; Association Agreements and preferential co-operation agreements with Mediterranean countries; non-preferential trading and co-operation agreements with developing countries in Latin America and Asia; and the General System of Preferences for the industrial exports of developing countries.

As far as the GDR's subsisting agreements with developing countries are concerned, they will in principle be incorporated into the above-outlined EC system, rather than being continued as separate agreements. The relevant ministries in Bonn and East Berlin had by August 1990 declared their intention to dissolve the network of supply contracts and trade agreements between the GDR and developing countries, with particular development-assistance elements of such agreements (e.g. technical assistance) being continued in modified form.

Conclusion

With the GDR's accession to the Federal Republic of Germany and the inclusion of the economic area of the former GDR in the European Communities, completely new conditions have arisen for firms in operating Eastern Germany. These will in the medium term lead to significant changes in the material and regional structure of foreign trade of the former GDR territory and in its external economic relations.

On the asset side, for many East German firms, is the fact that they have skilled workers and engineers at their disposal. Since the beginning of the currency union, all firms have been able to use the advantages of the internationally-valued convertible German mark. Now, with the status of EC firms, they have open to them all the possibilities of integration into the Western European internal market. Existing freedom of decision on investment and manufacturing programmes, on partners in cooperation and sales orientations allows flexible and effective work, with at the same time higher risk.

On EC terms, competition throughout the whole spectrum of goods and services on offer will intensify in the five new Federal **Länder** and in East Berlin. The pressure to reduce costs and improve efficiency in manufacturing and service firms will grow still further and be associated with social problems for many citizens in the economic sphere.

An important part of former GDR foreign trade today is now clearly taking on the nature of internal trade. At the same time, many new trade and co-operation relations will appear with firms in other EC countries and in EFTA countries. EC internal and West European internal trade will grow in importance on both the European and the world scale. Western and Central Europe are likely in the 1990's to become the growth centre for the world economy. Given consistent efforts at restraining protectionist tendencies, there is a chance to expand the world's biggest treaty area to date - the EC and EFTA countries, with some 375 million inhabitants - into a European free-trade area and make it a model for the future development of international economic co-operation. As one observer has put it: "The fundamental importance of the EC's 1992 internal market is that Europe has regained its self-confidence and that the Europeans are now resolved to determine their future themselves."[5]

It is to be hoped that - partly through exploiting the existing positions of the East German economy - commercial and economic relations between the united Germany and other West European states, as well as those of eastern and southern Europe, will develop into a powerful catalyst for European unification.

References

1. The author wishes to acknowledge the assistance of Rudi Hage and Gerhard Hofmann in the writing of this essay.

2. EC **Official Journal** L 166, 29 June 1990, pp. 1-2.

3. **Ibid**. pp. 3-4.

4. **Berliner Zeitung** , 25 July 1990.

5. M.E. Weinstein, "Washington und Europa 1992", **Europa-Archiv** 5/1990, p. 173.

Part IV

Challenges for European Integration

Extending the Structural Fund commitments to East Germany

Koldo E. Echevarria and Günther F. Schäfer

1. Introduction

This essay seeks to explore some of the basic issues in the potential application of the Community Structural Fund Programme to East Germany after unification and the GDR's simultaneous accession to the European Community.[1] Our aim is not to define a detailed model for the application of the Funds but to explore the factors that could make their application effective.

The German question cannot be seen in isolation. It is the most visible expression of a new European reality, one that requires a broad approach in the context of European political and economic integration. If the Community is to lead this process, rather than react to it, it needs to be endowed with new policy functions and a more sophisticated institutional framework. The initiatives for political and monetary union reflect the political will to make the necessary changes. But all reforms in the constitutional design of the European Community are fraught with difficulties. At a time when the Community is in the middle of implementing the most ambitious reforms since its foundation - the Single European Act with the completion of the Internal Market, the changes in the Structural Funds and the Common Agricultural Policy - it is faced with some of the most important strategic choices in the history of European integration.

In addition to the unexpected challenges the Community faces in its international environment, it is confronted with many internal challenges. One of these is the implementation of its own programmes. The programme for the completion of the Internal Market, while progressing well in the formal adoption of legal measures, is being delayed by member states at the implementation stage; technical harmonisation is being slowed down by the task of sorting out countless details; the removal of border controls for persons is being resisted by national governments; and the lack of a common understanding makes it difficult for tax authorities to co-operate against fraud.

Similarly, the reform of the Structural Funds is likely to encounter serious problems in meeting its objectives. Although the innovations in the planning phase have taken place on schedule, the real problems begin with implementation, when the plans must be applied. The uncertainties relate to the capacities of the Commission and national and regional administrations to ensure proper joint management. Major changes are not self-implementing and the limited capacity to manage change at the Community level is seriously strained by the complexities of national interests and cultural diversity.

The accession of East Germany to the European Community therefore takes place in the middle of political optimism and practical difficulties. In the coming years, East Germany will be confronted with unprecedented social, economic and political change. Economic actors will have to cope with a radically different environment. In this learning process, the ability to understand the new rules and take advantage of them could turn into a competitive advantage. If such massive and frenetic social change is not to produce profound imbalances between social groups and regional units, a system must be developed which is capable of anticipating problems and taking corrective measures. This would be a formidable challenge even for the most solid and stable of public authorities; yet East Germany will also have to be primarily concerned with setting up its own system of public authority on both the regional (**Länder**) and the local level. It is in this context that we propose to explore the possible extension of the Structural Funds to East Germany. This essay will concentrate on defining the framework in which the Structural Funds operate, while seeking to identify the factors that could help to achieve their effective application in East Germany.

2. The role of redistributive policies in the EC's evolution

The progress of the European Community towards deeper integration can be measured by its capacity to spread costs and benefits equally between member states. Its development has been characterised by a permanent effort to strike a balance between what member states give to the Community and what they receive from it. The problem of "dividing up the Community cake" is one of the key questions in the substantive design of the Community and part of the general debate about its distributive and redistributive functions.

The difficulties encountered by efforts to guarantee a proper distribution of costs and benefits can be traced back to the context in which the Rome Treaty was signed. The European Community was created to allow member states to increase trade with each other and gain competitive advantage vis-à-vis non-EC countries. Emphasis was placed on "negative integration" - the removal of barriers to free trade between member states. The main effort towards positive integration was represented by the Common Agricultural Policy. It was created with several objectives: food security, income-support for farmers and relatively low prices for consumers. Its practically single mechanism - price-support - turned it more or less into a distributive policy function. As a consequence, agricultural expenditure absorbed the largest part of the Community budget, making for rigidity and inequality in its distribution.

Redistributive policies were only marginally dealt with in the Rome Treaty. The declaration of the Preamble, advocating a "harmonious development" in the regions of the Community, was hardly further developed in the substantive part of the Treaty. Only a few provisions on regional aid, transport and agricultural policy and the creation of the European Investment Bank reflect some concern for regional development. The marginal role attributed to redistributive instruments can be explained by a general confidence in the future performance of the Community's economy and by the considerable degree of economic convergence between the founding member states. Moreover, the time was not ripe for a positive stance toward regional policy, given the precarious agreement reached by member states and the controversial character of redistributive policies. The dominant neofunctional perspective on European integration viewed it as an incremental process, based on the parallel development of economic growth and political trust.

However, progress in economic integration practically always requires a redistributive function to ensure an even spatial distribution of costs and benefits, otherwise distrust, unilateral decision-making and bilateral arrangements result. For many years, every proposal up for discussion in the Council of Ministers has followed the pattern of a zero-sum game in which governments of member states have seen themselves as either winners or losers.

The favourable economic environment of the 1960's allowed for closer convergence between member states, even with the lack of significant redistributive mechanisms. Nonetheless the Commission, recognising the weakness of the system and in anticipation of future needs, set up a Directorate-General for Regional Policy and made the first attempts to create a Regional Fund. At the end of the decade the Werner Report on Economic and Monetary Union stressed the need to develop regional policy instruments. With the 1970's came the economic crisis and the accession of new member states. The European Regional Development Fund was created, primarily in response to UK complaints about the prominence of agricultural expenditures. Designed to operate as a repayment mechanism, it could never achieve a real regional impact. The lack of meaningful spatially-redistributive measures, the uncontrollable growth of agricultural spending and the controversial system of calculating national contributions to the Community budget brought calls to change the rules and ensure a better distribution of the Community cake to the centre of Community policy concerns. The accession of Greece and the anticipated accession of Spain and Portugal further highlighted the inadequacy of the whole system. With these new members, territorial disparities in the Community doubled. A final impetus to achieve a more balanced framework for policy functions came with the programme to complete the Internal Market, which included the development of more effective redistributive mechanisms. The Single European Act and the ensuing reforms inaugurated a new role for redistributive policies in the European Community.

The "accession" of East Germany will be facilitated by these new policies. The Community has greater capacity and flexibility. The new redistributive policy framework considerably broadens the scope for manoeuvre in this rather unconventional "enlargement". The "status quo" of contributions and allocations of the Community budget will have to be revised. The German net contribution to the Community budget is likely to be reduced and other member states will share the costs of East German integration. Reaching an agreement on the new status quo will be crucial to designing a scheme for the application of the Structural Funds in East Germany.

3. The Single European Act and the reform of the Structural Funds

The Single European Act (SEA) is the most visible expression of the political will to change the framework in which the European Community has operated since its foundation. The objective is to give the EC the capacity in policy functions and decision-making processes to cope with an increasingly-heterogeneous and changing environment. Although the Act contains rather few truly innovatory provisions, it paves the way for strategic changes in the way the Community is run.

The Single European Act reformulates some of the central ideas of European integration. Instead of the "Common Market" it speaks of the "Internal Market", and "harmonious development" is replaced with "economic and social cohesion". The real challenge of the Act, however, lies in the implementation of the mandates and objectives stated. In fact, reaching agreement on the implementation of the reforms stipulated was more time-consuming than the negotiation of the Act itself.

The reforms envisaged were outlined by the Commission in its document "Making a Success of the Single Act: A New Frontier for Europe". This document presented the reforms as a coherent negotiation package to the European Council. The final objective was to strike a new balance between distributive and redistributive functions in the Community budget. The reforms can be divided into four major objectives: a) adapting the Common Agricultural Policy to the world market and reducing its burden on the budget; b) ensuring adequate, stable and guaranteed financial resources and aligning the collection system to the relative prosperity of the respective member states; c) strengthening budgetary discipline and establishing new rules for managing the budget; and d) designing common policies with a significant economic impact, in particular giving new operating rules and increased financial resources to the Structural Funds.

The approval of these measures by the European Council at the special summit in Brussels in February 1988 opened a new chapter in the evolution of the Community. It inaugurated a new substantive design in the Community's policy functions and gave redistributive instruments a new role in its budget. The Community is now finally endowed with the capacity to give member states confidence in a better distribution of the benefits that will derive from the Internal Market.

The provisions of the Single European Act on economic and social cohesion start by stressing the objectives of "harmonious development" and the need to reduce disparities. Regional policy instruments, already in force through the European Regional Development Fund regulation, were incorporated into the Treaty through Article 130. The existence of the Fund itself is given new recognition by Article 130 C. Finally, Articles 130 D and E provide the mandate for the reform of the Structural Funds, to clarify and rationalise their tasks in contributing to the achievement of economic and social cohesion and in reducing regional disparities.

The reform of the Structural Funds had been called for for some time by the Commission, the European Parliament and the Court of Auditors. The mandate of the SEA is the response to a widespread dissatisfaction with the functioning of the Funds. It provides for three major financial instruments offering grants and loans for investment in infrastructure, capital and human resources. They are:

i) The European Agricultural Guidance and Guarantee Fund (EAGGF) - Guidance Section, established under Article 40 of the EEC Treaty to contribute to "an increase in productivity through a rational development of agricultural production and an optimum use of factors of production, in particular the work-force".

ii) The European Social Fund (ESF), established under Article 123 of the EEC Treaty "in order to improve employment opportunities for workers in the common market and to contribute thereby to raising standards of living".

iii) The European Regional Development Fund (ERDF), which, according to Article 130 C of the SEA, is to help "to reduce the principal regional imbalances in the Community".

In addition to these, the Community has financial instruments offering grants and loans which are also included in the co-ordination mandate of the SEA. Among them are the loans of the European Investment Bank and the European Coal and Steel Community, the assistance provided by the Integrated Mediterranean Programmes and other structural measures, mainly in the fields of transport, energy, environment and technology.

This short description already suggests that fragmentation of objectives and duplication of aid schemes was a likely problem in the management of the Funds. In the view of the Commission, the European Parliament and the Court of Auditors, the "old" Structural Funds had serious shortcomings as effective instruments of economic and social cohesion. Among the most common criticisms were the following. First, there were insufficient financial resources and a lack of concentration on priority areas. Second, the allocating system was too flexible to reflect Community-wide priorities and policies. Third, there was a lack of co-ordination in the operations of the different funds and between national and Community authorities. Fourth, there were deficiencies in the operating procedures, in particular in the control and evaluation of projects and programmes. Fifth, there was a lack of global programmes providing consistency throughout the individual projects.

The reform of the Structural Funds came into force on 1 January 1989. It consists of a framework regulation, new regulations for each of the three funds and an operational regulation with common procedures and co-ordinating mechanisms. The key features of the reform can be summarised as follows:

a) Concentrating the activities of the funds on specific objectives, the main problem areas of economic disparity in the Community. They are as follows:

Objective 1: promoting the development of less-developed regions. The regions to be covered are those whose GDP per capita is below 75% of the Community average.
Objective 2: helping the reconversion of declining industrial regions.
Objective 3: combating long-term unemployment.
Objective 4: facilitating the occupational integration of the young.
Objective 5: with a view to the reform of the Common Agricultural Policy, speeding up the adjustment of agricultural structures and promoting the development of less-developed rural areas.

b) Providing the Funds with adequate financial resources to deal with problems. The volume of Community assistance is to be increased to ensure a real impact, especially in Objective 1 regions for which the funds will be doubled by 1992.

c) Establishing a new method of operation based on complementarity, partnership and programming. The objective is to make a more effective use of the Funds. Complementarity implies that Community structural action complements national measures. Partnership means that the management of the Funds' operations should involve co-operation between the Community, national, regional and local authorities. Programming tries to give structural action the necessary strength by grouping individual projects in coherent sets.

d) Simplifying procedures and improving co-ordination. This includes common procedures for the different instruments, improved and simple co-ordination mechanisms and more effective monitoring and evaluation systems.

With these innovations, the operating framework of the Structural Funds has undergone a profound change. The Commission and member states have started to implement the reforms. It is too early to judge their success or failure. It is clear, however, that these reforms have tackled one of the more serious deficits in Community policy functions. The fact that the Twelve agreed to double the financial resources dedicated to improving social and economic cohesion is an indication of the fact that more than lip-service to these objectives is intended. This in itself is more than a symbolic contribution to the effort to reduce regional imbalances.

4. The Structural Funds' objectives and their application to East Germany

The question of extending the present Structural Fund Programme of the Community to East Germany is not only one of how its objectives fit East German reality. It is also a highly political issue. In member states which currently receive a large share of the Funds, fears have been expressed that resources will be withdrawn from them and redeployed in East Germany. Even if this does not happen, and any funds from the Community flowing to East

Germany are additional resources specifically raised for that purpose, the fact remains that private investment, not only from West Germany, will certainly be partly redirected to East Germany and to all of Eastern Europe. The volume and extent of this is very difficult to assess.

Before examining in more detail the question of how the Structural Funds could be extended to East Germany, it is necessary to recall a few salient facts about the situation there.

Firstly, the former territory of the German Democratic Republic has become part of the present Federal German Republic by way of Article 23 of the latter's Basic Law allowing any German **Land** to join it. On 3 October 1990, five new German **Länder** officially joined the Federal Republic in this way (Mecklenburg, Brandenburg, Sachsen-Anhalt, Thüringen and Sachsen; East Berlin will be united with West Berlin). The first elections in these **Länder** were held on 14 October and all-German elections on 2 December.

Secondly, reliable statistics about the economic situation in East Germany are simply not available. Most experts estimate that the GDP per capita of East Germany is about 1/3 of that of West Germany, which places it somewhere between Greece and Portugal on the European scale. Moreover, there exist significant regional differences: the primarily agricultural north (Mecklenburg) and the industrial centre (Brandenburg, Berlin) and south (Sachsen) face different problems both with respect to the economic viability of their industry and their infrastructure. At the same time it must be pointed out that, due to the socialist economic system, there are as yet virtually no income disparities between the various regions and between rural areas and industrial cities. However one interprets these facts,[2] there can be no doubt that the whole territory of the former German Democratic Republic and each individual new **Land** created has a GDP per capita significantly below 75% of the Community average.

Thirdly, within the Eastern bloc, East Germany had the strongest economy. It does not stand comparison, however, with similarly industrialised economies in the West. Even in those sectors where productivity and output quality were relatively high, the level of technological capability is in no way comparable to the West. Production equipment is hopelessly outdated; some facilities predate the Second World War. One of the authors of this essay recently visited a medium-sized machine-tool company where the most recent equipment was built in 1971. Furthermore, practically all industrial activity in the former GDR fails to meet Western environmental standards. If EC environmental law were to come into force immediately, practically all East German industry would have to close down.

Fourthly, research and development efforts significantly lag behind comparable Western industrialised countries. Only 4.4% of total employment of industry is working in R & D and even if the staff of the Academy of Sciences is added to this number, it is in no way comparable to the R & D efforts of Western industrial countries. This puts the technological competitiveness of East German industry into serious question; without a significant technology transfer effort, there is no way that it can compete on Western markets in the foreseeable future.

Fifthly, the infrastructure of the former GDR is a shambles: road connections, telecommunications and energy supplies are characterised by practically pre-World War II standards. Large investment is required to improve and upgrade these facilities, which are essential for the proper functioning of a market economy.

Sixthly, agriculture is characterised by overmanning and low productivity and guided by bureaucratic plans rather than the needs of the market. In addition, there have been recent reports that many products do not meet EC minimal health standards.

Seventhly, the employment situation is potentially serious. In the early summer of 1990 unemployment figures were around 200-250,000. With the coming into force of German economic and monetary union, this figure rose significantly. Estimates as to how high unemployment will ultimately rise vary from a few hundred thousand to 2-3 million, in other words up to 25% or even more of the work-force. While there is considerable uncertainty as to how large unemployment will be and how long individual cases will last, there can be no doubt that a large number of people will have to be re-employed and will face at least temporary unemployment in the process. Estimates vary, depending on the industry in question, between 30 and 60% of the present work-force. It is difficult to assess how the economy will respond to the situation and how the social fabric or social peace will be affected. There can be no question, however, that East German society will have to undergo fundamental change and that unemployment is the key threat to social peace.

Finally, this situation is not primarily the result of underdevelopment or peripheral location, as in most of the other regions of the Community that are lagging behind economically; rather it is the result of the peculiar socialist economic practices of East Germany. Marketing and distribution functions are underdeveloped; production costs are unknown; financial markets are non-existent; consumer product industries were sacrificed in favour of heavy industry; a network of small and medium-sized firms - the backbone of West German economic strength - is almost completely absent; production-support services are extremely difficult to find; industrial relations was seen as a problem that only occurred in the West. The application of market rules and international competitiveness must produce a complete turnaround in the way industry is run. The transition to a market economy will raise many problems which are quite different from those faced by the underdeveloped economies of the Community.

In the face of these facts, there can be no doubt that on formal grounds the whole territory of the former GDR qualifies for Community aid under Objective 1. The need for redevelopment there is focused on the improvement of the infrastructure, industrial development and redevelopment, agricultural modernisation and above all human resource development. It thus fully accords with the objectives of the Structural Funds. If for some reason aid under Objective 1 should be excluded, several regions would qualify for Objectives 2 and 5b and the whole territory for Objectives 3 and 4.[3]

This conclusion brings us to the political issue of including East Germany in the present Structural Funds commitment. This certainly cannot be done without making additional financial resources available. It is hard to imagine the member states which at present benefit most from the Structural Funds - and which have a blocking minority in Council - being prepared to reduce their share in order to transfer some of the money to Eastern Germany. The financial resources for the Structural Funds Programme, moreover, have been committed up to the end of 1993, and German politicians repeatedly stated during the last few months of 1990 that they did not expect any fundamental change in European policies or a large share of EC funds to be given to help the East German economy. The cost of German unification is thus being viewed as a primarily German affair, with the West German economy strong enough to carry the burden.

The situation will be different when the continuation and revision of the Structural Funds Programme is negotiated in the Community in 1992-93. If we assume the same distribution key as for the year 1992 (for 77 million inhabitants in the Objective 1 areas, 8.2 billion Ecu will be available - that is 117 Ecu per inhabitant) then East Germany would be entitled to 1.8 billion Ecu.[4] Clearly this is only a hypothetical figure, but it is worthwhile to estimate the amount of Community resources that could then flow to East Germany. It would be roughly 22% of the total, more than the amount currently received by Greece, Portugal or Ireland.

Two other factors need to be considered. Firstly, the specific problems of redevelopment and change from a socialist system to a market economy faced in East Germany are quite different from those of the EC member states which now receive the largest share of the Funds appropriations and for which the strategies and methods of the existing Programme have been designed. Thus, while the situation in East Germany formally fulfils the requirements of the present Programme, its specific situation and resulting needs require a different approach and different instruments. More will be said about this question in the next section.

Secondly, the "accession" of East Germany is not only a question of economic redistribution. It is also a question of national identity. As noted above, West German politicians view the matter primarily as a German affair. West Germany has the strongest economy in the Community and many Germans consider the East German problem primarily as a question of national responsibility, which Germans have to solve together and to which Community programmes should probably not be applied. At the same time the fact cannot be ignored that East Germany is becoming an integral part of the Community, and the Community must assume the same responsibilities as it bears towards the distant regions of Portugal, Spain or Greece. The redistributive policy functions must be extended equally to all parts of the Community. The full integration of East Germany into the Community - not only into Germany - would definitely be enhanced if there were some Community involvement in its redevelopment efforts.

Taking these considerations into account, it would probably make sense to develop a transitional programme outside the existing framework of the Structural Funds, allowing for tailor-made instruments for regional development, adapted to the specific and unique development needs of East Germany. In the next section we shall discuss the management issue of the Structural Funds which will reinforce this conclusion.

5. Managing the Structural Funds: implementation problems

Designing the application of the structural funds to East Germany is not only a matter of matching objectives with economic reality. The implementation process is critical to an effective use of the resources available.

The management of the Structural Funds prior to their reform was subject to widespread criticism. Among the numerous deficiencies criticised, the lack of co-ordination in the operations of the three different Funds was considered the main cause of low effectiveness. Another frequently-mentioned weakness was the limited involvement of regional and local bodies in the management process, which was viewed as an obstacle to the forceful impact of the measures. Co-operation between national and Community authorities was considered largely insufficient, particularly with respect to monitoring and evaluation mechanisms.

As already mentioned in section 2, the reform of the structural funds was intended to improve the management process. The key concepts of the new operating system are complementarity, partnership and programming. These principles apply to all five objectives and they operate in a three-stage process. First, member states submit multi-annual development plans explaining their priorities and intentions with regard to Community aid. Then the Commission examines the plans and, in consultation with member states, regional and local authorities, responds in the form of a Community Support Framework, setting out the broad principles of the assistance to be provided by the Community. Finally, the assistance itself is managed through operational programmes, involving regional and local actors; other forms of assistance include general grants, part-financing of aid schemes and major projects. The new process is aimed at ensuring a co-ordinated action between the different funds and between Community, national and regional and local authorities, including private or semi-private bodies. In addition, procedures have been simplified and monitoring and evaluation mechanisms reinforced.

The new system for the management of the funds looks ideal on paper. It resembles a carefully-constructed machine for processing Community funds, encompassing all relevant actors and instruments. As in every comprehensive system, however, its Achilles heel lies in the administrative capacity of the authorities responsible for putting it into practice. An effective redistribution system is always management-intensive, requiring the appropriate capacities at both the centre and the periphery. The critical question is whether the Commission and national authorities can satisfy the co-ordination demands of the new process or not. A smooth functioning relies on a good level of understanding between different units of government. Regional and local authorities will have to increase their management capabilities to cope with a new role; paradoxically, such authorities in disadvantaged regions are not ideally-equipped for enlarged responsibilities. In fact, previous attempts to improve the co-ordination and management of the funds through the integration approach (integrated operations, integrated programmes and, finally, the integrated Mediterranean Programme) have not been very successful, precisely because of such problems.

The new system can only work given a high degree of stability on the part of national authorities and a good deal of previous experience in the operation of the Funds. These conditions obviously cannot be met immediately by the newly-created **Länder** in East Germany. The creation and consolidation of the new **Länder** and their local authorities will require time before they can become meaningful partners in the administration of the Funds, particularly as the tasks of restructuring the economy and the business sector have simultaneously to be faced. Recourse to the capacity and experience of the German Federal administration will be of only limited use, as the role of the **Länder** is essential in the German structure of government. In short, it will be extremely difficult to extend the Structural Funds Programme immediately to East Germany and to follow the procedures applied in other member states.

Moreover, the three-stage process established to manage the Funds will create additional problems for Germany. Given the necessary changes in the whole political and economic system and uncertainties about key economic developments, it will be difficult to elaborate multi-annual development plans. They will be outdated before support frameworks, programmes and projects can be approved. Although certain elements of the plans could be developed with a sufficient degree of certainty (infrastructure or environmental protection for instance), productive investment and human-resource development will need permanent and relevant strategic adjustment and revision at least during 1991-2. This is not to say that planning is impossible, but rather to stress the need for a flexible and constantly-updated effort. With existing management procedures, the actual implementation of development plans would be too complex, inflexible and slow.

To summarise, a strict application of the existing management procedures could seriously undermine the effective use of the Funds. It would probably lead to inflexibility and to a low capacity to respond to rapidly-changing conditions. In the previous section, we argued that the special nature of the circumstances in East Germany demands a transitional commitment outside the current framework. The management dimension of the Funds reinforces this argument. It has also been suggested that the Community has a definite interest in participating in the reconstruction of East Germany and not leaving it to the Germans alone. For this reason a flexible interim programme, outside the Funds and tailor-made to the needs of East Germany - possibly along the lines of the PEDIP programme for Portugal - could be initiated by the Community. This could include long-range contributions to infrastructure development and environmental protection, while support for productive investment and human-resource development would have to be short-range and flexible.[5]

Once the economy of the new **Länder** has gained sufficient stability, once new governmental institutions and procedures have become firmly established and a proper diagnosis of the economy has been made, the new **Länder** could confidently be included in the general revision and expansion of the Structural Funds due to be negotiated in 1992/93.

References

1. For the sake of simplicity we use the term "East Germany" to refer to the territory of the former German Democratic Republic (GDR), which now constitutes the five new **Länder** of the Federal Republic of Germany.

2. Despite the lack of reliable information on East Germany, the following recent publications have been consulted which give a general view:

Die Auswirkungen der Vereinigung Deutschlands auf die Europäische Gemeinschaft, European Parliament, June 1990.

Quantitative Aspekte einer Reform von Wirstchaft und Finanzen in der DDR, Deutsches Institut für Wirtschaftsforchung, April 1990.

DDR-Wirtschaft im Umbruch - Bestandsaufnahme und Reformansätze, SIW, January 1990.

The Global Economic Implications of German Unification, Board of Governors of the Federal Reserve System, Washington, D.C., April 1990.

DDR-1990, Zahlen und Fakten, Statistisches Bundesamt, April 1990.

DDR Perspektiven, Informationsdienst der Frankfurter Algemeinen Zeitung, May 1990.

DDR-Wirtschaft: Lage-Wandel-Zukunft, Deutsche Bank AG, January 1990.

Entwicklung in Deutschland - Manuskripte zur Umgestaltung der DDR, Jakob-Kaiser-Stiftung, January 1990.

3. The Commission is currently (October 1990) working on the hypothesis that 15% of the available resources will be allocated to Objective 1, 70% to Objective 2 and 15% to Objective 5b (compare G. Stahl in this volume). It is questionable whether this hypothesis can be realised and whether it is the proper response to the existing problems (see also note 5 below).

4. Europäisches Parlament, **Die Auswirkungen der Vereinigung Deutschlands auf die Europäische Gemeinschaft** (100355DE13/25-6-90), p. 140. Meanwhile, the Commission has proposed to allocate 1 billion Ecu per year from 1991-1993. No justification or explanation of why the amount was set at this level has been given (Com(90)400 endg-Syn 300, p.169 ff). Stahl has presented interesting calculations which suggest that rather different figures would be appropriate (see his essay in this volume).

5. Since the initial writing of this paper the Commission has chosen a different approach. The basic procedures of the new approach will be followed. Germany will have to submit integrated development plans for the five new **Länder** by 31 January 1991. Three months later Community Support Frameworks will have to be elaborated (see Com(90)II-400 endg-Syn300). The Commission recognised, however, that the procedures could not be rigidly applied.

German unification and the EC's budget and budgetary policy

Gerhard Stahl

1. The framework of budgetary policy

The budgetary policy of the European Community is clearly distinguished from that of the member states. This is true both of the goals of European budgetary policy and of the decision-making processes leading up to the annual budget proposals. Therefore, to assess the effects of German unification on the EC budget we must first look at particular aspects of European budgetary policy.

The Community budget, which in 1990 amounted to 46.7bn Ecu,[1] is the outcome of a - provisional - political compromise between the EC member states in the Council and the European Parliament. This compromise is aimed at striking a balance between various demands on the expenditure side, such as the funding of the Common Agricultural Policy, structural policy, common research and development policy and support for developing countries, and the constraints on the revenue side.

In the early 1980's, conflicts over the budget between the two arms of the EC's budgetary authority and between the member states were a routine feature of European politics. These disputes, characterised by rejection of the draft budget by the European Parliament, national demands for compensation - especially by the United Kingdom - and the inadequate financial resources of the Community, were provisionally terminated by the resolution on new "own resources" for the Community, agreements on budgetary discipline and the conclusion of an inter-institutional agreement involving the establishment of a binding five-year finance plan.[2]

The inter-institutional agreement

The inter-institutional agreement of June 1988 between the European Parliament, the Council and the Commission included a financial perspective for the years 1988-1992. At the same time agreement was reached on procedural rules for the adjustment and revision of this financial planning.[3] This financial perspective translated into budget estimates extending to 1992 the essential policy resolutions, such as those on doubling the Structural Funds, limiting agricultural expenditure and developing research policy, adopted by the Council in Brussels in February 1988 and approved by the European Parliament the following month. The figures contained in the financial perspective represent upper limits for the annual budget resolutions and are used by the Commission in formulating the preliminary draft of the annual budget.

The inter-institutional agreement has brought about a substantial change in EC budget procedure. Important decisions on budgetary policy, such as those concerning the financial consequences of German unification, first demand a revision of the financial perspective before decisions of detail can be taken within the framework of the budget procedure. Such a revision calls for a joint decision by both arms of the budgetary authority acting on a proposal by the Commission. It should remain within a margin of 0.03% of the Community's GDP and can be accepted by Council and Parliament with a qualified majority.[4] Any revision exceeding this figure requires an amendment of the inter-institutional agreement, for which unanimity is prescribed by the Council.

In accordance with the resolutions on the Community's own resources for 1992, Table 1 shows a top limit on own resources for the EC budget equal to a maximum of 1.2% of GNP. The expected budget trend based on the present financial perspective will not quite reach this top revenue limit. The ratio of budget size to GNP provides a pointer to the very limited significance of the Community budget compared with national budgets, which usually account for 25-50%+ of gross national product.[5]

Table 1 **Financial perspectives**
(m ECU)

	1988 (1)	1989 (1)	1990 (1)	1991 (1)	1992 (2)
1. Expenditure Resources for commitments					
European Agricultural Guidance and Guarantee Fund, Guarantee Section	27 500	28 613	30 700	33 000	33 750
Structural policy measures (eg Regional Fund, Social Fund, EAGGF Guidance Section)	790	9 522	11 555	14 054	15 598
Policy areas with appropriation of resources for several years (eg integrated Mediterranean programmes, research and technology)	1 210	1 708	2 071	2 516	2 820
Other policy areas including: non-compulsory expenditure (eg fisheries, education, energy, food aid, co-operation with Eastern Europe, the Mediterranean and developing countries)	2 103	2 468	3 229	4 255	4 823
	1 646	1 864	2 523	3 355	3 876
Repayments and administration including : stock disposal	5 741	5 153	4 930	4 559	3 936
	1 240	1 449	1 523	1 598	1 148
Currency reserve	1 000	1 000	1 000	1 000	1 000
Total	45 344	48 464	53 485	59 384	61 926
Means of payment Total	43 820	46 885	51 291	56 950	59271
2. Revenue Own resources required as % of GNP					
Proposal by Parliament and Commission	1.118%	1.099%	1.117%	1.157%	1.166%
Proposal by Council	1.118%	1.099%	1.106%	1.133%	1.138%
Upper limit of own resources as percentage of GNP	1.150%	1.170%	1.180%	1.190%	1.200%

Source: Preliminary draft of overall budget, Com (90) 121.
(1) At current prices
(2) At 1991 prices

2. The budgetary consequences of integrating the GDR into the European Community

2.1 The phases and time-frame of German unification

As the prospect of German unification became increasingly clear at the beginning of 1990, Community institutions began to examine its implications for European policy. As early as February the European Parliament set up a special German Unification Committee, and on the basis of the Committee's preliminary work stated its fundamental attitude to German unification in a resolution passed on 4 April 1990. This called upon the Commission and the Council to draw up an immediate programme for the GDR[6] enabling financial aid to be granted from the EC's 1990 budget prior to the GDR's unification with the Federal Republic of Germany and its concomitant membership of the European Community. At the special summit on German unification held in Dublin on 4-5 June 1990, however, the heads of government of the EC member states did not take up this proposal. It was merely agreed that the GDR was eligible for loans from the programmes of the European Investment Bank, the European Coal and Steel Community and the European Atomic Energy Community.[7] The Commission, for its part, in its preliminary draft for budget year 1991, submitted on 29 June 1990, earmarked no special budgetary resources for the GDR.[8]

In its second resolution on German unification (the Donnelly Report) of 12 July, the European Parliament regretted the reservations implicit in the Council's and Commission's positions and called upon the Commission to make a statement on the budgetary consequences of the integration of the GDR and submit a proposal for the amendment of the financial perspective. On 17 July Commissioner Bangemann complied with these requests before the Special Committee of the European Parliament. He explained that the Commission also assumed that German unification would take place before the end of 1990. By 12 September the Commission would therefore be submitting a package comprising both the legal adjustments regarded as necessary for the integration of the GDR and an estimate of the financial consequences together with a proposal for the amendment of the financial perspective.

2.2 Estimates of the financial effects on the EC budget of integrating the former GDR

Estimates of the financial effects of the integration of the GDR are at present attended by great uncertainties. Firstly, there are no reliable or comparable statistics.[9] Secondly, it is difficult at the moment to assess the economic consequences of economic and monetary union. This means that a great deal of uncertainty also surrounds estimates of the Community's own resources to be generated on the former GDR's territory (share of VAT income, duties and agricultural levies, etc.). Thirdly, it is likewise difficult to estimate the amounts payable under the Community's agricultural policy, given the likely structural changes in East German farming, in consumer prices and consumption habits and the associated uncertainties in assessing the production and consumption of farm products. Fourthly, there will probably be some EC budget appropriations which are decided not according to economic and social criteria but by way of political compromises.

Despite these uncertainties, some estimates have to be made of the budgetary effects of the decisions on the 1991 budget. We should also remind ourselves that following the occasion of earlier accessions to the EC, the statistics of the newcomers proved to be unsatisfactory.

Revenue
The figures given correspond roughly to the internal estimates of the Commission and the Federal German Ministry of Finance. In a statement to the special German Unification Committee of the European Parliament (EP 141 041/Part C), the Parliament's Budget Committee indicated a revenue increase of 1.4bn Ecu.

Table 2: **Budgetary effects of GDR integration - 1991 budget**
(mEcu)

1	Revenue [1]		500	
1.1	Duties, agricultural levies, etc		1 000	
1.2	Value-added tax			

1.3	Total		1 500	

2	Expenditure			
2.1	EAGGF guarantee payments [2]		800 -	1 100
2.2	Structural policy expenditure [3]		1 000 -	2850
	including ;			
	Objective 1 "Underdeveloped regions"		150 -	2 000
	Objective 2 "Regions with declining industrial			
	development"		700 -	700
	Objective 5b "Promotion of rural areas"		150 -	150
2.3	Other expenditure, esp. research [4]		100 -	200

2.4	Total		1 900 -	4 150
	"Net beneficiary status of GDR territory"[5]		- 400 -	-2 650

	For comparison		6 500	
	"Net performance of FRG" 1989[5]			

Source : European Parliament ; European Commission; Federal German Ministry of Finance; author's calculations.

Table 2 requires some detailed explanation.

These estimates do not include the possible increases in Community revenue due to greater economic growth. The statement by the EP Budget Committee assumes an increase of 0.5% in the average economic growth of the Community over the next few years due to GDR integration and the opening of Eastern European markets and, to repeat, derives from this a possible annual increment of 1.4bn Ecu in the revenue available for financing the EC budget. Even if the assumed impact on the growth of the Community is seen as very high,[10] calculations of this kind nonetheless point to the positive secondary effects of GDR integration on the financing of the EC's budget. It is also true, however, that this kind of increase in the Community's own potential resources does not automatically accrue to the EC budget, as these resources are used only to the extent necessary to finance the budget as it stands. Regardless of the extent of the Community's own available resources, the scale of the EC budget is restricted by the relevant budget strategy and, until 1992, by the financial perspective.

EAGGF guarantee expenditure
The present estimates of market-regulatory expenditure for the former GDR territory exhibit substantial disparities. 800m Ecu is the lowest figure according to an internal estimate by the Commission. In formulating the GDR budget for 1991, the FRG and (late) GDR governments earmarked a sum of DM 2.2 bn (about 1.1bn Ecu) for market-regulatory expenditure for the GDR. However, this estimate already allowed for set-asides in the GDR.[11] Original estimates made by the Federal German Ministry of Agriculture were higher. My own "status quo" estimate for the five most important market-regulatory measures suggests expenditure of 1.5bn Ecu for the former GDR territory.[12] The statement by the EP Budget Committee, referring to experts from the European Court of Auditors, even mentions a sum of 2bn Ecu.

Structural policy expenditure
On 17 July Commissioner Bangemann indicated to the EP special committee the Commission's target structural policy expenditure for the former GDR territory. The Commission does not intend the rules for the Structural Funds to be directly applied to the former GDR. In view of statistical difficulties which make it impossible to single out measures corresponding to the objectives of the structural-fund rules,[13] the structural-policy allocations until 1993 are globalised at 3bn Ecu. This amounts to 1bn Ecu a year. Commissioner Bangemann explained that the sum of 3bn Ecu for the Structural Funds was based on the working hypothesis that

15% would be used for objective 1, 70% for objective 2 and 15% for objective 5b.

To gauge whether this amount is appropriate for the former GDR, a more detailed calculation for objective 1 was performed, the result of which is shown in Table 2 (the Commission's figures were used for objectives 2 and 5b). Per capita GNP in the former GDR is 75% below the average for the Community.[14] As wages and prices in the GDR were controlled by the state until a short time ago, regional differences in income are virtually non-existent. It can therefore be assumed that for the time being the whole GDR region could be categorised as a development area for the purposes of objective 1, i.e., an underdeveloped region. However, in its provisional calculations the Commission seems to regard the region covered by objective 1 as being confined to the north of the GDR's territory. The draft budget for 1991 allocates a sum of 8,537m Ecu to objective 1. The geographical distribution of these resources has already been decided. The selected development areas have some 70 million inhabitants.

Per capita support in the GDR region corresponding to the Community average for developing regions would produce a theoretical claim for about 2,000m Ecu in 1991. The satisfaction of this claim is conditional on a corresponding increase in the financial perspective and in the 1991 budget appropriations in the forthcoming budgetary procedure and on the classing of the territory of the former GDR as a developing region under the rules of the Structural Funds. It would then be necessary to propose suitable co-funded projects for the territory.

Other expenditure

Following its unification with the FRG, the territory of the former GDR, like other Community regions, is eligible to participate in a large number of Community programmes.[15] Research-policy expenditure is likely to be of greater consequence here in terms of figures, but thoughts could also turn to EC co-funding when it comes to the restructuring of the fishing fleet or to the financial support required for maintaining trade relations with the Soviet

Union. The possible repercussions on the 1991 budget are estimated at between 100 and 200m Ecu.

Support by the ECSC

In addition to financial resources from the Community budget, the former GDR can call upon European funds which do not fall within the Community budget and are therefore not included in Table 2. Mention has already been made of loan facilities from the EIB, Euratom and ECSC, which are already available to the GDR. Following unification, the GDR territory belongs to the ECSC. This opens the way not only to ECSC loan facilities but also to economic re-adaptation aid. Under Article 56 para 2 b) of the ECSC Treaty, non-repayable grants may be made to help in the restructuring of coal and steel industries. These grants may be used both to finance compensation for workers affected by restructuring and for allowances to firms.

The former GDR has been an important steel producer, with an annual output of around 8 million tonnes of crude steel (compared with Belgium, 9 million tonnes, and the Netherlands, with 5 million tonnes). However, labour productivity is only 45% of that in the West German steel industry.[16] The need for restructu ing and a cut-back in manpower is plain. The ECSC re-adaptation aids for the steel sector are therefore specially important. The following calculation indicates the order of magnitude of the funding which may be involved in such measures:

If it is assumed that 40,000 employees in the former GDR's steel industry will be affected by restructuring measures, a sum of 3,000 Ecu per head produces an aid package of 120m Ecu. (For the purposes of comparison, the ECSC contributed a total of 85m Ecu between 1981 and 1987 for the restructuring of the Italian steel industry affecting some 26,000 beneficiaries [3,283 Ecu per head]).[17] If these measures are spread over, say, six years, annual payments of 20m Ecu will have to be made from the ECSC budget.[18]

The question admittedly has to be asked whether such a long period can be justified in the light of the massive structural changes which the GDR economy is already experiencing. If the programme is spread over the next two years in response to the urgent needs of the area, the annual outlays work out at 60m Ecu. Without extra funding, however, the ECSC will be unable to provide such large sums, even if unification results in the former GDR's coal, iron and steel industries participating in the funding of the ECSC via the output levy. It therefore has to be considered whether allocations to the ECSC from the EC budget can provide the financial means for comprehensive support of the former GDR's steel industry.

Net contributors and net beneficiaries

Net contributors and net beneficiaries constitute categories which provide only limited information. At the national level, the attribution of both the revenue and the appropriations of the EC budget are inadequate.[19] All the same, the net positions do give an indication of the inter-regional spread of the Community budget and therefore continue to play a significant role in the political debate.[20]

The preliminary work carried out by the Commission on the consequences for the EC budget of German unification also creates the strong impression that a decision was first taken, as a purely political calculation, to classify the GDR area as a net beneficiary to the tune of about 500m Ecu; only afterwards were decisions made regarding the orders of magnitude of the expenditure from the EC budget with due allowance for the estimated revenue from the GDR. Table 2 therefore shows the GDR region as having the status of a "net beneficiary", while the status of the FRG as a "net contributor" is also noted.

2.3 Is it possible, by analysing the net status and economic capacity of the EC member states, to derive criteria for the appropriate extent of EC support for the former GDR area?

The comparison of economic capacity and net status shows that the EC budget has a certain redistributive effect between economically strong and weak countries inasmuch as all countries whose per capita GDP is well below the Community average are net beneficiaries. The amounts paid out under the Common Agricultural Policy, which greatly favour "northern" farming structures, do, however, lead to distortions of distribution policy. This is why the Netherlands and Denmark are net beneficiaries in spite of their above-average economic performance and Ireland, as

Table 3 **Economic capacity and net status of EC member states**

Country	per capita GDP 1988 EC 12 = 100 in purchasing power parities 1)	per capita GDP 1988 EC 12 = 100 in Ecu 1)	net status 1988 in million Ecu + net payment - net receipt	net status 1988 + net payment - net receipt 2)
Luxembourg	127.4	121.4	+ 62	+ 169.3
FRG	113.2	133.5	+ 5 181	+ 84.8
Denmark	109.5	143.2	- 408	- 79.6
France	108.7	115.9	+ 937	+ 16.8
United Kingdom	105.7	96.5	+ 1 206	+ 21.2
Italy	104.8	99	- 994	- 17.3
Netherlands	103.2	105.7	- 1 373	- 93.6
Belgium	101.2	102.8	+ 844	+ 84.5
Spain	74.8	59.6	- 1 923	- 49.5
Ireland	64.6	62.1	- 1 213	- 342.36
Greece	54.4	36.7	- 1 643	- 164.5
Portugal	53.8	29.2	- 672	- 64.9
EC	100	100		
GDR 3)		56		

1) Figures from Commission's Annual Economic Report 89-90, in **European Economy** No. 42, November 1989.
2) Author's calculations based on figures given in the 1988 Annual Report of European Court of Auditors, OJ C 312, 31 Dec 1989.
3) Author's calculations using the estimate of DM 270 billion for GDR's 1990 GNP produced by the German Institute for Economic Research.

Table 4 **Model calculations for "appropriate" net status of the GDR area**

	Net beneficiary status of the GDR in m Ecu
With net per capita status of :	
Spain	834
Ireland	5 696
Greece	2 737
Portugal	1 080

an economically weak country, receives especially large payments out of the EC budget.

Although Table 3 does not provide the means for setting clear distribution-policy criteria for the management of the EC budget, it is nonetheless possible to draw a number of conclusions conducive to the plausible participation of the GDR area in the Community budget. Firstly, the former GDR area is an economically weak region and should therefore assume the status of a net beneficiary. Secondly, the lower limit for net receipts, based on the EC budget structure which has existed hitherto, is around 800m Ecu (by the yardstick of Spanish net receipts), while the upper limit is around 5bn Ecu (by the yardstick of Irish net receipts). If the matter is considered realistically, however, Ireland is eliminated as a reference value, as Greece and Portugal cannot be expected to put up with a situation in which, besides Ireland, another region of the EC with a higher per capita economic performance than these two countries fares relatively better. The fact that the former GDR area has a lower per capita GNP, which is likely to sink even further as a result of the drastic economic upheavals of 1990 and 1991, argues against equality of treatment with Spain.[21]

3. Difficulties in budget debates on integrating the former GDR

Even in the run-up to the debates on the 1991 budget it is clear that institutional difficulties and procedural problems impede a proper decision on the budgetary integration of the GDR area. Firstly, the increase in the 1991 budget to allow for the integration will necessitate an amendment of the financial perspective. This "GDR increment" will exceed the margin of 0.03% of GNP (around 150m Ecu) provided for unforeseen expenditure. This means that an appropriate amendment of the financial perspective demands a unanimous resolution by the Council. Secondly, the integration of the former GDR will also give rise to renewed discussion on the calculation of the agricultural guidelines. Those for limiting the outgoings on agriculture were laid down in the Council's resolution of 24 June 1988 on budget discipline and should ensure that agricultural guarantee expenditure grows less rapidly than the Community's GNP.

In view of the conflicting interests between Council members as to where the emphasis in expenditure should lie and because of the unanimity requirement, it is to be feared that the only 1991 draft budget to which the Council will agree will represent the lowest common denominator and be inadequate for the GDR area. This fear is reinforced by the political line so far taken by the Federal German government, which has consciously refrained from calling upon the Community to assume an appropriate share of financial involvement. Chancellor Kohl went so far as to write to Mr Delors, President of the European Commission, warning against higher expenditure for the GDR's integration.[22] It remains to be seen whether the European Parliament will be able in the budget debates to ensure that greater attention is paid to the interests of those living in what was the GDR.

4. Inferences for the future development of EC budget policy

The debates conducted to date have shown that the former GDR area will be excluded from full use of the Structural Funds in the next few years. The projected upper limits on the EC funding of measures for the area, and the Commission's tacit political decision in favour of a net negative balance of around 500m Ecu for the coming years, may lead to below-average contributions to the area from the non-agricultural outlays of the EC budget. As far as agricultural expenditure is concerned, the integration of the GDR will once again turn the budgetary burden of farming into a disputed issue. The former GDR area has "northern" agricultural structures and can therefore look forward to considerable inputs from the Community. It remains to be seen whether the available instruments of budget discipline (agricultural guidelines, quotas and stabilisers) will be sufficient to restrict the Community's farming outlays in such a way as to achieve the desired continued shrinkage of agriculture as an element of the EC budget.[23]

The ground rules of EC budget policy dictate that any increment in the Community's own-resource income due to a higher economic growth rate which the member states might enjoy as a result of GDR integration does not automatically accrue to the EC budget. This creates the danger that EC budgetary policy, despite any financial room for manoeuvre which may exist in theory, is placed in a position where it is unable to provide adequate funding for new functions like the integration of the GDR. This danger is aggravated by the clumsiness of the budget procedure and, in particular, by the Council's voting rules, which prescribe unanimity in the event of the financial perspective being exceeded.

These restrictions on EC budget policy may foster the resurgence of a nationalist approach to Community policy. If member states cannot count on a minimum amount of financial solidarity from the Community, they will be forced into the further development of national measures aimed at ironing out regional differences. However, a trend of this kind may conflict with the goal of reducing national subsidies, where these impair competition, in order to improve the conditions leading to a uniform European internal market.

The budgetary difficulties arising from the integration of the GDR are therefore one more reason for considering a reform of EC budget policy and for moving forward from the 1988 budget compromise. The Commission should include proposals for budget reform in the report on the implementation of the inter-institutional agreement and the future development of the financial perspective, which is due to be submitted by the end of 1991.

References

1. The EC's overall budget for 1990 authorises payments amounting to 46.7 bn Ecu and commitments amounting to 49 bn Ecu (cf Overall EC budget, OJ L 24 of 29 January 1990).

2. For demands for budgetary reform and budget conflicts see inter alia Gerhard Stahl, "Die Lösung läßt noch auf sich warten", in **Wirtschaftsdienst,** HWWA-Institut, Hamburg, vol 61, No 7, p.326 ff. For the financial resolutions of the Brussels summit of February 1988, see Dieter Biehl, "Ein substantielles, aber begrenztes Reformpaket", in **Integration,** Bonn, vol 11, 2/88, p. 164 ff., and Michael Shackleton, **Financing the European Community** (London: Royal Institute for International Affairs, 1990). For the Inter- Institutional Agreement see Gerhard Stahl, "Medium-term financial planning: an answer to the Community budget crisis?", in **Intereconomics,** Hamburg, January 1989, p. 36 ff.

3. For the text of the inter-institutional agreement on budget discipline and the improvement of the budgetary procedure see **Official Journal** 1988, L 185, of 15 July 1988, p. 33 ff. Para 3 of the Agreement makes it clear that there is no change in the budgetary responsibilities of the institutions as set out in the Treaty. However, under the inter-institutional agreement the Parliament, Council and Commission undertake to adhere to certain procedures when fulfilling their responsibilities. For the consequences of budget discipline in relation to the budgetary procedure and the classification of functions compare the report by the chairman of the EP Budget Committee, Thomas von der Vring, on the classification of functions, **EP** 139 310 (final), 1 June 1990.

4. There is admittedly a difference between Parliament, Commission and Council regarding the interpretation of the 0.03% limit. Whereas Parliament and Commission take the view that the 0.03% limit is available for each year, the Council argues that it applies to the entire duration of the Agreement. This

means, according to the Council's interpretation, that in 1990 the remaining latitude for unforeseen expenditure was a mere 0.006% of GNP.

5. For the tasks of EC budget policy and evaluative criteria see especially the report by the group of experts which examined the role of public finance in European integration (MacDougall Report), vols I and II, Brussels, 1977. A more up-to-date but less detailed discussion is to be found in L. Spaventa, G. Koopmann et al., **The future of Community finance**, CEPS Paper No. 30 (Brussels, 1986). Reflections on a federalistic reference system for assessing the EC financial system are contained in Dieter Biehl, "Outlines of an EC financial system along federalistic lines", in Ernst-Joachim Mestmäcker ed., **Eine Ordnungspolitik für Europa** (Baden-Baden: Nomos, 1987).

6. Paras E1 and E2 of the text of the resolution passed by the European Parliament on 4 April 1990 read as follows:
"1. considers that the Community must contribute to the costs of the restructuring of the GDR's economy, and that such a contribution is necessary in order to show solidarity with the population of the GDR;
2. calls for the rapid preparation of a special Community aid programme for the GDR during the interim period before unification is completed, and for this to be presented in time for the forthcoming Dublin European Council."

7. The European Council resolved in Dublin: "During this time (prior to unification) the German Democratic Republic is granted unrestricted access to EIB, EURATOM and ECSC credit facilities in addition to the support given by the Community in the framework of the co-ordinated action by the Group of 24 and together with participation in the EUREKA project."

8. Although the GDR would in theory qualify for assistance under the PHARE programme, which is especially aimed at Central and Eastern Europe, the Commission confirmed in para 5 of its communication Com (90) 257 final of 19 June 1990 that this was not contemplated in practice: "Actions on its [the GDR's] behalf will therefore mainly be undertaken within the framework of European Community internal procedures or by ad hoc measures."

9. Only recently did the German Institute for Economic Research succeed in converting the GDR's GNP, which is based on the Eastern-bloc concept of material production, to the National Economic Accounting System (cf **DIW-Wochenbericht**, No 26/90 of 28 June 1990).

10. For an estimate of the growth effects on the FRG and the EC, compare Broclawski and Kenigswald, "Allemagne, année zéro", in **Economie et Statistique**, No 232, May 1990; Olivier Passet, Murielle Fiole et al., "Evolution à l'Est: quel impact sur la croissance économique de l'Europe de l'Ouest?", in **Problèmes Economiques** No 2.165, 7 March 1990, p. 2 ff; and Klaus-Werner Schatz, "A single German market as economic growth factor for Germany and the EC", paper contributed to the CEPS seminar "The single German market", Brussels, 19 June 1990.

11. This estimate assumes, for instance, that a decline of about 20% takes place in milk and pig-meat production, that an area of 250,000 hectares is taken out of production and that the cereals output of around 12 million tonnes is consumed at home (close on 10 million tonnes for animal feed and 2-3 million tonnes for human consumption).

12. Status quo estimate of agricultural guarantee expenditure:

	Cereals	Meat, poultry 1)	Milk	Sugar	Protein, vegetable fat	Total agricultural market-regulatory expenditure
FRG in mEcu	983.9	662	1295	385.5	841	4167
GDR production as % of FRG production (1985/88 average)	43%	35%[2]	32%	35%	38%	
GDR in mECU	423	232	414	135	319	1946

1) Larger proportion of pigs in the GDR than in the FRG
2) 1981/85 Average

Source: Figures taken from the 1988 Annual Report of European Court of Auditors and **Landwirtschaft der DDR** by the German Institute for Economic Research, Study for the European Parliament, April 1990.

As the market-regulatory expenditure is to be paid out by the EC with a delay of 2 1/2 months, the 1991 budget year is affected by expenditure for only 9 1/2 months, ie about 1 500 m Ecu. Influencing factors which are not taken into account in a status quo prognosis are: changed selling-price structure due to reduction of subsidies; changed production-cost structure; rationalisation and increased productivity; arable set-aside and abandonment of autarky policy; changes in consumer habits; and intervention in 1991 of surplus agricultural products from 1990. If it is assumed that productivity increases take place with the result that the present disparity between the GDR and the FRG in yields per hectare and animal products is halved, then, other things being equal, a production increase of 1 million tonnes of cereals and 1 million tonnes of milk is, for example, likely with a consequent marked rise in market-regulatory expenditure. Compare "The consequences of German unification for the agriculture and fisheries policy of the EC" in **The consequences of German unification for the European Community,** European Parliament, Directorate-General for Science, working document No 1, 6-1990.

13. For the purposes of the Structural Funds cf Regulation 2052/88 in **Official Journal** L 185 of 15 July 1988, p. 9 ff.

14. Cf calculation for the GDR in Table 3.

15. For instance, see Gerhard and Maria Sabatil, **Förder programme der EG 1988** (Bonn: Economica, 1988).

16. Cf a brief appraisal by the German Institute for Economic Research in **The Consequences of German Unification for the European Community**, p.59.

17. For details of EC re-adaptation aid for the coal and steel industries, compare William Rees and R.Barry Thomas, **Study of the European Communities' Re-adaptation Aid in the Coal and Steel Industries** (Brussels: Commission of the EC, 1988).

18. The figures indicated coincide with the internal views of the Commission regarding the theoretical support requirement of the GDR area over the next few years.

19. In the case of customs revenue, for instance, the "Rotterdam effect" occurs, i.e., duties on imports into member state A arise in member state B, since that is where the goods are landed. Expenditure includes cross-border programmes, in which persons from a number of member states are involved or agricultural products from country A are dealt with under intervention arrangements in country B.

20. However, net status is not a suitable criterion for gauging the economic benefit which a country derives from EC membership. The redistributive effects of the EC budget can only be one element in an economic cost-benefit analysis of EC membership. Much more important are the effects of the allocation policy of the EC budget, the EC's legislative role and the "internal-market dynamic" conducive to higher economic growth.

21. The German Institute for Economic Research estimates that the GNP of the GDR area will shrink by 6.5% in 1990 and a further 2.5% in 1991. Cf **DIW-Wochenbericht**, No 26/90 of 28 June.

22. Cf **Financial Times** of 31 July 1990, page 2 of which contains a reference to this letter.

23. EC agricultural policy is in need of reform irrespective of the immediate budgetary implications. See, for example, D. Biehl, G. P. Cesaretti et al., **The Common Agricultural Policy, European Integration and the International Division of Labour** (Bonn: Europa Union, 1987).

The free movement of persons

Lammy Betten

1. Introduction

One of the questions raised by German unification that concerns all EC member states is the possible effect on the Community labour market, in particular in view of the right to free movement of workers of all the member states.[1] In addition, the labour market of the new German **Länder** will be particularly affected by EC law on the free movement of persons.

The question has legal as well as political aspects. Even though the legal problems are quite fascinating, their solutions are - as so often is the case - far more a matter of political will than of legal argument. Legal obstacles can either be used to conceal political reluctance or swept aside by political energies. Indeed in the matter of German unification, there has at times been a dazzling disregard for legal aspects.

One of the crucial questions with regard to the free movement of persons is, obviously, whether governments in member states will seek (and be able) to protect their own labour markets against the influx of a large number of former East Germans. In view of the high numbers of unemployed in most member states as well as the alarming increase in the numbers of their underprivileged citizens, that worry is well-founded.

How far German unification will actually lead to increased cross-frontier migration, however, remains to be seen. For most of those workers there will be hardly any settled jobs available in other member states. In view of the existing rules of the free movement of workers (as will be explained below), this means that the East German job-seekers will not obtain the right to stay in other member states. But that would put the entire burden of coping with these extra millions of job-seekers on the government in Bonn. In fact, German constitutional law has never drawn a clear legal distinction between Germans residing in the Federal or in the Democratic Republic. Intra-German problems will not, however, be discussed here, apart from those which touch upon EC provisions with regard to the accession of the new workforce to the Community labour market.

A second problem is the question of protection of the East German labour market against an influx of employees from other EC member states. The latter, indeed, might in time take over key positions in industry in the former GDR as it is regenerated and integrated into the Community.

Thirdly, the full implementation of Community law on the free movement of persons poses some problems for the protection of migrant workers to and from the former GDR, with regard to their social security rights.

In this contribution, some aspects of these problems will be analysed. I will start with explaining the rules of the free movement of workers; in this regard I will concentrate on the law of the European Community. I will then discuss the consequences of a united Germany in view of the free movement of persons. The latter includes an analysis of the way in which a united Germany is "received" in the European Communities, as this might determine to some extent the possibility of transitional measures. The analysis is not an economic one and focuses on the legal problems, although it should again be stressed that the solutions to the problems will be mainly political.

2. The principle of the free movement of persons in the European Community

The free movement of workers is one of the "four freedoms" of movement, which, together with common agricultural, fisheries and transport policies, are the major instruments for realising the Community's goals. (The other three freedoms are the free movement of goods, capital and services). The free movement of persons is divided into the free movement of workers and the freedom to exercise a trade or profession. The means to which these instruments belong is the establishment and functioning of a common market.

2.1 Basic legal provisions

The basis for the free movement of workers is to be found in Articles 48 to 51 of the EC Treaty; the right to establishment (in order to exercise a trade or profession) is laid down in Articles 52 to 58.

The basic principle of the free movement of persons is that they must be treated equal to nationals, not only as regards their labour rights, but also as regards their rights to social security and assistance, taxation, housing, etc.

The principle of the free movement of workers is given practical scope by - amongst others - Regulation 1612/68 and Directives 64/221, and 68/370. It contains the right a) to enter another member state in order to take up employment; b) to stay or to move freely in a member state in order to carry out the accepted employment, and to remain in the territory of a member state after having been employed there.

Apart from these provisions, an important aspect of the free movement of workers is obviously the safeguarding of the right to social security. If migration within the Community were to lead to a loss of acquired rights or benefits, that would be a major obstacle to any migration at all. The basic provisions on social security of migrant workers will be discussed briefly in paragaph 2.4 below.

The right to enter. Before an EC member state national can enter another member state, he or she must have the right to leave his or her own country. Directive 68/360 establishes, therefore, that a person seeking employment in another member state must be admitted on the basis of a passport or equivalent travel document.[2] The residence permit which must be given to that worker for a period of five years does not, however, constitute the right to stay, which is ultimately governed by national law. The worker's rights extend to certain members of his or her immediate family, irrespective of their nationality.[3] The only condition for the admission of the family members is that the worker must have the disposal of a home for the family in the state where he or she is going to work.[4] These rights are given only to workers who already have accepted a job in another member state. Members of the family have full rights to seek and accept jobs in the territory of this member state.[5]

The right to reside. The right to reside also applies to a situation in which, having worked in a member state, a worker is no longer employed there. Indeed, if the worker becomes unemployed, he or she enjoys exactly the same social security rights as national workers, which include unemployment benefit, social assistance and assistance in finding new employment. The residence permit cannot be withdrawn for reasons of unemployment. The situation is different when the permit has to be extended after five years. If a worker has been unemployed for a period of longer than twelve months, a new permit can be given for a period of only one year.[6] Directive 68/360 does not provide what happens after that year. It seems to be reasonable to suggest that, if the worker has found employment during that period, he or she will be given a new residence permit for five years, and if not, no new permit will be given. If the worker dies, the members of the family maintain the right to stay in the member state.

It should be borne in mind that these rights apply only to workers with an employment contract for an indefinite period. Workers with contracts for a definite period receive a residence permit for that period only, while job-seekers receive a residence permit for a period of three months. If they have not then succeeded in finding a job (for which they are entitled to the same assistance from Labour Offices as national job-seekers), they must leave the member state.

The rules of the free movement of workers apply in principle only to the private sector, but a foreign worker who is or has been employed in the public sector comes under private-sector rules.

2.2 Legal restrictions on the freedom of movement

The most important legal restriction on the free movement of workers is that allowing a residence permit to be refused or withdrawn for reasons of public policy, security or health. Such an action must be based, however, on the personal conduct of the migrant worker. The fact that he or she has previously committed criminal acts cannot be a motive for refusing a permit or for expulsion.[7]

The European Court of Justice has been called upon several times to interpret provisions relating to such restrictions. One of the first problems to be solved was the question of whether the term "public policy" should be interpreted according to national or Community law. As the latter does not explicitly provide for an interpretation of this term, the Court has decided that it has to be defined primarily by national law, but that the limitations on the provisions with regard to the free movement of persons must be strict and in accordance with Community law.[8]

In other words, Community law limits the freedom of national authorities to interpret the grounds for expulsion; the latter must be within the limits laid down in Directive 64/221. In the first place the limitations may not have a discriminatory effect. This became most clear in the case of two French women working as prostitutes in the city of Liège in Belgium, who were expelled on the grounds that they attracted criminal elements, and thus formed a serious threat to public policy. As the Belgian authorities did not prohibit Belgian prostitutes from carrying out their work (with, presumably, the same social consequences in the eyes of the authorities), the expulsion of the two French women was found by the Court to be a violation of Community rules with regard to the free movement of persons.[9] The Court has elsewhere made clear that restrictions on freedom in the European Convention on Human Rights, which forms part of the general principles of law as applied in the Community, cannot go further than is necessary in the interests of public order in a democratic society.[10] The threat to public policy must be genuine and sufficiently serious and affecting one of the fundamental interests of society.[11] The Court, moreover, has pointed out several times that the measures taken must be proportionate to the nature of the offence committed during the stay of a member state national in another member state.[12] Expulsion is not justified, for instance, to "set an example" to other migrant workers.[13]

Whereas there are a considerable number of cases with regard to restrictions for public policy reasons, there is no case-law on restrictions based on public health. Directive 64/221 mentions a number of diseases which can endanger public health, such as tuberculosis, syphilis, and diseases for which a person can be put into quarantine. Another category of diseases which may constitute a reason for refusing a permit includes those which can endanger public order or safety, such as addiction to drugs and alcohol as well as serious mental disorders. How authorities are to establish that a person is dangerously addicted to drugs or alcohol is, however, somewhat unclear.

2.3 Practical restrictions on the freedom of movement

Apart from the legal restrictions there are the probably more important practical restrictions, among which the most obvious are restrictions based on national authorities' failure to recognise certificates and training, and prospective workers' lack of knowledge of languages. With regard to the first, the Community has recently made considerable progress in removing obstacles. There are a number of Directives dealing with the mutual recognition of certificates and training, based on the principle that, if a certificate entitles one to carry out a certain profession in one's own member state, one can do so in another member state as well. Additional conditions demanded of nationals may be demanded of migrant workers as well. For instance, if a lawyer qualified to practise must pass a specific bar examination of his or her home state before being able to actually start practising, this condition must be fulfilled by a migrant lawyer in that state as well.

It is far more difficult to remove the obstacle of the lack of language-knowledge, in spite of Community efforts (e.g. the

LINGUA and ERASMUS programmes) to remedy this problem. These programmes are mainly meant for university students, while whole categories of workers do not qualify for participation in them, which implies that the free movement of persons will be made easier for higher-educated persons only. In fact, even though languages do not always constitute an obstacle to exercising one's profession in another country, in many professions it is a very real obstacle (e.g. for nurses and doctors). Even where it is not an obstacle, it constitutes a social problem, as one lacks a basic means of communication.

There are also, of course, cultural problems. It is not easy for a Greek worker and his family to adapt to, or be accepted by, societies such as that of Denmark. The danger of creating "second-class" citizens is very real, as studies of the problems of Turkish migrant workers in Germany have shown.

It would seem that these practical problems, in combination with a lack of a migratory tradition on the part of European workers, explain why there has in fact been very little movement of workers in the EC since the establishment of the rules on the free movement of persons.

Statistical data from Eurostat do not indicate a drastic increase in migration between the member states since 1973, when the transitional period for the establishment of a common labour market ended, and, moreover, the United Kingdom, Ireland and Denmark became member states. From 1973 - 1978 the highest number of foreign workers was employed in the Federal Republic of Germany. Of those, 621,000 came from other member states, while 1,974,000 came from outside the Community (of whom, however, 525,000 came from the future member states of Greece, Spain and Portugal). As the figures in the annexes to this essay show, this number has steadily decreased to a total of 1,557,100 in 1987, of whom 483,500 came from other member states (now including Greece, Spain and Portugal). In France, too, which has the second largest number of foreign workers (but the biggest number of Community workers) the number of employees from other member states decreased from 694,100 in 1984 to 589,600 in 1986. [14]

In other member states, the number of employees from the Community appears to be much lower. In some member states the figures are stable or show a slight increase (the Netherlands, Denmark, Greece, Luxembourg) or decrease (Ireland, Belgium). The data on the United Kingdom are inconclusive. [15]

Even though the figures shown in the Eurostat statistics are neither complete nor very reliable, it seems possible to draw two conclusions from them, which may be relevant here. The first is that there has been a far bigger movement from the "poorer" to the "richer" member states than vice versa. The second is that the labour market of the Federal Republic of Germany has attracted the most foreign workers (although not most from other member states; this number is slightly higher in France). These two conclusions suggest that with the influx of East German workers, the labour market of the Western **Länder** could come under heavy pressure. (To this it could be added that there seems to be a tendency in the other countries of former communist Eastern Europe to see the labour market of the Western part of Germany as a land of milk and honey.) This problem will be discussed below.

2.4 Migrant workers and social security

The reasoning behind the regulation of the social security of migrant workers is that the free movement of persons cannot be realised if it leads to the loss of acquired rights or benefits or to the possibility of not being insured in the member state in which one has found a job. This is quite a different question from the worries expressed in some member states claiming to have a much better social security system than others, to the effect that they may become over-attractive to nationals of other member states. This fear has been expressed several times in connection with moves towards the completion of the internal market in 1993. Since the establishment of the common labour market, that is to say, since the rules on the free movement of persons have been fully applicable, workers from all member states have in theory been able to take advantage of better social security systems. But so far, such a phenomenon has been hardly observable, for as noted above, there has been remarkably little movement of labour in that period due to other than economic circumstances.

Social security in Community law has a function only with regard to the full application of the free movement of persons. It does not, in fact, aim at (even though it may result in) the approximation of social security policy in the member states.

There are four issues to be distinguished in EC social security law: applicable legislation, equal treatment, aggregation of insurance benefits, and the "export" of benefits.[16] The basic application of this law is very simple: the law of the member state in which the migrant worker has found employment must be applied, and there may be no discrimination as regards this application between national workers and workers from other EC-member states. Acquired rights are not affected and periods of insurance spread over two or more member states must be cumulated; in each of the member states the worker is entitled to a pro-rata benefit. The pro-rata rule does not necessarily apply, however, if a more favourable outcome were to result from applying one national legislation only or from applying one national legislation in combination with a pro-rata rule in another member state. Finally, benefits may be "exported". Thus, for instance, an Italian who has built up in the Netherlands the right to an old-age pension is entitled to take the right to that pension with him or her back to Italy. The application of this rule is more complicated with regard to, for instance, unemployment benefits. Most member states demand that persons who enjoy unemployment benefit remain available for the labour market. Under Community law this can also mean, of course, the labour markets of other member states. Here the right to unemployment benefit is not affected if an unemployed worker tries to find a job in another member state over a period of three months, but there are certain conditions to be met.[17]

Thus, while the basic rules of EC social security law are as such relatively simple, their application is extremely complicated, leading to extensive case-law by the Court of Justice.[18]

3. The implications for a united Germany of Community law on the free movement of workers

As suggested earlier in this essay, one consequence of German unification could be an influx of a not inconsiderable number of workers onto the Community labour market, and not only that of West Germany, as well as a movement from the west towards the former East German labour market.

The widely-publicised bankruptcy of the former GDR's industry, together with its at times catastrophic ecological effects, can be expected to set off two movements. The first, which we have already been witnessing, is of former East Germans to the West, and is obviously due not only to industrial bankruptcy, but also to various other factors. The second is a movement of capital, services and persons (mainly from the West) to the East in order to rebuild its economy and infrastructure. The movement of capital (investments) also has already begun and will logically be followed by persons engaged in the rebuilding of the former GDR.[19] It may be safely assumed that business investment policies are not totally "disembodied". That is to say, if a firm decides to invest in a certain country, the firm's employees are sent to see to it that these investments are properly handled.

These movements beg two questions in the framework of Community law: can (and/or should) labour markets be protected against a destructive influx of foreign workers and can those workers be properly protected as regards their labour and social security rights?

3.1 The protection of labour markets

Four main movements on the various labour markets have to be distinguished, causing different problems and calling for different solutions. These are: the migration of East German workers to Western Germany; the migration of East German workers to other EC-member states; the migration of West Germans to East

Germany; and the migration of nationals of other EC-member states to East Germany.

Migration within the united German state falls outside the scope of Community law on the free movement of persons, which deals only with cross-frontier migration. The problems caused by this migration have to be solved within the context of German law and employment policy.

The first option of East Germans who want to leave their part of the country and seek employment elsewhere is to go to West Germany. Once the Berlin Wall had fallen, the Federal labour market experienced a stream of hundreds of thousands of East Germans seeking employment. A logical conclusion at first sight was that, in view of existing unemployment in West Germany, this development would cause a rise in unemployment figures. This, apparently, has not happened so far; on the contrary, West German unemployment figures went down recently, while unemployment figures in East Germany went up, reaching a level in September 1990 of no less than 5 million unemployed. These developments were allegedly due to an enlargement of the West German market following the fall of the Berlin Wall. In a speech at CEPS in September 1990, Carlo Trojan, Deputy Secretary-General of the European Commission, related the strong preference of East Germans for West German products. On the other hand, investment in the East German economy did not nearly come up to expectations. Many East German companies were not at all equipped to compete on their "own" market with their western counterparts. The result is well known: tens of thousands of East German companies have had to close down, and millions of East German workers have lost their jobs.

Some economists have predicted that there will be no further significant migration from East Germany to the West. Others, however, pointed out that in the border areas, many East Germans were thought to be seeking employment in West Germany, while continuing to live in their own homes.

Whatever the exact scope of the present developments may be, it seems that nobody is able to predict with accuracy what movements of people there will be in the future. This justifies an examination of the question (theoretical as it may seem at the moment) of whether other member states could - if the necessity were to arise - protect their labour markets for a transitory period against a possible influx of East German workers and job seekers.

A similar problem faces the East German market: can it be protected from an influx of employees from other EC member states taking over key positions? These problems must be re-phrased into what is in fact the crucial question facing the Community, namely, can the law on the free movement of persons be delayed in view of the process of unification of Germany?

The treaties of accession of the newest member states (Greece, Spain and Portugal), provided for a transition period with regard to the application of certain parts of Community law, including that on the free movement of persons. As such, therefore, transition periods are possible, and are not considered discriminatory but simply a consequence of later accession. The transition period with regard to the free movement of persons was necessary in order to give new member states as well as old time to adapt to the new situation, in which their markets have been enlarged.

In the situation of German unification, however, this was far more complicated. The "introduction" of the former GDR was not considered to be its accession, in the usual sense, to the European Communities. According to experts in international as well as Community law, the former GDR was "absorbed" by the Federal Republic of Germany (an unprecedented situation); hence, the territory of the FRG was simply extended. According to the 1978 Vienna Treaty on State Succession in respect of Treaties (which, however, has not yet received sufficient ratifications for its entry into force), the treaties applicable in the incorporating (or absorbing) state automatically extend to the incorporated (or absorbed) state.[20] In this context, Community lawyers pointed to Article 227 of the EC Treaty, in which it is stated that the Treaty is applicable to (amongst others) the Federal Republic of Germany. If the territory of the Federal Republic is extended, the Treaty becomes applicable to the extended FRG.

There are, of course, many arguments to be put forward against this point of view. What is important here is that the general trend of thought seemed to be that there would be no amendments to the Treaties; primary Community law would become applicable to the extended FRG from the moment of unification onwards; the concept of "direct effect" would not be touched; and the concept of **acquis communautaire** would be upheld. In simple terms, this meant that only with regard to secondary Community law, as far as it does not have direct effect, would transitional measures be possible . It could be argued that the concept of "direct effect" will be upheld only in as far as it concerns primary Community Law. With respect to secondary Community Law the rule could be that in as far as the application of secondary law is delayed, its directly effective provisions are delayed, too. In this case, the application of not only secondary law with no direct effect (e.g. Directives) but also directly-effective secondary law (Regulations) could be postponed for a certain period.

In terms of the free movement of persons, if the first option were to be selected this would mean that Articles 48 - 51 of the EC Treaty, Regulations 1612/68, 1408/71, 1390/81 etc., would become directly applicable throughout the territory of the FRG after its incorporation of the former GDR. Only the application of the Directives on free movement could be delayed for a certain period.[21] If the second option were selected this would imply that only Article 48 would become directly effective over the entire German territory, while the application of the Regulations as well as the Directives would be delayed.

If one examines the basic instruments on the regulation of the free movement of persons, it is hard to imagine how Treaty provisions as well as Regulations can be applied while Directives are not. Or vice versa: it is hard to see how Directives 64/221 and 68/360, which regulate the practice of the free-movement rules, cannot be applied if the basic rules are applied. It would mean, for instance, that a worker from the former GDR would have the right to take up a job in Belgium and be accompanied by members of his or her family, while the provisions on obtaining a residence permit were not applied. If that were the case, it would mean that rights under the Treaty and the Regulations could not be exercised, which would clearly be a violation of the Treaty itself. The same applies if only Art. 48 of the EC Treaty were applied, but not the Regulations or the Directives.

Apart from these legal problems, it may be added that it seems that it will be practically impossible in future to distinguish between East and West Germans. They will come to the border with a passport from the Federal Republic, whose Constitution does not recognise a difference between them. The place of birth mentioned in the passport will be a useless reference, as many citizens living in the West since the division of Germany were born in the former GDR.

It was this practical argument which led to the conclusion that the Community rules on the free movement of persons must be applied lock, stock and barrel from the moment of German unification and that no transitional measures were possible. Thus, there can be no protection of labour markets on either side. In any case, one could argue that there is no real necessity to do so. In view of the limited movement of workers throughout the Community in the past, it seems somewhat unrealistic to expect that the entire labour force of the former GDR will spill over onto the labour markets of other member states. The labour market of the Federal Republic may come under some pressure, but that problem cannot be solved by Community law since it results from German unification itself and has, therefore, to be solved within the context of that - national - labour market.

The problem of the protection of the East German labour market is somewhat different. It will, of course, be possible to identify non-Germans coming onto that market. In that case, the application of the whole of Community law on the free movement of persons could be delayed for a certain period as far as the territory of the former GDR is concerned. In view of the options put forward by the Communities, however (see above), this is not going to happen, in spite of suggestions to that effect by the late GDR's government. Moreover, it is questionable whether such a delay would help the process of rebuilding the German economy as a whole, which is badly in need of investment and restructuring; and, as noted above, the capital involved in investment and restructuring will be followed by an influx of people. It seems, therefore, unwise to delay rules on the free movement of persons as far as the East German labour market is concerned, even though this will cause problems there, in view of the already-high unemployment, and even though there is a danger that East German employees who have stayed in their own country may lose their jobs to foreigners. It is, however, impossible to say whether this will actually happen and, if so, to what extent it will create problems.

In sum, from 3 October 1990 onwards, the entire body of law on the free movement of persons has become applicable. That means that there are no legal obstacles (other than those inherent in the present law) for persons from the present EC member states to move to the territory of the former German Democratic Republic, nor are there any such obstacles for the East Germans to move to any EC member state of their choice.

3.2 The protection of workers

The second problem to be discussed is how far Community law will protect workers migrating in either direction. The movement of workers from West to East will cause no major problems in this regard, once the provisions of the first **Staatsvertrag**[22] are implemented. This treaty entails a number of provisions with regard to labour and social security rights (**Sozialunion**). The principle is laid down in Article 17 that fundamental labour rights are recognised in the GDR in accordance with the law of the Federal Republic. The various obligations arising out of this, relating to such areas as job-security, unemployment, accident and sickness insurance, and health care are laid down in Annexes II and III.[23] It is not entirely clear from the treaty exactly when these systems have to be established. Different dates are mentioned in the various provisions, or none at all.[24]

The second treaty, or **Einigungsvertrag**, adopted at the end of August 1990, specifies the social security provisions of the first **Staatsvertrag**. It entails a much more detailed regulation (the labour and social security measures cover more than 300 pages) of the methods by which social security measures and social assistance law and practice have to be harmonised. An important difference between the two treaties is that the aim of the first was to achieve German unity at a time when it was not clear how the two systems were to be integrated. The second **Staatsvertrag** deals in detail with the concrete measures to achieve integration. Yet in the latter too, different periods are mentioned over which integration has to be completed.

For as long as the systems have not been beaten into one, and for as long as differences in the levels of benefits and salaries remain, it is likely to be an unattractive proposition for most Community citizens to move the territory of the former GDR, since it would involve a considerable drop in the standard of protection they are used to.

Another problem resulting from the differences between the former GDR's social security system and those of the EC in general concerns East German workers moving outside Germany to other states of the Community. The protection of collective as well as individual labour rights causes no problems. EC Regulation 1612/68 provides that the rights of migrating former East German workers will be protected on the same basis as national workers. That goes, of course, in principle for social security rights, too, but problems will be caused by the notion of "acquired rights". Social security rights acquired in other member states have to be taken into account when the migrant worker can lay claim to unemployment, disability, old-age and other benefits (see para. 2.4 above). However, an East German worker migrating to other member states did not acquire his or her rights - if any - in "another member state". At the end of August 1990, the Commission adopted a proposal to the effect that from the day of unification onwards, Community principles governing social security for migrant workers would be applied to migration from and to the territory of the former GDR. That means that the rights to benefits, to pro-rating, to accumulation of periods, etc., exist for all from 3 October 1990 onwards. The question remains, of course, of those East German workers who acquired certain social security rights before unification, especially as the level of benefits acquired over those years may be considerably lower than the level in other member states.

Towards workers who acquired their social security rights in the GDR before unification, the Community will act on the assumption that the GDR has always formed part of the Federal Republic, although, again, the level of benefits will be based on the actual East German rates. This concerns East German workers as well as workers from other member states who worked in East Germany before unification. In the above-mentioned Commission proposal it is provided that the Council will take measures in order to solve the practical and technical problems in the area of social security law.

4. Conclusion

The handling of the problems caused by German unification for the European Communities is a clear demonstration of the superior influence of politics over law. While lawyers were left gasping on the touch-lines, overcome by the enormity of the legal consequences of this historic process, politicians rode over complicated problems as if they did not exist. The key phrase has undoubtedly been "political pragmatism", overruling any desire for legal purism. Whether that is good or bad is another issue. It has been, and still is, fascinating to witness such an important process being dealt with in what, from the legal point of view, seems to be an almost off-hand way.

From the point of view of the free movement of persons in the Communities, one could argue that this pragmatism has resulted in sensible solutions. Some pressure on labour markets may occur, but while it is difficult to forecast how many East Germans will flow onto other member states' labour markets, it is hard to see how this could have been avoided. Such access cannot be controlled if the purpose is to reject any distinction between East and West Germans. Thus the wish apparently expressed by the late GDR government to protect its labour market could not be granted, since it would have been an undesirable violation of the principle of reciprocity. Moreover, if the new German **Länder** wish to attract foreign investment to rebuild their economy it is clear that they must also accept the people that come with that investment. But the migration of workers to the former GDR who will become dependent on its social security system will probably be slowed for the time being by the lower standard of protection for social security rights in general. Once the Federal social security system becomes applicable in the whole of the "new" Germany, however, this obstacle will cease to exist.

References

1. By the term "Community labour market" is meant the labour markets of the member states before 3 October 1990.

2. EEC Dir. 68/360, Article 3.

3. EEC Dir. 68/360, Art. 3. EEC Reg. 1612/68, Art. 10.

4. **Ibid.**

5. EEC Reg. 1612/68, Art. 11.

6. EEC Dir 68/360, Art. 7, para 2.

7. EEC Dir. 63/221, Art. 3.

8. See, e.g., the case of Yvonne van Duyn v. Home Office, Case 41/74, (1974) **European Court Reports**, pp. 1337 et seq.

9. Adoui and Cornuaille v. Belgian State et. al., Cases 115 and 116/81, (1982) **European Court Reports**, pp.1665 et seq.

10. Rutili v. Minister for the Interior, Case 36/75, (1975) **European Court Reports**, pp. 1219 et seq.

11. R. v. Bouchereau, Case 30/77, (1977) **European Court Reports** pp. 1999 et seq.

12. See, e.g., the case of Watson and Belmann, Case 118/75, (1976) **European Court Reports**, pp. 1185 et seq.

13. Bonsignore v. Oberstadtdirektor der Stadt Köln, Case 67/74, (1975) **European Court Reports**, pp.297 et seq.

14. As the figures given for 1987 for France are exactly the same as for 1986, there is some doubt as to whether the figures for 1987 are correct. The statistical reports from 1973-78 give only the data for 1975 as far as France is concerned. In that year, only 300,000 employees from other member states were counted, while 1,600,000 workers came from outside the Community, of whom, however, 745,000 came from Greece, Spain and Portugal.

15. The same figures are published over 1985, 1986, and 1987. It is clear, however, that the great majority of Community workers in the UK come from Ireland. It is therefore questionable how far this figure can be related to the effect of Community law on the free movement of persons.

16. See Lawrence W. Gormley (ed.), P. Kapteyn and P. Verloren van Themaat, **Introduction to the Law of the European Communities After the Coming into Force of the Single European Act**, 2nd edition (Deventer: Kluwer, 1989), p. 423, quoting earlier distinctions made by Van der Ven.

17. See Articles 69-71 of EEC Regulation 1408/71.

18. See Art. 51 EC Treaty and the important Regulation 1407/71, supplemented by Regulation 1390/81 which expanded the scope of the former to cover not only employed persons but also the self-employed.

19. This may not always have to be so, as was shown by publication in several newspapers of a case in which a number of very rich Hong Kong Chinese allegedly agreed to invest huge amounts of capital in the former GDR, in exchange for its citizenship, a proposal which was accepted by the then government of the GDR. The concern of these Hong Kong citizens was suggested to be to keep their money out of reach of the Chinese government once Great Britain hands Hong Kong back to the People's Republic of China in 1995. As it later turned out, the case was made up by a number of imaginative journalists. This, of course, could have been an extraordinary case. It is not often that people are willing and able to openly "buy" the nationality of another state (let alone that a state is willing to sell its nationality) although it is not an unknown practice for people to buy the protection of another nationality to escape the consequences of a highly criminal background.

20. At the same time, the treaties applicable in the incorporated state do not automatically cease to be applicable, which causes a number of very interesting problems which will not be discussed here.

21. This goes also for the Directives on equal treatment of men and women, insofar as their provisions have not been declared to be directly applicable by the EC Court of Justice, and other (social policy) Directives, that concern workers.

22. **Staatsvertrag über die Schaffung einer Währungs-, Wirtschafts- und Sozialunion zwischen der Bundesrepublik Deutschland und der Deutschen Demokratische Republik**, 18 May 1990.

23. Annexe II obliges the GDR to incorporate a number of Federal labour acts such as those on co-determination, collective agreements and protection against dismissal. Annexe III obliges the GDR to amend or abolish its labour laws insofar as they are in violation of the **Staatsvertrag**. Article 18 provides that the Federal Republic will introduce a system of social security on the basis of the Federal Republic's system. Article 19 provides the same for a system of unemployment insurance, Article 19 for rehabilitation, invalidity, old age and death, Article 21 for illness, Article 24 for accidents. Article 22 provides that a system of health care will be introduced on the basis of the Federal system. Article 25 demands a system of social assistance also in accordance with the Federal system.

24. Article 18 mentions the first of January 1991, Article 20 mentions a transitory period of five years, while the present systems were to be closed down on the first of July 1990; the other provisions mention no date; the health care system having to be changed, according to the Federal system, "step by step" (Art. 22).

Annexe 1
Foreign workers in EC member states, 1973-1978 (x1000)

	1973	1974	1975	1976	1977	1978	Origin
D	621	483	433	400	400	407	All EC
of whom	450	341	298	274	275	282	Italy
	1974	1848	1658	1538	1475	1442	Non-EC
of whom	525	466	416	363	325	302	GSP[1]
F	n.a.	n.a.	300	n.a.	n.a.	n.a.	All EC
of whom	n.a.	n.a.	230	n.a.	n.a.	n.a.	Italy
	n.a.	n.a.	1600	n.a.	n.a.	n.a.	Non-EC
of whom	n.a.	n.a.	745	n.a.	n.a.	n.a.	GSP
I	22	23.8	23.9				All EC
of whom	8.6	8.9	9				D
	32.7	34.6	35.1				Non-EC
of whom	4.5	4.8	4.8				GSP
NL	51	50	47	50	51		All EC
of whom	23	22	19	18	18		Belgium
	70	67	67	50	39		Non-EC
of whom	17	15	12	8	6		GSP
B		125	130	169	n.a.	169	All EC
of whom		83	90	91		90	Italy
		82	100	128		141	Non-EC
of whom		24	44	43		45	GSP
L	28.7	30.5	31.3	31.2	31.5	31.7	All EC
of whom	10.7	10.9	11	10.9	10.8	10.7	Italy
	13.2	14.9	15.1	14.9	15.1	15.6	Non-EC
of whom	11.5	12.8	12.9	12.8	12.9	13.1	Portugal
UK	301		316				All EC
of whom	224		232				Ireland
	376		475				Non-EC
of whom	19		31				GSP
IRL			11		11.8		All EC
			2.1		2.1		Non-EC
DK	8	8.5	12.9	12.5	13.3	14	All EC
of whom	3.6	4.1	5.3	5.2	5.3	5.3	D
	28.6	27.4	28.3	26.9	27.5	28.9	Non-EC
of whom	0.9	1.4	1.4	1.3	1.3	1.3	GSP

1. Greece, Spain, Portugal

Annexe 2
Foreign employees in EC member states, 1984-1987 (x1000)

	1984	1985	1986	1987	Origin
GERMANY	1636.7	1555.3	1546.5	1557.1	All countries
	560.6	519.9	498.3	483.5	EC only
from:					
F	44	40.9	39.1	37.3	
I	220.2	199.9	187.7	177.3	
NL	33.9	30.3	27.8	25.5	
B	8.6	7.8	7.2	6.6	
L	1.2	1.1	1	0.9	
UK	29.8	30	30.4	31.8	
IRL	1.4	1.3	1.3	1.3	
DK	3.1	2.8	2.5	2.4	
GR	105.6	103.4	101.3	101.1	
E	69.5	76.2	65.4	64.2	
P	43.2	35.2	34.6	35.4	
FRANCE	1306.4	1259.7	1172.5	1172.5	All countries
	694.1	640.1	589.6	589.6	EC only
from					
D	13	15.4	14.9	14.9	
I	109.8	94.1	84.8	84.8	
NL	3.9	2.7	1.2	1.2	
B	12.8	12.5	12.4	12.4	
L	0	0	0	0	
UK	11.7	488.9	11.9	11.9	
IRL	1.4	0.7	1	1	
DK	2	1.1	0	0	
GR	1.6	1	1.7	1.7	
E	418.2	400.1	110.5	110.5	
P	119.3	98.3	350.9	350.9	
ITALY	57	57	57	57	All countries
	14.1	14.1	14.1	14.1	EC only
from					
D	1.7	1.7	1.7	1.7	
F	4.1	4.1	4.1	4.1	
NL	0.2	0.2	0.2	0.2	
B	0.8	0.8	0.8	0.8	
L	0.1	0.1	0.1	0.1	
UK	1.8	1.8	1.8	1.8	
IRL	0	0	0	0	
DK	0	0	0	0	
GR	0.3	0.3	0.3	0.3	
E	2	2	2	2	
P	3.1	3.1	3.1	3.1	

	1984	1985	1986	1987	Origin
NETHERLANDS	166.7	165.8	168.6	175.7	All countries
	74	76.2	76.2	86.1	EC only
from					
D	15.1	16.3	16.1	18.7	
F	2.2	2.5	2.6	3.1	
I	7.3	7.2	7	7.9	
B	20.9	21.3	22	24.6	
L	0.1	0.1	0.1	0.2	
UK	14.3	14.9	14.6	16.5	
IRL	0.9	0.9	1.2	1.5	
DK	0.4	0.4	0.4	0.5	
GR	1.6	1.6	1.5	1.7	
E	8.2	3.2	7.6	8.1	
P	3.1	7.8	3.1	3.4	
BELGIUM	199.5	199.5	187	187	All countries
	151	151	140.7	140.7	EC only
from					
D	6.3	6.3	6.1	6.1	
F	25.7	25.7	24.1	24.1	
I	66.4	66.4	61.2	61.2	
NL	18.8	18.8	17.9	17.9	
L	1.4	1.4	1.3	1.3	
UK	6.7	6.7	6.2	6.2	
IRL	0.4	0.4	0.5	0.5	
DK	0.7	0.7	0.7	0.7	
GR	4.4	4.4	3.9	3.9	
E	3.7	3.7	15.3	15.3	
P	16.4	16.4	3.6	3.6	
LUXEMBOURG	53	52.6	54.9	58.8	All countries
	50.4	49.9	52.1	55.7	EC only
from					
D	5	5	5.6	6.1	
F	10.3	10.4	11.3	12.6	
I	8.5	8.2	8.3	8.4	
NL	0.8	0.8	0.8	0.8	
B	8.4	8.5	9.1	10	
UK	0.5	0.5	0.5	0.6	
IRL	0	0	0.1	0.1	
DK	0.1	0.1	0.2	0.2	
GR	0.1	0	0.1	0.1	
E	0.9	0.9	0.9	0.9	
P	15.7	15.3	15.3	16.1	

	1984	1985	1986	1987	Origin
UK	757	820.9	820.9	820.9	All countries
	361	398.2	398.2	398.2	EC only
from					
D	19	17.6	17.6	17.6	
F	13	16.8	16.8	16.8	
I	55	56.5	56.5	56.5	
NL	7	9	9	9	
B	1	3.3	3.3	3.3	
L	0	0	0	0	
IRL	236	268	268	268	
DK	6	3.2	3.2	3.2	
D	3.5	3.7	3.7	4	
UK	2.7	4.4	2.8	2.6	
DK	12.7	12.7	12.7	12.7	
GR	3	7.3	7.3	7.3	
E	15	14.5	14.5	14.5	
P	5	2	2	2	
IRELAND	21	20.3	20.5	19.9	All countries
	17	16.7	16.1	16.2	EC only
from					
D	0.7	0.5	0.7	0.9	
F	0.4	0.3	0.4	0.4	
I	0.2	0.3	0.5	0.5	
NL	0.5	0.4	0.4	0.4	
B	0.1	0.1	0	0	
L	0	0	0	0	
UK	14.9	14.7	13.7	13.5	
DK	0.1	0.2	0.1	0.1	
GR	0	0	0	0	
E	0.1	0.2	0.2	0.1	
P	0	0	0	0.1	
DENMARK	37.5	39.5	39.3	42.5	All countries
	11	11.6	11.6	12.4	EC only
from					
D	3.5	3.7	3.7	4	
F	0.7	0.7	0.7	0.8	
I	0.7	0.8	0.8	0.9	
NL	0.8	0.8	0.8	0.9	
B	0.1	0.1	0.1	0.1	
L	0	0	0	0	
UK	4.2	4.4	4.4	4.6	
IRL	0.3	0.4	0.4	0.4	
GR	0.2	0.2	0.2	0.2	
E	0.4	0.4	0.4	0.4	
P	0.1	0.1	0.1	0.1	

	1984	1985	1986	1987	Origin
GREECE	24.3	24.3	24.4	24.9	All countries
	6.1	6.4	6.9	6.6	EC only
from					
D	1.1	1.2	1.4	1.4	
F	0.8	0.8	0.8	0.7	
I	1.1	0.8	1.2	1.2	
NL	0.2	0.8	0.3	0.3	
B	0.1	0.1	0.2	0.1	
L	0	0	0	0	
UK	2.7	4.4	2.8	2.6	
IRL	0	0	0.1	0.1	
DK	0	0	0.1	0.1	
E	0.1	0	0.1	0.1	
P	0	0.1	0	0	
EUR 10	4259.1	4259.1	4259.1	4259.1	All countries
	1939.3	1939.3	1939.3	1939.3	EC only
from					
D	65.4	65.4	65.4	65.4	
F	101.2	101.2	101.2	101.2	
I	469.2	469.2	469.2	469.2	
NL	66.1	66.1	66.1	66.1	
B	52.8	52.8	52.8	52.8	
L	2.9	2.9	2.9	2.9	
UK	86.6	86.6	86.6	86.6	
IRL	240.5	240.5	240.5	240.5	
DK	12.7	12.7	12.7	12.7	
GR	116.8	116.8	116.8	116.8	
E	518.1	518.1	518.1	518.1	
P	205.9	205.9	205.9	205.9	

Source (Annexes 1 and 2): Eurostat.

EC transport policy: the consequences of German unification

Albrecht Frohnmeyer

1. EC transport policy: objectives and state of development

For many years the common transport policy provided for in the Treaty of Rome was seen as a live Community issue, and indeed until well in the 1980's the rules introduced had hardly any directly visible effects as far as the citizen of Europe was concerned. They chiefly related to the transport industry and focused mainly on those engaged in the carriage of goods. The great mass of car-drivers and bus, rail and aircraft passengers was not directly concerned. Movement towards a consumer-orientated policy developed only recently.

The reasons for the character of past transport policy stem from the fact that the Treaty of Rome dealt with this topic under only the few very summary provisions. The introductory Article (74), states that "the objectives of this Treaty shall... be pursued by Member States within the framework of a common transport policy". The organs of the Community - the Commission, the European Parliament, the Economic and Social Committee and the Council - were to act in concert to lay down, before the end of the transition period (i.e. 1970): a) common rules applicable to international transport between member states (Article 75 para 1a), and b) the conditions under which non-resident carriers may operate transport services within a member state (Article 75 para 1b). The Council may also lay down any other appropriate provisions.

Discriminatory freight rates and different conditions for the carriage of goods are to be abolished, at the latest, before the end of the transition period (Article 79); rates involving any element of support or protection are also to be prohibited before this time limit unless the Commission gives exceptional authorisation (Article 80). Until the provisions referred to in Article 75 have been laid down, the member states are not to take measures which place foreign carriers at a disadvantage in relation to domestic ones (Article 76). Finally, the Council may decide whether, to what extent and by what procedure appropriate provisions may be laid down for sea and air transport (Article 84, para 2).

At the time the signatories to the Treaty were unable to agree on more detailed provisions, as they held widely differing views on the extent of competition and the instruments for controlling the market. Over the 30-year development of the European Community's transport policy these concepts have, however, come closer together and in many areas coalesced into a uniform approach. Two facts have been of crucial significance here. Firstly, the ruling of the European Court of May 1985 under which the Council, in response to a plea by the European Parliament, was required to implement within a "suitable period" the freedom to provide transport services in compliance with the mandatory provisions of Article 75, paras 1a and 1b. Secondly, the agreement of the signatories to the Treaty on the amendments under the Single European Act which came into force on 1 July 1987, and also include transport, aimed at the creation by 1 January 1993 of the European internal market.

The most important results in the area of a common transport policy to date can be summarised as follows: the transport user is entitled to a free choice of carrier in all areas. Government intervention in goods traffic between member states will largely cease, so that genuine competition can determine the division of labour between carriers and transport undertakings. A precondition for competition of this kind is the alignment of those parameters which depend on government intervention (the harmonisation of tax, social and technical regulations and the rules governing public transport firms which are relevant to competition).

Road haulage

In the road haulage field, success has been achieved in laying down framework regulations on this basis, to operate from 1 January 1993, for transport activities between the member states of the Community. These regulations cover the conditions for access to the profession and to the market as well as the most important social and technical conditions, but abolish government rules on pricing and restrictive quotas.

Success has not yet been achieved, however, in agreeing a common taxation system aimed at covering road costs. This deficiency prompted the Federal German government to devise special road-use charges, which were to be introduced on 1 July 1990. It was further planned that the GDR would introduce the charges on 1 January 1991. However, these plans were abandoned when the European Court, before which they were laid by the European Commission, ruled them illegal. Another issue which remains open is the extent to which vehicles from one member state will be allowed to participate in the internal transport of another (**cabotage**). The Council has been able to come to an agreement only on a quota-based transitional arrangement running until 31 December 1992. Complete freedom from restriction from 1 January 1993 and any conditions relating to this are likely to be the subject of further debate and may also require a legal ruling by the European Court.

Inland waterways

With regard to international goods traffic on inland waterways, the 1868 Convention of Mannheim and the ensuing regulations have established complete freedom of navigation of the Rhine for enterprises domiciled in and "genuinely linked" to the Community. However, restrictive regulations to the east of the Dortmund-Hamm line and on the canals between the Netherlands, Belgium and France have not yet been removed. The purpose of a 1989 scrapping arrangement was, as a first step, to remove the existing overcapacity which stood in the way of a properly-functioning competitive system. In addition,

Community conditions were laid down governing entry into the inland shipping industry.

Goods transported by rail
Imposed tariffs have been removed from goods transport by rail between the member states. Furthermore, the financial disadvantages arising from competition-distorting charges on the railways (public service obligations, pension charges, infrastructure costs, etc.) are to be offset in accordance with Community rules. With regard to the restructuring of railway undertakings to take account of the requirements of competition in goods and passenger transport, the Council has before it a proposal of December 1989 which calls for further detailed discussion, especially in view of the financial consequences for member states.

Passenger transport
There are to date few legal instruments governing passenger transport between the member states of the Community, and these are mainly concerned with motor buses and coaches. While services for special occasions and shuttles (holiday coaches) have been largely liberalised, international scheduled passenger services are subject to verification of need by the authorities. In other words, there is no free access to the market. The enterprises already in operation are thereby protected against duplication of services. Railways are able to compete in international transport without having government-sanctioned prices imposed on them. However, prior to agreement of the Council of Ministers on the structural proposals already referred to they are prohibited from providing services outside their national network.

All the Community regulations referred to so far relate solely to market arrangements for the three land-based modes of transport. It is a peculiarity of this transport that each mode requires a route provided by the state in addition to the activity of the transport undertakings. This public function is performed by the railways themselves.

Against the background of increasing market deregulation, transport policy can cater for all public and private interests only if decision-makers have at their disposal such tools of infrastructure policy as exist in each state. At the Community level, however, an infrastructure policy of this kind is only at the preparatory stage. The member states remain sovereign with regard to their infrastructures. The Commission merely has the possibility, with the help of a special committee of senior civil servants from the member states, of "co-ordinating" national projects with important implications for the Community, but it cannot make decisions on priorities which are binding on the member states. A more powerful influence is possible only to the extent that the Community is able to take a financial share in certain investments. In economically-disadvantaged areas, particularly those in outlying regions, the Community's regional policy is already capable of effective intervention. Outside these areas, the Community has so far had only modest resources to devote to transport policy, and these amounts have been allocated from year to year without the Council of Ministers being able to reach agreement on a multiannual programme. In the autumn it will perhaps be possible for the first time to adopt a three-year programme comprising seven main projects.

Air and sea transport

As far as air and sea transport is concerned, the Community's transport policy has been relatively slow to take concrete shape.The first regulations adopted related to sea transport and focused on two objectives: the protection of Community interests in relation to developing countries (the code for liner conferences); the protection of Community interests in relation to non-EC countries conducting, from the Community's standpoint, unfair pricing practices; and safety in sea transport and protection of the maritime environment. In order to detect unfair practices, the Community has set up a monitoring system aimed primarily at vetting the pricing policy of maritime transport firms operating from centrally-planned economies in eastern Europe.

The freedom to provide maritime shipping services between the member states of the Community was introduced in 1986, but the regulation of cabotage is still outstanding. The application to maritime shipping of the Treaty's rules on competition was settled from 1986 onwards with due regard for the special needs of the sector. The same applies to a co-ordinated procedure for protecting freedom of access to cargoes.

In the field of air transport the Community's policy has been aimed not so much at providing protection against external factors as at improving and reducing the price of the scheduled services operating between member states. The need for common principles has been rendered particularly acute by the prospect of the internal market in 1992. Of the rules promulgated to date, the following deserve mention in the light of the problems arising from German unification: the specification of a maximum permissible noise-level under a directive on the lowering of noise emissions; a directive on inter-regional air transport; special competition rules for air transport (with group exemptions); and capacity and pricing rules aimed at increasing liberalisation.

Taken as a whole, this enumeration of the Community's principal regulations for the transport sector demonstrates that the Community has been primarily concerned to bring about the internal integration of the various areas of the transport industry. With a few exceptions it has not yet been possible to give comprehensive treatment to relations with other European and non-European countries, which are very important to transport. The exceptions chiefly comprise the negotiations on transit traffic with Switzerland, Austria and Yugoslavia; agreements on motor bus transport concluded by the European Conference of Ministers of Transport; the negotiations on sea transport conducted in UNCTAD and with major world trading partners; and limited contacts on air transport policy with the large government-owned and non-governmental air-transport organisations.

2. The GDR's transport policy and its consequences for the future of East German transport

In common with all other sectors of industry, the transport sector of the GDR was managed according to the principles of the centrally-planned socialist economy. Its objectives were essentially determined by the resolutions of the party congresses, and the operation of the transport system was controlled by central organs which were at the same time directly responsible for managing the large state transport undertakings (Deutrans). The allocation of transport operations to individual carriers and enterprises had to conform to national economic priorities. The rail system, for instance, as a collective means of transport capable of using domestic primary energy resources, was given a high priority (approximately 70% of goods transport). In trade with Western countries, precedence was given to domestic road-hauliers and shippers in order to husband convertible currencies. In passenger transport the tariff-levels for rail and bus travel were geared to the incomes of the populace without noticeable regard for any calculation of costs. Private-car ownership was held in check by the high purchase price of vehicles and restricted development of the infrastructure.

The situation of the transport sector after forty years of existence of the German Democratic Republic is characterised mainly by a very deficient infrastructure. The funds which will be required to renew and update the railway, road and inland-waterway networks are estimated at between 200 and 300bn DM. As far as vehicles are concerned, the disparities are not so drastic, although here too there is a considerable need for modernisation by Western standards.

3. Initial measures by the Federal Republic of Germany, the German Democratic Republic and the EC to prepare for German unification

At the beginning of 1990 the two German governments opened negotiations aimed at creating, in parallel with German economic and monetary union, a special transport union as a preliminary to unification. Agreement was reached on the following measures: immediate steps at the internal German border to cope with the greatly increased passenger and goods traffic; co-ordination of route-planning with a view to the creation of an overall network; harmonisation of traffic laws; introduction of market-economy principles into the GDR transport sector; institutional integration of organs belonging to the two German states; and financial assistance for investment and the establishment of essential facilities.

The transport union was to come into being in two stages. Stage 1, to 1 July 1990, comprised an increase in the number of border-crossing points (from 20 to 200); an increase in the number of rail links (to date, from 60 a day to 200); and development of the roads and railway tracks necessary for this purpose (closure of gaps). A plan for inland waterways was to come later.

In the second phase the principles of the treaty between the two German states of 18 May 1990 also extend to transport. Market-economy principles operating within a free constitutional order will supersede "socialist legality" and "central planning". Private entrepreneurs will have an increasing place on the market, laws will be passed to allow freedom of investment, and the large state corporations, with the exception of the **Reichsbahn** and **Interflug**, will be broken up and partially placed in private hands. The operation of the transport system will be largely based on statutory arrangements established in the Federal Republic of Germany - it being assumed, of course, that these are also in line with EC regulations. Finally, joint administrative units will be set up hand-in-hand with the restructuring operation.

In the Commission's view, the internal German negotiations on the transport union fall within the category of measures which, under the terms of the Protocol on German Internal Trade, lie outside the purview of Community law. Nevertheless, representatives of the Commission have taken part in the negotiations to ensure that account is taken of Community interests.

With the conclusion of the Co-operation Agreement with the GDR the Community had a second transitional instrument pending unification. In its formulation this text corresponds to the co-operation agreements concluded with Poland and Hungary. The transport sector is one area covered. With regard to its content, however, this agreement has little impact on the transport sector, and with German unification it has become obsolete.

A further institutionalised basis for EC/GDR relations was established by the decision of the Council of Ministers of 4 July 1990 to include the GDR together with Czechoslovakia, Bulgaria and Yugoslavia in the expanded PHARE programme (Pologne-Hongrie, Assistance à la Restructuration Economique). Unfortunately, it was not possible to allocate funds from this programme for projects in the transport field. As a result of German unification, the programme can no longer be applied to the former GDR.

The transitional programmes referred to, in fact, had a mainly symbolic character during the period leading to German unification. The measures actually taken to incorporate the territory and economy of the former GDR into Community policy must go much further. They are at present in the course of intensive preparation by all concerned, especially by the Commission acting in collaboration with the German institutions concerned. The European Parliament, too, is considering special reports relating to EC transport-policy measures necessitated by German unification.[1]

4. Incorporation of the former GDR into EC transport policy

At the time of writing, this subject was under discussion between the European Commission, the Federal German goverment and the (late) government of the GDR. In considering this complex of questions a distinction is to be made between four constituent elements: details relating to the adoption of Community regulations; conditions governing the manner in which international agreements concluded by the GDR with member states or third countries are to be dealt with henceforth; ancillary supporting measures for the GDR concerning infrastructure and transport undertakings; and the possible reorientation of Community transport policy in response to the particular circumstances of the new German **Länder**.

The consequences for the ex-GDR of adopting Community regulations

In examining this complex of questions a distinction has to be drawn between the Community's basic principles and individual regulations. In their present form, the basic principles of common transport policy encompass the following aims: promoting a division of labour between carriers and transport undertakings at Community level which is determined by genuine competition; safeguarding the free choice of transport-users; co-ordinating investment in the transport infrastructure with due regard for the public interest; the phased recovery of infrastructure costs from user categories; and the allocation of responsibilities relating to public transport functions according to the principle of subsidiarity.

It follows from this synopsis that all former GDR regulations aimed at national transport prerogatives must be set aside, in particular the allocation of transport functions to specific carriers or transport undertakings. It is more difficult to answer the question of the extent to which corporate structures in the GDR need to be adapted to the requirements of competition. How far does the dismantling and possible privatisation of the state monopolies of the past have to proceed to meet the requirements of the Community? Under Article 222, the EEC Treaty should in no way prejudice the rules in member states governing the system of property ownership.

It follows that privatisation of the large state railway or air-transport companies does not flow from the Treaty. There should therefore be no objection to the **Deutsche Reichsbahn** and **Interflug** remaining in the public sector (or with the public **Treuhandanstalt**), although the removal from the main corporate body of certain elements such as airports and air-traffic control would be desirable in the interest of approximating to Community corporate structures. In the Community the vast bulk of road haulage is in private hands. The regrouping of the 100 or so state-owned road-haulage operations of the GDR into 12 regional road-haulage companies should meet with no serious objections. On the other hand the interpretation under competition law of a voluntary merger of these companies into a "German Transport Corporation" is dubious, although this form of organisation would counterbalance the activities in former GDR territory of large and medium-size West German road-hauliers. The organisation of passenger road services by local or regional bodies is regarded as standard practice, but arrangements should be made to ensure that private entrepreneurs also have access to operating rights. With regard to maritime transport, harbour operations and inland navigation, which were also in the hands of state-owned monopolistic combines, the German institutions concerned have given notice of organisational changes consistent with the requirements of competition.

The principles of public-sector infrastructure policy practised in the Community can henceforth be upheld by the government of the united Germany. As for investment, the practical content of the election decisions will be that greater importance than hitherto is attached to carrier-specific demand. A requirement here is to gear the contributions made by transport-users to the internal and external costs of route provision and maintenance. It is important that, following the principle of subsidiarity, decision-making on transport issues should be decentralised to a greater degree than in the past. The creation of new **Länder** in the East was a first step in this direction.

As far as the regulation of German domestic transport is concerned, the fact is that the Community has so far instituted only a few market-regulating measures with a direct impact on countries' domestic transport, such as the regulations on cabotage. However, the internal measures for regulating the transport market have to be gradually adapted to EC principles for international transport. The Community's harmonisation measures are also due to be applied to domestic transport.

Clearly, the accession of the GDR to the EC by unification with the Federal Republic will demand technical adjustments of Community law in exactly the same way as previous accessions. This applies, for instance, to regulations in which the national enterprises of member states are enumerated and to which the names of corporations such as **Interflug** or **Deutsche Reichsbahn** must be added. It is, however, questionable how long these two enterprises will retain their existing identity. In the case of the **Deutsche Reichsbahn**, a reasonable period up to the merger with the West German **Bundesbahn** is likely to be involved, but with **Interflug** it is not yet possible to predict whether and when capital participation by **Lufthansa** will be followed by further steps towards a merger which might need to be examined under competition law. Other "technical" adjustments relate, for example, to Community regulations with annexes containing details of the geographical extent or regions of the Community, which will, of course, have to be brought up to date. Finally, attention must be turned to the quantitative regulations which have hitherto been geared only to economic conditions in the Federal Republic of Germany and the Europe of the Twelve and will have to be extended accordingly.[2]

It is necessary to make a distinction between these technical adjustments and those regulations whose immediate adoption by the GDR would give rise to very considerable legal, economic or social difficulties and which can therefore be adopted only after the expiry of a transition period. There will probably be periods of two to three years for the application of a number of regulations: firstly, the professional and financial conditions for access to the profession of road-haulier or passenger-vehicle operator. These conditions might impede the desired establishment of new firms. Secondly, the introduction of the relatively-expensive monitoring instrument (tachograph) for commercial vehicles, and regulations regarding the introduction of the EC driving licence. Thirdly, adoption of the regulations for a structural cleansing operation in inland navigation, on a equitable basis, as proposed by the Commission. Fourthly, adaptation of the GDR's Sea Transport Agreements containing cargo-sharing clauses.

The list of Community regulations enumerated above is not exhaustive. It is conceivable that further adjustments will have to be made which can be executed in a simplified way.

Adjustments to the GDR's bilateral and multilateral agreements

There is a considerable number of such agreements relating to transport. However, many of them have never been published, especially if they were concluded within the Council for Mutual Economic Assistance or bilaterally in the context of friendship treaties. The most important - especially those multilateral agreements concluded within the CMEA - concern road, sea and air transport and inland navigation. In principle, the validity of international political agreements is extinguished when a legal signatory ceases to exist. With commercial agreements, however, the legal successor has to decide on the continuing validity of agreement. Because of German unification the new Federal Government will therefore have to clarify whether, as the legal successor to the GDR, it wishes to maintain, terminate or renegotiate the agreements. Apparently, the majority of them have to be terminated on 1 January 1991.

The European Community itself may also raise issues of legal authority for the new negotiation of agreements regarding commercial issues. In the past the Community, acting in accordance with the rulings of the European Court (principally the "AETR judgment"), has claimed powers of this kind for the negotiation of agreements between the Community and non-EC countries on all matters for which it had already created, or was under an obligation to create, secondary legislation. With regard to transport too, the Community has recently claimed, under Article 113 of the EEC Treaty, exclusive powers for all external relations (deemed to be commercial) relating to transport services. In view of the large number of bilateral and multilateral agreements to which the GDR is party, efforts will have to be made to achieve practical solutions in which Community representatives participate in the negotiation of new regulations and the conclusion of new agreements between the Community and the co-signatories concerned.

The agreements between the GDR and member states of the Community have been transferred to the Federal Republic following German unification. The agreements with the member states of the European Free Trade Association will also have to l taken into account in the framework of the negotiations on the creation of a European Economic Space.

The agreements with Central and East European countries belonging to the CMEA generally contain preferential clauses for traffic with the former GDR. These will continue to operate for the former GDR territory for the time being, but will have to be renegotiated on Community principles when their validity expires. In this process account must be taken of the goals of the development programmes and of these countries' subsequent associate membership of the Community. The extent to which existing preferential rights can be maintained will largely depend on their progress towards a market economy. The agreements between the GDR and the USSR represent another special case whose solution is connected with the Community's willingness, in the framework of the existing Co-operation Treaty with the

Soviet Union and the planned assistance programmes, to adopt a posture particularly conducive to the creation of genuinely pan-European solutions. In essence, Soviet-(former) GDR agreements which have only a short time to run will be allowed to stand, while longer-term agreements will be renegotiated on the basis of **Vertrauensschutz** (the protection of trust).

Regarding agreements between the GDR and non-EC countries, the target is likely to be those solutions which already govern the relations between the Federal Republic of Germany and the countries in question. One should also note, in this connection, that the agreements of the 'Two-Plus-Four' negotiations have restored full sovereignty to the Federal Republic, which extends, after ratification, also to air transport in Germany.

Even this brief survey reveals the complexity of the task facing the authorities. If a "common European house" is the aim, questions of law should not occupy the foreground (as an impediment), but should be magnanimously subordinated to political, economic and social goals.

Accompanying support programmes for the former GDR's transport system

After unification, the success and speed with which the GDR can be integrated into the Community transport system will depend first and foremost on the practical measures which can be taken to assist the restructuring of transport in this part of Germany. In the programme for the creation of a German transport union the Federal government has already outlined the measures to be organised and funded from its existing resources: the creation of common organisational structures for transport, the institution of a common transport law, the transfer of know-how and private capital for entrepreneurial activity and the transfer of budgetary means for undertakings in the interest of Germany as a whole which cannot be funded - or be wholly funded - from private capital. The first thing to be considered here is the urgently-needed investment in infrastructure.

The Community is called upon to supplement these German domestic programmes in the interests of the Community. These interests flow from the general objectives of the Treaty - balanced economic growth, accelerated improvement in standards of living, etc. - and from the aims of the Community's specific policies, including not only transport but also regional and social policy.

For particular transport sectors, effective support can be provided by Community loans from the European Investment Bank or the ECSC Fund, together with loans from the World Bank or the future European Bank for Reconstruction and Development, as well as funds from private financial institutions. Such loans would allow the procurement of vehicles of all kinds, providing the administration and enterprises with modern, computer-controlled instrument systems and, in extreme cases, even the creation of new routes, provided that government guarantees are given and/or appropriate user-charges are introduced (toll roads, airports and air-traffic control systems).

However, other investment demands budgetary appropriations on the part of the Community, as the likely interest burden arising from the invested capital will rule out any purely private-sector funding. This applies to transport-development studies, training and exchange programmes for transport workers and, above all, the bulk of the necessary infrastructure investment.

Following German unification, the Community's resources for transport projects will have to be provided either through special programmes, the Regional Fund or special budgetary appropriations for the transport infrastructure. It is obvious that these resources will have to be topped up to meet the requirements of the former GDR. It must be borne in mind here that the experts are predicting a far above-average increase in passenger and goods traffic between the two parts of Germany and with Eastern Europe.

According to the applications submitted, the initial phase will involve the contributory funding of immediate programmes for the restoration of an effective rail transport system and for plugging the obvious gaps in German domestic transport (rail,

Estimated increase in passenger traffic 1985-2010

FRG - GDR: from 27 to 228 million journeys
FRG - E. Europe: from 38 to 289 million journeys

Estimated increase in goods traffic 1985-2010

FRG - GDR: from 918 to 1581 million tonnes
FRG - E. Europe: from 45 to 450 million tonnes

road and inland navigation). Apart from basic renewal of the railway-track infrastructure, the urgent projects are: construction of the Hanover-Stendal-Berlin high-speed link by 1997; development and electrification of the Hamburg-Berlin line; the Brunswick-Helmstedt-Magdeburg (-Leipzig) line; the (Frankfurt)-Bebra-Neudietendorf (-Erfurt) line; and the electrification of the (Nuremberg-) Probstzella-Camburg (-Halle/Leipzig) line.

As far as the road system is concerned, the Bad Alsfeld-Eisenach gap has already been provisionally closed, but just as urgent is the closure of the motorway gap between Hof and Plauen.

Nor is there any lack of second-phase projects: Berlin must be provided with modern rail links with South Germany via Frankfurt (Main) and Nuremberg. It will also be necessary to examine the electrification of the Regensburg-Hof-Plauen links and in the North the Lübeck-Rostock link.

Considerable resources are also earmarked for the development of the road network. In the view of the Federal Minister of Transport, private funds should also be used for new stretches of motorway. Apart from link roads within Germany, the connection of Dresden to Czechoslovakia's Prague-Brno-Bratislava trunk road seems to be a priority. With regard to inland navigation, urgent requirements include an effective through bridge over the Elbe on the Mittelland Canal. In air transport, in the light of the forecast growth in traffic it seems that further expansion of the Schönefeld airport and the provision of a central airport in South Berlin is essential to meet future needs.

Reorientation of transport policy

The unification of the two German states has begun to take place at a time when Community transport policy is undergoing a profound reappraisal (e.g. the work of the "2000 Group") in the light of future requirements in terms of demand growth, the environment and energy. While road and air transport have experienced above-average development in the recent past, the limitations on the space available for further expansion and construction suggest that rail-networks, which are both space-saving and environmentally friendly, should be more heavily promoted than in the past by the creation of additional facilities, including in particular high-speed traffic and combined transport - accompanied by simultaneous commercialisation of corporate structures.

In the former GDR the railways carried the bulk of traffic, but are now run-down. As in the West, the people's first demand will be an efficient road network. However, those with responsibility for policy can resolve the inevitable conflicts of purpose only if both the positive and negative experiences of Western Europe are placed in the balance and a transport policy is evolved which is geared to the long-term requirements of the densely-populated areas of the continent.

Conclusion

The unification of Germany will considerably increase the tasks facing the European Community in the transport sector. The Community has to ensure that, after a brief period of transition, the territory of the former GDR is included in its transport market, so that Community firms can participate in the expanded range of activity under the same conditions as in the former Federal Republic. At the same time, structural measures will be needed in order to enable transport firms in the fomer GDR to develop rapidly along market-economy lines throughout the Community and, in accordance with existing agreements, in the neighbouring countries of eastern and central Europe.

A precondition for this is, first, an adequate level of both state and private investment in the transport sector in the former GDR, in order to achieve the necessary modernisation of vehicles and infrastructure. Secondly, personnel in the transport sector must be trained or retrained for the new tasks in national and international transport; in order to achieve this, seminars and exchange activities in particular are required. Cost-accounting and marketing, above all in international transport, will be the main themes of such training programmes, in which all transport firms, both public and private, should be included.

Insofar as retraining and privatisation bring about social problems, especially in the fields of road transport, inland waterways traffic and harbour operations, these must be resolved with the aid of the EC's Social Fund.

For the extensive investment required to modernise the former GDR's infrastructure, in addition to EIB Loans the maximum possible use must be made of the Regional Fund (objective 2 and, where possible, objective 1) and Budget Chapter 580 (transport infrastructure). These budgetary appropriations should be used, above all, to rebuild and create a modern rail infrastructure and trans-shipment facilities for combined transport. Road-building must be largely financed by loans, with public guarantees if necessary, or by the introduction of user-levies (tolls or motorway taxes).

Finally, in shaping transport agreements with the countries of central and eastern Europe, including the Soviet Union, the Community should take into account the principle of confidentiality, in order to counteract the creation of new transport barriers between the Community and these countries, and so as not to obstruct their route to the market economy. Similarly, particular attention should be devoted to expanding the transport infrastructure between Poland and Czechoslovakia and the former GDR.

References

1. See the report by Mr Anastassopoulos on co-operation with Central and Eastern European states and the report by Mrs von Alemann concerning the aspects of transport policy connected with German unification.

2. For example, the size of the Community quota or cabotage quota for road haulage (until 1 January 1993).